Interpretation: Theory and Practice

The Johns Hopkins Humanities Seminars

The Seminars are sponsored by the Humanities Center of The Johns Hopkins University. Each year these interdisciplinary programs bring distinguished scholars from other institutions to take part in the study of some particular period or subject. To date the following books have come from the Seminars:

Aspects of the Eighteenth Century
    Edited by Earl R. Wasserman (1965)

The Individual and Society in the Middle Ages
    by Walter Ullmann (1966)

Art, Science, and History in the Renaissance
    Edited by Charles S. Singleton (1967)

Interpretation: Theory and Practice
    Edited by Charles S. Singleton (1969)

INTERPRETATION
THEORY AND PRACTICE

EDITED BY CHARLES S. SINGLETON

THE JOHNS HOPKINS PRESS, BALTIMORE

Preface

This fifth Seminar of our series is dedicated, for the first time, to the study of a topic rather than a single historical period: *Interpretation,* not the theory, alone, but also the practice, exegesis as well as hermeneutics in three fields—history, art, literature.

Again, and chiefly for the record, this briefest of prefatory notes: the Seminar met regularly throughout the year and, needless to say, the discussions which followed these lectures were always lively. Each of our distinguished visitors was left humanistically free to choose his own subject and manner of exposition, nor was he asked to attempt to say what his own particular theory and practice might have in common with that of other speakers. But many who attended the entire series as lectures and discussions came certainly, at many a point, into new awareness of what some of the common denominators as well as some of the radical differences between these expositors of method might be. And now that the lectures are these several published papers, there will no doubt be readers of the whole volume who will in turn have glimpses, perhaps even more than glimpses, of what the basic agreements and differences of approach among our "theorist-practitioners" finally amount to, in these three fields of study, history, art, literature, which remain so essential a part of our humanity.

For their dedicated labor in the production of this volume, special thanks are due to my colleague Richard A. Macksey of The Humanities Center and to Miss Penny James of The Johns Hopkins Press.

CHARLES S. SINGLETON

The Humanities Center
The Johns Hopkins University

Contents

1

ARNALDO MOMIGLIANO

The Origins of the Roman Republic

I

WHEN Professor Singleton honored me with an invitation to contribute to this volume on Interpretation, it became obvious to me that I had to resist the temptation to write on wide issues of ancient history, such as the spreading of Hellenism after Alexander, the rise of the Roman Empire, or its decline and fall. These are, no doubt, issues of general interest in which conflicts of interpretation abound. But they do not lend themselves to a demonstration of how an ancient historian interprets his own evidence, if the demonstration has to be confined to a brief discussion. The evidence is too vast, the variety of interpretations is too dependent on presuppositions which in their turn must be made explicit and analyzed. If we speak of the cosmopolitanism of Hellenistic civilization, of the imperialism of republican Rome, of the conflicts between pagans and Christians or between Romans and barbarians in the late Empire, we must define what we mean by cosmopolitanism, by imperialism, by paganism, by Christianity, by Romans, by barbarians. We must interpret both the terms we use and the events to which we attach these terms.

It seems to me that the origins of the Roman Republic are a more suitable subject for our purpose. The evidence is limited. Indeed, it is so limited that it can illustrate one of the distinctive features of the study of archaic societies: the poverty of evidence. Furthermore, the evidence is varied: it raises the problem of how to interpret various types of evidence within the same historical context. Finally, at least the literary evidence about early Roman history is still the common patrimony of educated people. Even if we have not read our Livy, we know what Livy tells us about the tyranny of Tarquinius Superbus, about the rape of Lucretia, the reaction of the Etruscan Porsenna on behalf of the Tarquinii, and his ultimate failure. Brutus, Horatius Cocles, Mucius Scaevola, and Cloelia are still part of our classical heritage.

We have here a well-known story. It is exactly dated (509 B.C.). It assumes that Rome was a powerful city under the kings who ruled an extensive territory in Latium and Etruria. It describes the revolutionary change from monarchy to an aristocratic constitution with two annual consuls. Our task is to decide whether this story makes sense within the context of our present knowledge of early Latium and Etruria and within the terms of reference of our present methods in source criticism.

The credibility of the traditional account has been challenged from every point of view. In very recent years authoritative scholars have maintained that Rome was never a powerful state under the kings, that the transition from monarchy to republic was gradual and took at first the form of replacement of the king by an annual dictator. Early Roman historians have been accused of being forgers and liars. Even the date of the fall of the monarchy has been transferred from 509 B.C. to a later year—either 475 B.C. or 450 B.C. circa.

A. Alföldi has submitted the literary evidence to a searching negative analysis in his *Early Rome and the Latins* (1965). E. Gjerstad has thoroughly re-examined the archaeological evidence in his *Early Rome* (1953–67). The constitutional facts have been reinterpreted by S. Mazzarino, *Dalla monarchia allo stato repubblicano* (1945); Krister Hanell, *Das altrömische eponyme Amt* (1946); R. Werner, *Der Beginn der römischen Republik* (1963); etc.

Before I go into these recent theories, however, I must glance back to the end of the nineteenth century, when a new phase of the study of Roman archaic history began.

II

In 1898 Ettore Pais published his *Storia di Roma*, in which he tried to prove that the kings of Rome had never existed; they were all old gods. One year later Giacomo Boni discovered in the Roman Forum the so-called *Lapis Niger*, an archaic inscription in which there was the word *regi*. The inscription was found in a place which according to an ancient tradition was the tomb of Romulus. The discovery caused a sensation. The tradition about the ancient kings seemed to have been vindicated. Pais seemed to have been refuted overnight. From the point of view of strict logic all this was nonsense. The inscription, or rather the fragment of an inscription, was and still is almost unintelligible, but certainly had nothing to do with Romulus. It is not even certain that the word *regi* is the dative of *rex* rather than the infinitive passive of the verb *regere*. Yet the emotions roused by the discovery were not misplaced. For the first time archaeology was intervening in the centuries-old controversy about the origins of Rome. Soon the discovery of very archaic tombs in the Forum was to confirm the possibility of studying the origins of Rome with the help of archaeology. Giacomo Boni did for Rome what Schliemann did for Troy and

Mycenae. Both, incidentally, were inspired by the same romantic faith in the truth of the tradition.

But after the first discoveries of about 1900 there was an interruption in research: there was an even worse interruption in the publication of the finds. It would take us too far to explain this interruption. The First World War and fascism had something to do with it. The fascists encouraged exploration of the imperial Fora rather than of the old monuments of primitive Rome. The discovery of the archaic temples in the area of the Church of Sant'Omobono, not far from the Capitol, happened in 1938, but became generally known only twenty years later.

The exploration of the Forum and the Palatine started again about 1947 under the able guidance of Sopraintendente Pietro Romanelli. The discovery of the archaic huts on the Palatine, of new and even more archaic tombs on the Forum, was the most important result. In the less nationalistic climate of the years after the Second World War, international co-operation developed in these studies. The Swedish archaeologist E. Gjerstad was allowed to make new soundings for stratigraphical purposes and, what was more important, was allowed to publish much that had remained unpublished of the old explorations. His masterly archaeological survey of early Rome has now been completed in four volumes, and he has already outlined his theory about the origins of Rome, which is to be developed in two further volumes. Gjerstad's account is very different from the traditional one, especially in matters of chronology. Gjerstad thinks he can prove that Rome was founded, not in 753 B.C., but about 575 B.C. He also believes that the monarchy ended, not about 509 B.C., but about 450 B.C.

His theories have given rise to lively controversy. In its turn this controversy has inspired new archaeological research. For the moment I want to mention only the exploration of the building of the *Regia* in the Forum by Frank Brown of the American Academy in Rome, because it has yielded new essential data about the origins of the Republic. Indeed, what has become clearer in the last years is that the history of the origins of the Republic is much more directly affected by the new discoveries than is the nebulous age of the kings. I shall therefore mainly deal with the beginnings of the Republic.

Another point has emerged from all these recent discussions. It is that it would be too simple to speak of a confrontation between literary tradition and archaeological data. Linguistic data are equally important. Furthermore, literary tradition is an inadequate label for a very complex conglomeration of data. What we call literary tradition includes data about religious ceremonies and political institutions which cannot be treated in the same way as one would treat the account of a battle, an embassy, or a conspiracy. The element of conservatism in political and religious institutions is too obvious to need further elucidation. On the other hand, archaeology, too, is a conglomeration of different elements. Some stones speak more intelligibly than others. Those which speak most intelligibly, because they are inscribed, have much in common with literary tradition. In many cases inscriptions contain lists of magistrates, mention political and religious institutions, allude to battles and embassies and conspiracies, just as much as literary texts do. In these cases there is no a priori reason to conclude that what an inscription says is invariably more credible than what literary texts say. In the last years Greek historians have been disputing whether it is Herodotus or the newly discovered Themistocles inscription which is more credible with regard to the events that led to the battle of Salamis.

Historians of antiquity who believe in weighing the claims of archaeology against the claims of literary tradition can be dismissed as too naïve members of their profession. The real task of the historian is to analyze all the data he has and to try to account for all of them. But the process of analyzing data is never an individual performance. It is invariably, though in varying degrees, a collective enterprise of scholars of different countries, different academic traditions, different generations—indeed, different centuries. Especially in the study of classical antiquity, we cannot lightly ignore the fact that the texts we study, the inscriptions we read, the monuments we see, have for the most part been known to previous generations of scholars and in some cases have been studied uninterruptedly since antiquity. The editions we use, the meaning we attribute to the texts, the identification and the description of ancient monuments, are the result of the work of centuries. Any new interpreter must be aware of past interpreters: he who is not aware of past interpreters will still be influenced by them, but uncritically, because, after all, awareness is the foundation of criticism. The historian must therefore be able to account not only for all the data he possesses but also for all the interpretations he is aware of.

There is a basic similarity between accounting for ancient data and accounting for modern, or less than modern, interpretations of ancient data. The historian is not supposed to produce all the data or all the modern interpretations of ancient data. He must produce those he considers most important—and he may add those he has good reason to believe are less well known to his readers. For the rest, he must be ready to answer questions if challenged. Complete collections of sources can hardly be expected, except where the sources are few. Complete bibliographies of modern works are normally useless. But every historian must be prepared to explain why he has not mentioned a certain source or a certain modern interpretation.

My task is therefore to give my own interpretations, with as much support from ancient data and as much background of previous interpretations as I consider necessary. I hope that I shall be challenged both on ancient data and on modern interpretations. What I am trying to show by an example is how a modern historian must treat a traditional account of a period for which tradition is obviously unsafe. As for the tradition itself, I shall only remind you that Roman history began to be written in Rome under Greek influence about 200 B.C. When Fabius Pictor, the first Roman historian, wrote about the beginnings of the Republic, he claimed by implication to know what had happened 300 years before him. We do not know what his sources were. In fact, so little of his work has come down to us that we can only form a vague idea of what it was. Professor Alföldi's recent indictment (in *Early Rome and the Latins*) of Fabius as a liar and a forger falls to the ground simply because we have not enough of Fabius to justify any precise opinion about his honesty—let alone his reliability, which is a different matter. Later historians enlarged, corrected, modified, and even transformed his account to an extent which we cannot easily assess. What we read in Diodorus, Dionysius of Halicarnassus, and Livy is the result of two centuries of writing and rewriting Roman archaic history after Fabius Pictor. What we call Roman tradition about the origins of the Republic is in fact what we read in Diodorus, Dionysius, and Livy. It is safer to discuss Diodorus, Dionysius, and Livy, who have come down to us, than Fabius, who has not.

III

As Thucydides was pleased to tell his readers twice (1. 20; 6. 59), it was not Harmodios and Aristogeiton who put an end to tyranny in Athens. It was the Spartan army four years after the murder of Hipparchos. In Rome there was no Thucydides to expose the story of Lucretia's suicide as the immediate cause of the fall of the monarchy. But even in Rome the truth did not remain entirely concealed from the students of history who during the early Empire had some access to Etruscan sources. Pliny the Elder (*N.H.* 34. 139) and Tacitus (*Hist.* 3. 72) knew that after the fall of the Tarquinii another Etruscan king, Porsenna, had occupied Rome for a while and inflicted heavy conditions on the Romans. The heroic feats of Horatius Cocles, Mucius Scaevola, Cloelia, did not persuade him to abandon the siege of Rome, which was the Roman version of the story. Even if Porsenna had not formally made himself king of Rome as successor to Tarquinius Superbus, there could have been no freedom in Rome so long as Porsenna was there to impose his will.

We can go further than Pliny and Tacitus did. Greek and Roman historians record that the tyrant Aristodemus of Cumae in conjunction with a Latin army defeated Porsenna at the battle of Aricia about 505 B.C. (Dionys. 5. 36; Liv. 2. 14; Fest. *ep.* 487 L.). We may infer that this defeat was the real cause of Porsenna's retreat from Rome after having occupied it. The coalition of the Cumaeans and of the Latin League against Porsenna is the likely explanation of why Rome emerged to freedom after having fallen from the hands of Tarquinius into those of Porsenna.

This is all we can state or reasonably guess about the immediate circumstances of the transition from the monarchy to the Republic. In Rome, as in Athens, a love affair, a personal offense, may well have contributed to the end of the tyrannical government. There is no reason to deny the substantial truth of Lucretia's story. But only military defeat inflicted by a third power brought about the "liberation."

Yet our inquiry about the transition from the monarchic to the republican regime begins just at this point. The whole study of archaic Rome has entered a new stage characterized by new systematic collections of the evidence, by new important discoveries, and by new revolutionary theories. At first only the monarchic period was affected by the new research. But soon it became obvious that our evaluation of the transition from the monarchy to the Republic also was involved. Indeed, the progress of research has brought about new discoveries which are perhaps more relevant to the early years of the Republic than to the last period of the monarchy. Such are the discoveries in the sanctuaries of Pyrgi and Lavinium, not to mention again the *Regia* in Rome. We are, then, faced by two orders of questions regarding the origins of the Roman Republic:

1. Have the chronology and the interpretation of the events that led to the establishment of the Republic been affected by the new facts and the new theories concerning the Roman monarchy?

2. What is the significance of the new facts directly bearing on the origins of the Roman Republic?

I shall have to face both questions. But there is a third point to which I attribute even more importance and to which I shall try to give due attention. Recent discussions on the origins of the Roman Republic may not have been concerned with the most interesting problems. We have heard a great deal about

Etruscan rule in Rome, about the interruption of Greek imports, about the relation between patriciate and cavalry, about Fabius Pictor, who has been presented
to us as the archforger of Roman pseudo history. As we might expect, we have
also had a revival of the old discussion about the authenticity of the *fasti*, that is,
of the official list of the consuls. But according to Roman tradition the first fifty
years of the Republic were a period of struggle between patricians and plebeians.
There is very little about plebeians in recent books, such as those by A. Alföldi.
There is place for a few pertinent questions about the rise of the *plebs* within
the context of the young Republic. In asking them I am carrying a step further
the revision of accepted views on the social structure of the early Republic which
I started in my article "Procum Patricium" in the *Journal of Roman Studies*,
1966, and continued in my contribution to the 1966 *Entretiens* of the Fondation
Hardt. The 1966 *Entretiens* were entirely devoted to the origins of the Roman
Republic. The discussions were of considerable interest, and my debt to the
other members of that "symposium" is obvious. Naturally enough, Gjerstad's
admirable work on the archaeological evidence and Alföldi's penetrating analysis
of the literary tradition were at the center of the discussion. By dealing with the
origins of the *plebs* I seemed at first to be outside the mainstream of the discussion. But it soon became apparent from the debate that no clear understanding
of the origins of the Roman Republic is possible without taking into account
the implications of the surprising organization of the Roman *plebs*. After so much
talk on the Roman patricians, it is the Roman *plebs* that have to be put back on
the map.

IV

I begin with the chronological question. Contemporary scholars have produced various objections against the traditional date for the beginning of the
Roman Republic in or near 509 B.C. Alternative dates of about 475 and even 450
B.C. have found authoritative supporters. It has been said that archaeology shows
that the Etruscan monarchy survived for another fifty years after 500 B.C. But it
is not evident how archaeology can help in questions of this kind. There is no
obvious connection between the political regime and the importation of Etruscan
terra cottas and Greek vases. What is true is that Rome became poorer in the
fifth century B.C. because of internal struggles and external wars. This almost
certainly explains the interruption in the building of new temples after 480 B.C.
—and may well explain more generally the reduction in luxury imports from
Greece and Etruria. Gjerstad also tried to show that buildings attributed to

7

Servius Tullius belong to the period around 500 B.C. He argued that, if Servius Tullius has to be dated according to the date of his buildings, the end of the monarchy must be placed fifty years later, about 450 B.C. But buildings have often been attributed to the wrong man; and there is in this case an additional factor of doubt in the very nature of the evidence for dating early Roman buildings. Terra-cotta revetments had a short life. The terra cottas we find in a building are not necessarily the earliest revetments of the building itself.

I shall not dwell on these arguments, because I have already discussed them elsewhere, in the *Journal of Roman Studies*, 1963. However, we must be clear in our minds about the nature of Roman chronology for the early Republic. An examination of the main facts indicates elements of doubt which I shall duly point out, but it also leaves us reasonably reassured about the basic soundness of the Roman traditional date of the end of the monarchy. Indeed, in my opinion, the discovery of the Pyrgi inscriptions reinforces the claims of tradition.

The Romans had two chronological systems. One was based on lists of their yearly magistrates, the consuls; the other was dependent on the *clavus annalis*, the nail which every year at the ides of September was planted into the wall of the temple of Jupiter Capitolinus by whoever was the supreme magistrate in Rome (Liv. 7. 3. 5–7). The dating by consuls was supposed to have started with the beginning of the Republic. The dating by nails presumably started with the inauguration of the temple of Jupiter Capitolinus, though the only explicit statement on the subject is concealed in a corrupt passage of Livy. What we are told by the Romans themselves is that the Republican era and the Capitoline era were in practice identical, because the temple of Jupiter had been dedicated in the first year of the Republic. This belief in the identity of the Republican and Capitoline eras already existed in 304 B.C., when Cn. Flavius dedicated his *aedem Concordiae* as *CCIIII annis post Capitolinam dedicatam* (Plin. N.H. 33. 1. 19). The date which he implied for the temple of Jupiter was 507 B.C., which is practically identical with the date of the foundation of the Republic, as stated in the *fasti*. It is unnecessary to labor the point that differences of a few years in the reckonings of the beginning of the Republic are of no consequence. It would be pleasant to believe that Cn. Flavius, before writing his dedication, went to the temple of Jupiter and made certain that there were 204 nails in the wall. This is what Professor Alföldi believes. But it is more sensible to assume that Cn. Flavius accepted as true the identification of the Capitoline era with the Republican era, and that he ascribed to the Capitoline era the period of 204 years which he had derived from consulting the consular *fasti*. In fact it is not even certain that the planting of the annual nail was still going on in the time of Cn. Flavius.

8

We can of course doubt the correctness of this equation between Capitoline era and Republican era, even if we know that it was accepted as early as 304 B.C. We can for instance argue that the temple of Jupiter Capitolinus had been dedicated under the kings before the beginning of the Republic and/or that the *fasti consulares* had already started under the kings. Professor Hanell in fact maintains with considerable ingenuity that in Rome, as in Sparta and in Assyria, there were eponymous yearly magistrates under the kings.

The theoretical possibility that both the Capitoline era and the consular *fasti* started under the kings and therefore do not define the beginning of the Republic must be granted. But one would have to explain why the Romans went so wrong over their own chronology. One of the new facts that have apparently emerged from the inscriptions of Pyrgi is that the local king or tyrant Tiberius Velianas dates his own dedications according to the years of his own reign. The Phoenician text says "in the third year of his kingdom." If we accept the date of about 500 B.C. for these inscriptions, we have a chronologically suitable analogy of what to expect in Rome under the kings: neither a Capitoline era nor consular *fasti*, but plain regnal years. Now, we know of one Roman religious document of the early third century B.C. which was dated by the *rex sacrificulus* L. Postumius Albinus (Plin. *N.H.* 11. 186). Though we cannot be certain that this type of dating is a survival from the monarchic period, such survival seems still to be the most natural explanation. It will be conceded that a date according to the *rex sacrificulus* is more likely to be monarchic in origin than a date according to the consuls.

We can furthermore produce two independent confirmations of the theory that the Romans preserved a fairly correct date of the end of the monarchy. One confirmation is provided by the recent American excavations in the Forum. As we shall later see in greater detail, Professor Frank Brown has been able to show that the *Regia* was built *de novo* about 500 B.C., not as a house for an ordinary king, but as an office and place of cult for the *rex sacrificulus*. In other words, the house for the republican substitute for the king goes back to the traditional date of the beginning of the Republic. The agreement between the date of the *Regia* and the beginning of the *fasti*, even if inevitably an approximate one, cannot be fortuitous. Second, it was observed long ago that the historians of Cumae knew that the tyranny of Aristodemus was contemporary with the end of the monarchy in Rome; and the tyranny of Aristodemus has been independently dated in the last years of the sixth century B.C. This synchronism with the history of Cumae is the strongest single argument for the correctness of Roman republican chronology.

9

From whatever angle one considers the chronology of the early Republic, it is clear that the difficulties in accepting the traditional dates are far less great than the difficulties in replacing them by newly made ones. It does not follow from this that the names of the consular *fasti* should be accepted without reservations. But it seems at least probable that there was never any need to interpolate the *fasti* in order to make them agree with the Capitoline era. The two eras must have coincided naturally. In this matter of interpolations no dogmatic statement is of any use. If better arguments against the authenticity of the *fasti* are produced in the future, we shall accept them gladly. The arguments which one used to hear from Ettore Pais or which nowadays one finds in R. Werner's *Der Beginn der römischen Republik* amount to a *petitio principii*: the critic decides what to expect from the *fasti* and expunges names that do not come up to expectation. The *petitio principii* is particularly flagrant in the case of the so-called plebeian names because on the one hand it is not certain that they were plebeian and on the other hand it is not certain that plebeian names deserve to be rejected from the *fasti*.

v

The main benefit to be derived from taking a date of about 500 B.C. as the beginning of the Republic is that it leaves a space of more than fifty years between the end of the monarchy and the decemvirate. This period of time seems to be necessary to make sense of the very involved constitutional developments which led to the decemvirate. But this advantage is partly offset by the obscurity of Italian history in the second half of the sixth century B.C. One simple example indicates the conflict of opinions among modern historians on this matter.

There is a strange story in Theophrastus, *Historia Plantarum* (5. 8. 2), that the Romans tried to establish a colony in Corsica and failed. Theophrastus has romantic details. Now, it is interesting to compare the comments by two Italian historians on this strange story. In 1907 G. De Sanctis stated in his *Storia dei Romani* that in the fourth century B.C., when Theophrastus wrote, or before the fourth century, the Romans could not think of colonizing Corsica: he suggested, therefore, that Theophrastus had wrongly attributed to Rome something done by an Etruscan city such as Caere. De Sanctis' advice was: read *Caere* where Theophrastus writes *Rome*. About sixty years later Mazzarino re-examined the passage in his *Il pensiero storico classico* (1966). He found the story of Rome's attempt to colonize Corsica perfectly credible, but did not place it in the fourth century B.C. He linked the alleged Roman attempt with the struggle

10

between Phocaeans and Etruscans for the rule of Corsica which culminated in the battle of Alalia about 540 B.C. According to Mazzarino, Herodotus forgot to tell us that the Etruscan, and especially Caerite, struggle against the Phocaeans had been organized in Rome by King Tarquinius Superbus. The battle of Alalia becomes a Roman victory. Mazzarino's advice is: read *Rome* where Herodotus (1. 167) writes *Caere*. The Roman failure to plant the colony in Corsica was only a less fortunate development of the same struggle. Mazzarino and De Sanctis represent two diametrically opposed interpretations of early Roman history. De Sanctis attributed little importance to the rule of the Etruscan kings in Rome, did not believe that the Romans were in a position to have a pact with Carthage about 500 B.C., did not even believe that the Romans were able to venture upon the Tyrrhenian sea in the fourth century B.C. Mazzarino takes the Tarquinii who ruled Rome to be the center of a great Etruscan coalition against the Greeks and of course has no difficulty in accepting the Polybian date for the first treaty with Carthage, about 500 B.C. In his view the Romans were the leaders of a great confederation under the last kings.

The discrepancy between De Sanctis and Mazzarino is wide enough, but it is nothing in comparison with the gulf that separates both from the view recently propounded by Professor Alföldi with his customary boldness and skill. Alföldi believes that Rome became an independent power only with the end of the monarchy. During the last 150 years of the monarchy (that is from 650 B.C.) Rome was under the rule of one Etruscan city after another. The rule of the Tarquinii was literally a rule of the city of Tarquinia over Rome. Other Etruscan cities, such as Caere, Vulci, and Veii, would have ruled over Rome in other periods.

Such startling conclusions deserve close scrutiny. The result, in my opinion, is that none of Alföldi's suggestions can survive. His only evidence for the rule of Caere over Rome is the story of Cato (fr. 12 Peter) and other sources about King Mezentius of Caere. What the sources say is that during a war the Latins promised to consecrate each year's vintage to Jupiter if they did not fall under the rule of Mezentius. Being victorious, they kept their promise. Alföldi interprets the story to mean that "Mezentius . . . is said to have imposed on the Latins the humiliating obligation to deliver to him each year the wine they produced" (*Early Rome*, p. 210). It is clear that the texts say the opposite of what Alföldi reads into them. They imply that Mezentius of Caere failed to conquer the Latins. Incidentally, Rome was not thought to have existed at the time of King Mezentius: so the story does not apply to Rome in any case.

Less flimsy, but not therefore convincing, are the arguments produced by

Alföldi to show that Vulci had its turn in ruling over Rome. Alföldi quotes the well-known popular etymology of the Roman *Capitolium*'s deriving its name from the head—the *caput*—of a man called *Olus* which was found there: *Capitolium* from *caput oli*. As Olus is another form of the name Aulus, some scholars (among them M. Pallottino) have rightly identified this Olus with Aulus Vibenna, the brother of Caele Vibenna from Vulci, an Etruscan warrior connected with the legend of early Rome. The identification is probable because Olus is called *Vulcentanus*, a man of Vulci, by Arnobius (6. 7). But if the head of Aulus Vibenna from Vulci was supposed to have been discovered in the Capitol, it does not follow that Vulci ruled Rome—it does not even follow that Aulus Vibenna ruled over Rome. In the main tradition the brothers Vibenna seem to have been kingmakers rather than kings. Only the so-called chronographer of the year 354 B.C. calls Olus a king (p. 114 Frick = 144 Mommsen). I do not see any reason to agree with Alföldi's assertion: "the statement of a late chronicle calling him *rex*, derived from old roots" (*Early Rome*, p. 217). It is more likely that either the chronographer of the year 354 B.C. or his source decided that the man who gave the Capitol its name must have been a king: in any case neither the chronographer nor his source seems to have known that Olus was Aulus Vibenna. Alföldi tries to combine his theories about the alleged King Aulus Vibenna with a new interpretation of the well-known Vulci paintings of about 300 B.C. in order to prove that "not long after the middle of the sixth century, a Vulcentane army, vanquished by a coalition of Etruscan powers, was nevertheless able to capture Rome whose king, Gnaeus Tarquinius, fell in the war against Vulci" (*Early Rome*, p. 230). The relevant paintings show, as we all remember, a Marce Camitlnas successfully attacking a Cneve Tarchu[nies] Rumach, a Gnaeus Tarquinius Romanus. There is no evidence that that Cneve Tarchu[nies] was a king of Rome, and even less evidence that his conqueror, or anybody else from Vulci, became king of Rome instead of Cneve Tarchu[nies]. But if we were to accept the hypothesis that the paintings of Vulci allude to an episode of the Roman monarchy, the natural consequence would be to take Marce Camitlnas as the successor of Tarquinius, not Aulus Vibenna. I fear that Alföldi—in making Aulus Vibenna a king of Rome—is adding a new myth to the many myths of early Roman history.

Finally, Alföldi advances the theory that Veii also ruled over Rome. I cannot summarize his evidence, because it simply does not exist. The fact that archaeological evidence shows Veii to have been powerful and well connected by roads with Latium and Etruria has no relevance to the alleged control of Rome. Alföldi adds that "the visit of the Veientan king Vel Vibe in Alba Longa in the *Lupus* of Naevius [fr. 3 Ribbeck] is a mythical paraphrase of the encroachment of Veii on Latium in the late sixth century" (p. 234). Even if we knew more about Naevius' tragedies and their sources, Alföldi's inference from a tragedy of the late third century to the history of the late sixth century would remain a wild guess. But what can we really deduce from two partly corrupted lines such as

> Vel Veiens regem salutat Vibe Albanum Amulium
> comiter senem sapientem. Contra redhostis . . . ?

To sum up, there is no evidence that Rome was under the control of any other city during the monarchic period, except for a short time under Porsenna, when monarchic institutions were crumbling in Rome. The rule of the Tarquinii was a rule by foreigners, but was not a foreign rule in the sense that it implied subservience of Rome to another city. The rule of the Tarquinii was not the rule of Tarquinia. An elogium found at Tarquinia (*Not. Scav.* [1948], 266, n. 77) may be construed to say that somebody from Tarquinia did something to nine Latin places, but Rome would never be anonymously included among such places. The rule of kings of foreign extraction is a sociologically well-defined phenomenon not to be confused with foreign rule.

The point is important. The end of the monarchy in Rome would have a different meaning if we had to envisage it as the end of a foreign rule which had lasted for 150 years. In my view Rome was an independent and comparatively powerful city during the sixth century B.C. and fell under foreign rule only in the very process of transition from the monarchic to the republican regime. This view involves two consequences. First, there is no reason to reject the tradition which was supported by epigraphical evidence that Servius Tullius organized a Latin center in the Aventine temple of Diana. Dionysius of Halicarnassus had epigraphical evidence for his attribution of the *Foedus Latinum* to Servius Tullius (4. 26). We do not know how good this evidence was, but it shows at least that the notion of the *"grande Roma dei Tarquinii"* was not invented by Fabius Pictor and willfully spread by Giorgio Pasquali, as Alföldi implies. Second, there is no reason to deny what tradition partly states and partly implies, namely, that at the end of the monarchy the Roman army included six centuries of knights and sixty centuries of footmen. The existence of a federal center in Rome and the conspicuous size of the Roman army go together. Both point to the same conclusion—which archaeology confirms: Rome was rich and powerful at the end of the monarchy.

The power of the Latins under Roman leadership in the sixth century is probably confirmed by the lines of Hesiod's *Theogony* 1011–16 which are now taken as a sixth-century addition to the original Hesiodic text. These lines speak of Agrios and Latinos as rulers of Etruria. Agrios may or may not be Silvius, a legendary Latin figure. Latinos, as far as we know, can only symbolize the power of the Latin League under the Roman leadership. I cannot find any other historical situation of the sixth century or earlier which fits this statement. The Greeks of the sixth century must have known the power of the Latins over the Etruscans.

Alföldi's seven arguments against the Polybian date of the treaty between Rome and Carthage (*Early Rome*, pp. 350ff.) are so weak as to make it unnecessary to discuss them in detail. But even the more pertinent objections by R. Werner, based as they are on speculations about the power of Carthage about 480 B.C., are not cogent. The fact is that the recent discovery of the dedications by Tiberius Velianas at Caere has provided unexpected support for the Polybian date which cannot be overestimated. The date of these inscriptions is approximately fixed about 500 B.C. by the archaeological context. Can it be simple coincidence that Polybius placed the first treaty between Rome and Carthage around 500 B.C., at a time when the Carthaginians were in a position of extraordinary prestige and influence in neighboring Caere? Alföldi assumes that Polybius was deceived by Fabius Pictor, "the only possible author of this forgery" (*Early Rome*, p. 352). But the Fabii were traditionally well acquainted with Etruscan affairs, even with the Etruscan language. The date of about 500 B.C. for the treaty with Carthage would gain in authority if we could assume with Alföldi that Polybius derived it from Fabius Pictor. Unfortunately, we have no good reason for making such an assumption. We do not know which date Fabius attributed to the first treaty between Rome and Carthage.

VI

I am therefore a traditionalist where the chronology of the end of monarchy in Rome is concerned. I believe that the end happened about 500 B.C., more or less where the Roman historians put it. But I am even more deplorably conservative in my constitutional history. Roman historians thought that when the Tarquins were thrown out the Romans began to elect two magistrates every year with powers equivalent to those of the old king. These magistrates were called *praetores* or *consules,* and the latter name prevailed. But, according to the same historians, certain religious functions of the kings (in relation, for instance, to the calendar) were not considered capable of being transferred to the new *praetores.* They were vested in a man chosen for life under the official name of *rex sacrorum* or the unofficial one of *rex sacrificulus.*

What I am going to argue is that these two elements of the traditional account—the replacement of the king by two yearly *praetores* and the creation of a life-priest called *rex sacrorum*—are perfectly credible, more credible than the many modern theories which claim to be better than Roman tradition. I am also going to argue that these and other elements of the traditional account confirm that Greek influence was at work in central Italy in the period 500–450 B.C. Traditional chronology and traditional constitutional history support each other.

The first question to be asked is how the Romans could have gone wrong over the most elementary facts of their constitutional history. Legends could easily develop about the men and the women who brought about the end of the tyranny: Brutus, Lucretia, Cloelia, Mucius Scaevola. We shall not be concerned with them further. But why should the Romans say that two yearly *praetores* or *consules* replaced the king, if that was not the truth? How could they forget the character of the momentous change from monarchy to Republic? Did they have ulterior motives to conceal the truth? If so, what motives? These are questions which have never been satisfactorily answered by the modern historians who believe that the Roman historians either did not know the true facts about the creation of consulship or concealed them.

Let us begin with the *rex sacrorum*, because his presence has been regarded as a proof that there was no abrupt ejection of the kings from Rome. The *rex sacrorum*, whose existence is documented in Rome not only in republican times but even under the emperors, has been taken by some scholars to be the original king in a state of extreme decline, not (as tradition states) a priest appointed for the specific purpose of replacing the king. It is contended that little by little the king lost his political and military power and was relegated to a few and not very important religious functions under the supervision of the new head of the Roman religion: the *pontifex maximus.* This is a theory which found favor even with so prudent a critic of Roman tradition as my teacher G. De Sanctis. Not surprisingly, for De Sanctis had been a historian of Athens before becoming a historian of Rome; and Athens offered the best analogy for the alleged progressive decline of the *rex* in Rome. The evidence, as far as we have it, seems to indicate that the Athenian king, the *basileus*, had been progressively stripped of his powers, had become an annual magistrate, and had been included in the college of the nine archons as the *archon basileus*—a man with religious prestige but no military powers. Yet the Greek world also offers examples of kings stripped of their powers and reduced to the position of harmless priests, not by evolution, but by revolution. The best-known example is that of the king of Cyrene who, according to Herodotus, was transformed overnight into a *rex sacrorum* by a revolution in the sixth century B.C. (4. 161).

Thus the Greek analogies do not help us to decide whether in Rome the monarchy slowly declined or was replaced by revolution. What the Greeks do help us to understand, however, is the meaning of the replacement of a real king by a priest, the *rex sacrorum*. What we observe in Greece amounts to a separation of religious functions from political and military power. We observe a tendency to get rid of kings as political and military leaders and to avoid endowing their successors with religious powers. Certain specific religious ceremonies were considered inseparable from kingship and therefore had to be left in the hands either of the natural descendants of the kings (such as the *Basileidai* in Ephesus) or of elected officials who were called kings for the sake of continuity. But this religious respect for certain functions of the kings intensified the separation of political life from religious life and, no doubt, was exploited for that purpose. The movement toward the separation of political power from religious power was not confined to the Greeks. It also developed among Etruscans and Latins, and we may legitimately suspect that Greek influence was not absent. Etruscans and Latins were receptive to Greek ideas, and the Greek colony of Cumae—a great center of political and religious movements at the end of the sixth century B.C.—was not very far from Rome.

The *rex sacrorum* was not an isolated phenomenon of Rome. It is to be found in several other Latin cities, such as Lanuvium, Tusculum, Velitrae. The equivalent of a *rex sacrorum* seems to appear in Etruscan inscriptions. There is no reason to believe that in all these cases the *rex sacrorum* was an imitation of the Roman *rex sacrorum*. We must rather acknowledge that other cities developed on parallel lines to Rome. There is indeed one aspect of the evolution of certain Latin cities which cannot be related to Roman models. We find that in Lanuvium and (probably) Alba Longa a *rex sacrorum* and a *dictator* regularly coexisted as annual officials: the institutions of Alba Longa, as is well known, were preserved by the Romans after the destruction of the city. The *dictator* was not a regular magistrate in Rome, but some Latin cities appointed an annual head called *dictator*: *dictator* was also the name of the annual leader of the Latin League. We must therefore assume that in Lanuvium, in Alba Longa, and, no doubt, in other Latin cities the old king was replaced by an annual *dictator*, except for certain religious functions which were attributed to a *rex sacrorum*.

The way in which the *rex sacrorum* was chosen in Rome confirms that there was no constitutional continuity between the old king and his *Ersatz*.

Though many details are unknown, what is certain is the negative fact that the *rex sacrorum* was not chosen by the *comitia* as the old king must have been. The *pontifex maximus* selected the *rex sacrorum* from a list of patrician names submitted to him, as it seems, by the college of the pontiffs (Liv. 40. 42; Dionys. 5. 1. 4). A ceremony of inauguration followed before the *comitia calata*, that is, before the *comitia* in their passive function as witnesses. It is at least clear that the founders of the Roman Republic did their best to prevent the kind of proper election of the *rex sacrorum* which might become politically important. Furthermore, they declared the position of the *rex sacrorum* incompatible with that of an ordinary magistrate of the Roman state. This restriction was unusual. Ordinary pontiffs, even the *pontifex maximus*, did not suffer from any such restriction. Only the *flamen dialis* was debarred from a political career. The imposition of a ban on the political and military career of the *rex sacrorum* implies the firm determination to keep him powerless. In later times the office of the *rex sacrorum* was used to provide a young patrician with a dignified position that would keep him out of mischief.

Archaeology appears to confirm that the *rex sacrorum* was not a decayed king but, as tradition states, a priest created about 500 B.C. to replace the king in some of his functions. As I have said, the American Academy in Rome, under the leadership of Frank Brown, has now thoroughly explored the building of the *Regia* in the Forum. The results have just been made public by Brown in Volume 13 of the *Entretiens* of the Fondation Hardt. At the end of the Republic the *Regia* was occupied by the *pontifex maximus*, but in earlier times it had belonged to the *rex*, as the name indicates. The previous occupation by a *rex* was confirmed by the discovery of a *bucchero* vase (sixth or fifth century B.C.) in the building, with the name *rex* inscribed in it. The question which was often asked by modern scholars was whether the *rex* occupying the *Regia* had originally been the monarch of Rome or whether the *Regia* had been built as the official residence for the *rex sacrorum*. Frank Brown has been able to answer all these questions fairly conclusively. The *Regia* was built toward the end of the sixth century B.C. over the ruins of a temple which had been destroyed by fire in the third quarter of the sixth century. The *Regia* was built not as a dwelling but for the performance of sacred ceremonies. Hence, as F. Brown writes, it "was built not for a rex, but for a rex sacrorum." It was contemporary with the establishment of the Republic.

We can therefore conclude that the revolutionary aristocrats who threw out the Tarquinii had definite ideas, probably of Greek origin, about the separation of religious leadership and military command. They embodied their ideas in the creation of the *rex sacrorum*. In doing this they probably followed the example of other Latin cities, such as Lanuvium and Alba Longa. I shall not discuss here the possibility that in Alba Longa the *rex sacrorum* had been introduced by the Roman king Tullius Hostilius when he destroyed Alba Longa as a political and military center but wanted to keep it alive as a religious center. This interesting possibility—a *rex sacrorum* of Alba established by a real *rex* of Rome—would take us too far.

I have now to defend the other point of my traditionalism. I believe, as I said, that two annual magistrates replaced the life-king exactly as tradition has it. In the middle of the nineteenth century W. Ihne and A. Schwegler suggested that monarchy in Rome was replaced at first by one annual *dictator* and only later by two annual consuls. Mommsen disapproved of their theories and his authority prevailed for a long time. But E. Kornemann and K. J. Beloch returned to Schwegler's conception, and over the years what was an aberrant opinion has now become orthodoxy. K. Hanell and the whole Swedish school of Roman history, A. Alföldi, R. Werner, my friends S. Mazzarino and A. Bernardi in Italy, and very recently J. Heurgon have supported the notion that there was an intermediate stage in Roman constitutional evolution represented by an annual dictatorship.

What is the basis for this opinion? Chiefly, it is the result of two convergent orders of consideration. On the one hand, the study of Etruscan, Latin, and Osco-Umbrian institutions has shown that the institution of two equal magistrates governing the state for one year or more is unusual. It is more common to have one supreme magistrate accompanied by one or more magistrates with less power. The system of two contemporaneous heads of state is a difficult one to handle: we are surprised that Sparta managed to have one for centuries. On the other hand, it has been observed that Livy 7. 3. 5–8 quotes an archaic Roman law according to which every year at the ides of September the *praetor maximus* was ordered to drive a nail into a wall of the temple of Jupiter Capitolinus. The meaning of this ceremony (probably to mark the passing of one year) does not concern us here. What this passage seems to document is the existence in Rome of a *praetor maximus* as the head of the state. The name *praetor maximus* is otherwise only found in ancient attempts to interpret what this law said: evidently the Romans themselves had no clear idea of why this particular law should mention the head of the Roman state as a *praetor maximus*, not as a simple *praetor* or *consul*. It was easy for modern scholars to observe that *maximus* implies: (*a*) the existence of more than two praetors—otherwise the text would say *praetor maior*; (*b*) the existence of one *praetor* ranking above the others.

18

The passage of Livy seemed therefore to bring Rome into line with the rest of central Italy. Historians concluded that there had been a time in which one *praetor maximus* stood above the other magistrates in Rome. This conclusion did not solve all the difficulties. The date of the law remained uncertain. Some scholars would even put it in the monarchic period: the *praetor maximus* would have been an officer of the king prior to becoming the head of the Republic. It was also difficult to decide whether the *praetor maximus* could be identified with the dictator. The identification of the *praetor maximus* with the *dictator* implied that Rome, like other Latin cities, had passed through a stage of annual dictatorship before turning to the double consulate. But this identification also had its obvious disadvantages. It did not explain the transition from the annual dictatorship to the exceptional dictatorship of later times. It did not explain why the *dictator* should be called *praetor maximus*. We know that the Roman *dictator* had a second name, *magister populi*, which was complementary to that of his subordinate, the *magister equitum*, the commander of the cavalry. A third name, *praetor maximus*, would be hard to account for, the more so because in the circumstances we should expect the *dictator* to be called *praetor maior* rather than *praetor maximus*. As the consuls, *ex hypothesi*, did not yet exist, he had only the *magister equitum* under him: he was *praetor maior*, not *praetor maximus*.

In the face of these difficulties some scholars have turned to the alternative theory that the *praetor maximus* was really something different from the *dictator*. He was a regular magistrate, while the *dictator* was an emergency commander. Thus the *praetor maximus* would appear to be the first of several *praetores*, though it is not quite clear who the other *praetores* were and what they did. J. Heurgon explains the situation in the recent volume of the *Entretiens* of the Fondation Hardt, to which I have already referred, by saying that the Roman aristocrats hurriedly elevated one of themselves to the position of *praetor maximus* when they threw the Tarquinii out.

What matters to me is that the whole theory of the *praetor maximus* as the single head of the Roman state is founded upon quicksand. The Roman tradition knows nothing of a supreme regular magistrate of this kind. All we have is a law of uncertain date saying "*ut qui praetor maximus sit idibus Septembribus clavum pangat.*" As Mommsen observed long ago, at the ides of September of any given year of the Republic, Rome could be governed by two consuls, by one *dictator* (if there was a military emergency), or by an *interrex* (if both consuls were dead or had resigned). If a law wanted to say in Latin "whoever is the head of the state at the ides of September," it had to say *qui praetor maximus sit idibus Septembris*. It has been objected that archaic Latin was not capable of this degree of abstraction. But we know too little about the Latin of the fifth century B.C. What we know is that archaic Greek could express this degree of abstraction. An inscription of Elis, which is dated in the middle of the fifth century B.C., says ὅρ μέγιστον τέλος ἔχοι καὶ τοὶ βασιλᾶες, which seems to correspond to *qui praetor maximus sit* (E. Schwyzer, *DGEE*, 409).

If Mommsen's interpretation of *praetor maximus*, which seems to me the best, is not persuasive, there are other possibilities to be considered. The Greeks called each of the Roman consuls στρατηγὸς ὕπατος. This seems to be a natural translation of *praetor maximus*. In any case what the formula στρατηγὸς ὕπατος proves is that each of the two consuls could be qualified by a superlative. Neither στρατηγὸς ὕπατος nor *praetor maximus* necessarily implies that there was only one *strategos* or one consul.

Furthermore, it is by no means certain that *maximus* in archaic Latin indicated the greatest of at least three. The differentiation of comparative and superlative is a notoriously complex process in Latin. Terence uses *maximus* for the older of two brothers (*Adelphoe* 881). Ennius calls *summus* the higher of two Oscan magistrates: "*Summus ibi capitur meddix, occiditur alter*" (*Ann.* 298 V.). The "alter" makes it clear that Ennius speaks of two *meddices* only. *Praetor maximus* may have meant nothing more than what is elsewhere called *consul maior*. We know what a *consul maior* was. In Roman constitutional practice the two consuls took turns in being accompanied by the *lictores* with all the twelve *fasces*: the consul who had the twelve *fasces* either for the day or for one month was called *maior consul* (Fest., *s.v.* "maiorem consulem," 154 L). If we remember that the consul was also called *praetor*, all that the old law about the nail may say is "which of the two consuls happens to have the *fasces* on the ides of September will drive the nail into the wall of the temple of Jupiter."

Enough has been said to show that there is a gross disproportion between the text of this law, with its mention of the *praetor maximus*, and the inferences drawn from it. The words *praetor maximus* may just be a designation of the ordinary consul or may be a way of indicating whoever was the supreme magistrate at Rome on a certain day, whether *consul* or *dictator* or *interrex*. If we prick the bubble of the *praetor maximus*, nothing is left to show that Rome was governed by annual magistrates before the two consuls were instituted.

We can go back to good old Livy, who thought that the two consuls replaced the kings. We have gained from our discussion of the term *praetor maximus* the awareness that the double consulate was not a usual form of government and implied a certain maturity. It is the maturity of the men who created the *rex sacrorum* in order to isolate and therefore sterilize the sacral power of the kings. We see an alert and ruthless aristocracy at work at the beginning of the Roman Republic.

VII

The problems of foreign policy which the Roman aristocracy inherited from the monarchy were of course modified by the fall of the monarchy but could not change overnight. Relations with the Latin League and with the Etruscan neighbors and their Carthaginian allies remained the dominant problem of the early years of the Republic—until the progress of the Volscians about 490 B.C. introduced new elements of concern, and soon of panic. The Carthaginian treaty presupposes a Rome which was still in control of a part of Latium. The *Foedus Cassianum*—the pact between the Romans and the Latins of about 490 B.C.—presents a different picture. Rome by now has recognized the independence and the equal status of the Latin League (Dionys. Hal. 6. 95. 2). The very discrepancy between the two documents shows the authenticity of both. Alföldi's attempt to disprove the early date and perhaps even the reliability of the *Foedus Cassianum*, which was preserved on a bronze tablet in Rome (Cic-Pro Balbo 23. 53), is no more convincing than his arguments against the Polybian date of the first treaty with Carthage. We know from Festus (166 L.) that the *Foedus Cassianum*, or at least a *foedus Latinum*, contained the word *pecunia*. Alföldi concludes that the word *pecunia* points to a date after 269/268 when the Romans, according to him, began to mint coins. Whatever the date of the beginnings of Roman coinage, *pecunia* is a word which originally had nothing to do with coins—it indicated cattle. What is interesting is that the Romans preserved documents about their relations with Carthage and the Latin League dating from the beginning of the Republic. They appear to have had no documents about their relations with the Etruscan cities. We must assume that the treaty with Porsenna was preserved outside Rome rather than in Rome—for reasons only too obvious. But the treaty with Carthage shows that Rome managed to remain on good terms with the principal ally of the Etruscans—and therefore with the Etruscans themselves.

The Roman aristocracy which succeeded the kings was too much involved in internal problems to attempt an adventurous foreign policy. The change in Rome from monarchy to Republic was in tune with the elimination of kings and tyrants which we know to have been a feature of contemporary Greece and which we suspect occurred in Etruscan cities more or less at the same time. Tradition makes sense when it attributes the *comitia centuriata* to Servius Tullius. The *comitia centuriata* may have contained one or more *centuriae* reserved to the patricians. This is perhaps what is meant by the very mysterious allusion of Cicero (*Orat.* 46. 156) and Festus (290 L.) to the *proci patricii.* The centuriate organization as a whole was not, however, based on the distinction between patricians and plebeians. This is a good reason for inferring that the centuriate organization cannot have been introduced in the period between 500 and 366 B.C., when the patricians ruled the Roman state. On the other hand, it is impossible to believe that the *comitia centuriata* are later than 366 B.C.—later than the *comitia tributa.* In some simple form the *comitia centuriata* must be earlier than the Republic—which is exactly what tradition says.

The struggle of the orders is therefore a feature of the new republican regime. The elimination of the kings was both cause and consequence of the rise of the patriciate. But we have no right to think that the antithesis between patricians and plebeians developed overnight with the fall of the monarchy. Nor can we assume that the contrast between patricians and plebeians was the only one existing in the early days of the Republic. There were other antithetic pairs in early Rome (such as *equites – pedites, patroni – clientes, patres – conscripti, populus – plebes, adsidui – proletarii*). All these pairs are well attested in archaic formulas. Attempts have been made to show that the *patricii* were also the *equites* and the *patroni,* whereas the *plebei* were identical with the *pedites* and the *clientes.* It has also been assumed that the *conscripti* were plebeians; and arguments have even been produced for an original identification of *populus* with patricians. But these various identifications are more easily stated than proved. The very fact that nobody would nowadays dare to identify the patricians with the *populus* (which was Mommsen's opinion) shows that the whole picture of the stratification of Roman society at the beginning of the Republic appears far more complex than the historians previously admitted.

To begin with the military aspect of the situation, I have tried elsewhere to show in detail that the usual identification of patricians with *equites* is fraught with difficulties. Taken in its crudest form the theory leads to absurdity. When Alföldi maintains that the three hundred knights of the bodyguard of the kings became the three hundred *patres* of the Senate after the end of the monarchy (*Early Rome,* p. 44), he is bound to visualize his senators as bold young men who specialized in somersaults from one to the other of the two horses the state gave them (Fest. 247 L.). But, even if we take the identification between *patres* and *equites* in the more sophisticated sense that service in the cavalry was reserved for the members of those families whose heads were called *patres*, the identification is still open to serious objections. In emergencies, the Romans elected a *magister populi*—or *dictator*—who in turn chose a *magister equitum*. The first commanded the infantry, as the second commanded the cavalry. The *magister populi* was not allowed to mount a horse, except by special authorization. The same prohibition applied to the most important priest of archaic Rome, the *flamen dialis*. It is difficult to imagine an aristocracy of horsemen in which cavalry is rigorously subordinated to infantry and in which neither the commander of the infantry nor the chief priest is allowed to mount a horse. Furthermore, the six earliest centuries of cavalry, the so-called *sex suffragia*, voted in the *comitia centuriata* after the first class. Here again we see the subordination of the cavalry to the first class. The full significance of this fact becomes clearer if one reflects that in the archaic language of Roman law the first class was called simply the class (Gellius *N.A.* 6. 13). The "class," or first class, must originally have been identical with the whole infantry. If so, the cavalry voted after the infantry. This argument, to my mind, is sufficient to exclude the possibility that the Roman *patres*—that is, the patriciate—were ever identical with the Roman *equites*.

Alföldi involves himself in a further difficulty when he accepts the theory that at the beginning of the Republic Rome was governed by one annual dictator. As the dictator was the commander of the infantry, the cavalry could not be the dominant part of the Roman army and society. Alföldi puts together two theories that are mutually incompatible and, in my opinion, both wrong. The Roman army was always an army in which the infantry prevailed—in number, in efficiency, and in authority. The leaders of the infantry, not the knights, were the masters of the Roman state. The real question is how the *patres* controlled the infantry, because obviously there were not enough of them to fill it.

The Roman cavalry is a minor problem in comparison. The cavalry, which was probably a mercenary one during the monarchy, was no doubt given an attractive status under the republican regime. It was progressively reserved for young members of the upper class, but never to the point of separating the aristocracy from the infantry. A young aristocrat served in the infantry without feeling that he was *déclassé*.

Thus the *patres* cannot be identified with the cavalry, but even less can they be identified with the Senate. It would be pleasant to imagine the Roman revolution of about 500 B.C. as the work of a compact group of gentlemen called *patres*, who filled the Senate; but this is not possible. The Roman Senate, as we know it, was made up of two groups: the *patres* and the *conscripti*. The formula for the roll-call in the Senate was *"qui patres qui conscripti"* (Liv. 2. 1. 11; Fest. 304 L.). It was an empty formula by the end of the Republic, and therefore must have been a significant one at an earlier stage. What did it imply?

Our tradition leaves us in no doubt about the fact that the *patres* were the senatorial members of a hereditary aristocracy. Certain families were called *patriciae* because they gave *patres* to the Senate. The *patres* were senators of a special kind. They were the only ones entitled to elect the *interrex* when there was no curule magistrate *cum imperio* left; they were the only ones entitled to give *auctoritas* to the deliberations of the *comitia*; they also wore a special kind of shoe to distinguish them from the other senators, the *conscripti*. The mere fact that the *patres* were the only senators to elect the *interrex* seems to indicate that the distinction between *patres* and *conscripti* must have existed during the monarchy. The *interrex* of the Republic is a pale imitation or continuation of the *interrex* of the monarchy. We must, I think, assume that by the time the monarchy was overthrown the Roman Senate was already divided into two groups, the *patres* and the *conscripti*. The *patres* belonged to a privileged group of families which had exclusive access to the priesthoods and which had special rights in the Senate. It is probable that originally the heads of these families, the *patres* par excellence, had an automatic right to belong to the Senate, but we do not hear of this automatic right during the Republic. The *conscripti* were a group of senators added to the *patres* by individual registration: hence their name of *con-scripti*. Some antiquarians of the late Republic managed to calculate that at the beginning of the Republic there were in Rome 136 *gentes patriciae* and presumably as many *patres* in the Senate (Fest. 304 L.; Plut. *Popl.* 11). The basis of the calculation is probably nothing more than a list of names of patrician *gentes*. Even so, it gives some idea of the even proportion between *patres* and *conscripti* in the Senate. The ruling class of the early Republic, in so far as we can visualize it in the Roman Senate, was probably divided between a powerful group of patricians who had a right to sit in the Senate and a tame group of *conscripti* who followed the lead of the patricians and were chosen by them *ad hominem*.

Can we now call the *conscripti* plebeians? If we assume that at any time those who were not patricians were necessarily plebeians, we have obviously no alternative. But I very much doubt that about 500 B.C. all those who were not patricians were plebeians.

We have seen that the Romans used sacred formulas in which *populus plebesque* were mentioned. The most striking is in the *Carmina Marciana*: "*iis ludis faciendis praesit praetor is qui ius populo plebeique dabit summum*" (Liv.

25. 12. 10). *Populus* in archaic Latin meant the citizens in their military and political capacity. *Populari*, to lay waste, is the destruction brought about by an army. *Pilumnoe poploe* is the archaic formula of the *Carmen Saliare* to indicate the Romans "*velut pilis uti assueti*," as Festus explains (224 L.). If *plebs* is added to *populus*, the most natural inference is that *plebs* indicates those who do not belong to the *populus*, because they have no regular admission into the army and consequently to the *comitia centuriata*—in other words, those who did not serve in the legion, that is, the *infra classem*, in the likely original meaning of this expression.

I do not want to claim that the equation between *plebs* and *infra classem* is certain. What I would suggest is that the possibility of the *plebs* being the *infra classem* must be explored in connection with the other possibility that the *conscripti* were an intermediate group between patricians and plebeians. My suggestion offers certain clear advantages for the interpretation of the evidence. One of the great puzzles of the Roman tradition for the period from 509 B.C. to 445 B.C. is that the *fasti* contain names of consuls who do not belong to those *gentes* we know to have been patrician. There are Sp. Cassius, P. Volumnius, several Sempronii, Minucii, Genucii, not to speak of the otherwise problematic Brutus. In the traditional view any man who was not a patrician was a plebeian, and therefore these names had to be regarded as plebeian. We know the consequences. Either these names had to be considered interpolations in the *fasti* just because it was inconceivable that plebeians could be consuls—or the plebeian character of these names had to be explained away in some form in order to keep them in the *fasti*. In recent years the view seems to have prevailed that after all there may have been plebeian consuls in the first half of the fifth century B.C. But tradition states that there was no plebeian consul before 366 B.C.; and common sense would lend support to the opinion that plebeian consuls were unlikely during the most violent struggles between patricians and plebeians. My suggestion opens up another possibility. What we call plebeian names in the early *fasti* were plebeian if seen from the point of view of later times, when all those who were not patricians were plebeians. Seen from the point of view of the early fifth century, however, they may have belonged to an intermediate group between patricians and plebeians, namely, to the *conscripti*. I do not see why members of families which were admitted to the Senate in the subordinate position of *conscripti* should not occasionally have been chosen as consuls. We must take the families of the *conscripti* as families of protégés of the *patres*. I would therefore maintain that, when we meet so-called plebeian names in the *fasti* of the early Republic, we have to see in them names of *gentes* which gave *conscripti* to the

Senate. But there is no reason to identify the *conscripti* with the *minores gentes* of the patriciate. True enough, the Roman antiquarians were divided among themselves about the nature of the *minores gentes* and the date of their creation. Tacitus made them contemporary with the beginning of the Republic (*Ann.* 11. 25); and Suetonius even implied in a tortured and dishonest passage *à propos* of the *gens Octavia* that the *minores gentes* were not patrician (*Aug.* 1. 2). But the main evidence seems to be strongly in favor of the notion that the *minores gentes* were patricians. Indeed, we must admit that there is nothing in our evidence to indicate that the *conscripti* were ever connected with the *minores gentes*.

VIII

We have so far tried to make a case for taking the *patres* and the *conscripti* as the two groups which composed the aristocracy of the early Republic. On the other hand, we have suggested that the plebeians may originally have been the *infra classem*, that is, those who did not serve in the legion. We were skeptical about the customary identification of the patricians with the cavalry, but we were of course unable to go back to the identification of *populus* with patricians. We have now to explain who the people who filled the *classis* were if the patricians were not numerous enough to fill it, and if the plebeians were *ex hypothesi infra classem*, outside the legion.

We all remember two of the most famous stories of the early Republic. One is that the Claudii arrived in Rome with their retinue of *clientes* after the overthrow of the kings (Liv. 2. 16. 5; Dionys. Hal. 5. 40. 5). Professor Alföldi (*Early Rome*, pp. 159ff.) presents the picture of the hated Claudii as deserters and latecomers as a malicious invention by Fabius Pictor, who belonged to the rival clan of the Fabii. It is very doubtful whether poor Fabius Pictor ever had anything to do with the tradition of the arrival of the Claudii; it is even doubtful whether the Fabii acted according to the rules of prosopographic research and dutifully hated their rivals, the Claudii. But in any case the image of the great clan of the Claudii arriving in Rome just as the fortunes of the new Republic were in the balance impressed itself very favorably on the Romans. During the Republic nobody thought any the less of the Claudii because they had not been companions of Romulus. Only in imperial times was the well-established tradition of their migration to Rome in 504 B.C. modified to make them "Ur-Römer" (Verg. *Aen.* 7. 707; Suet. *Tib.* 1). The republican date is obviously the correct one and must have been the genuine tradition of the Claudii themselves. The same can be said of the tradition about the Fabii going to their death with their clients in the battle of the river Cremera: it was the Fabian tradition and must be genuine. Diodorus noticed that certain Roman historians took the defeat of the Cremera for a defeat of the whole Roman army, not only of the Fabian *gens* and their clients (11. 53). But the *fasti* confirm that the Fabii were almost wiped out in the defeat. The historians who "normalized" the battle of the Cremera into an ordinary battle of the whole of the Roman army spoiled the archaic features of the episode. The arrival of the Claudii with their *clientes* and the defeat of the Fabii with their *clientes* give us some idea of what Roman society—and consequently the Roman army—must have been like in its early republican stage. The *clientes* were led by their *patroni*; and the *patroni* could afford migrations and battles of their own. Consequently, we may visualize the army of the early Republic as having been filled by the *clientes* of the great patrician families and to a lesser extent by the *clientes* of the *conscripti*.

In Etruscan cities an army of clients must have been a normal feature for centuries. There was apparently very little middle class of the Greek type in Etruria. More than once our sources talk of the "most powerful men of Etruria" marching with their dependents to the battlefield. There is no reason to believe that the clients, either in Rome or in Etruria, were poor. It is very difficult to distinguish between fact and fiction in the traditional obligations of the Roman clients. But the rule by which the clients were to provide ransom for their patron or a dowry for the patron's daughter presupposes that the clients were, or at least included, well-to-do individuals. There is no radical incompatibility between such an army of clients and a primitive centuriate organization. When the patricians managed to overthrow the monarchy, they were free to fill the *centuriae* with their clients. I still assume that Servius Tullius must have created the *comitia centuriata* in order to check the expansion of such an army of clients. But the success of his enterprise depended on a strong monarchy. The great *gentes* of the early Republic could not have upheld their regime if they had not filled the *classis* with their retinue.

In a republic of warriors the men who are outside the army are also those who have no political power. The plebeians must have been the men outside the *clientelae*: small landowners too poor to qualify for the *classis*, artisans, petty traders. If they encountered the rich, it was through debt-bondage (*nexum*). The *plebs* must have provided the majority of the *nexi*; and in its turn the *nexum* was one of the causes of discontent among plebeians. We must, however, add that we know far too little about the nature and frequency of the *nexum* —nor do we know whether *nexi* could be turned into *clientes* under certain conditions. Our tradition knows or purports to know of refusal of military service by plebeians and therefore implies that the plebeians were or might have been soldiers. I have no intention of denying that the plebeians were liable to auxiliary service and might even be drafted into the *classis* in emergencies. But I doubt whether the army provided the nucleus of the *plebs* or played a very significant part in the mounting resistance of the *plebs* to patrician oppression. A few negative aspects of our tradition have to be taken into account. First, we know of no battle between patricians and plebeians, as we should expect if the *plebs* had been a conspicuous part of the *classis*—and even more if it were true that the patricians were the cavalry and the plebeians the infantry. Second, the plebeian organization is not founded upon the *classis*. The plebeian *tribuni*—whether they were two or four or ten—bear no relation to the *classis* with its six *tribuni militum*. The assembly of the *plebs* was founded upon the local tribes, not upon the *centuriae*, the fighting units. The very nature of the plebeian organization seems to prove my point that the *plebs* were originally outside the *classis*. What explains the initial success of the *patres* and their allies, the *conscripti*, is that they managed for some time to keep the plebeians outside the army. They filled the *centuriae* with their rather prosperous clients while oppressing the indebted *plebs*. If we want to attribute any reality to the mutinies of the army against the patricians, we must either postulate special emergencies during which the plebeians were drafted or turn to that transitional period in which the clients began to detach themselves from the patricians and to feel like plebeians. The second alternative is worth bearing in mind. We shall try to give more substance to it by our next question.

IX

We are now ready to attempt to answer the most difficult question: If the clients and the *conscripti* were originally outside the *plebs*, how can their absorption into it be visualized and explained? It must be emphasized that the scarcity of our evidence hardly allows us to give an entirely satisfactory explanation of this process of absorption. We do not know when the *classis* was broken into several *classes*—a reform which obviously facilitated the penetration of the *plebs* into higher spheres, and perhaps also the descent of *conscripti* and *clientes* into lower ones. Nor do we know the mechanism of the election of the *tribuni militum consulari potestate*, which contributed to greater social mobility in Rome and perceptibly reduced the patrician strangle hold on the Roman state. Above all, what we cannot measure is the impact of the continual wars of the fifth century on the social and economic life of Rome. We have to envisage the progressive pauperization of the less wealthy senatorial families as a consequence of the continuous and not very successful wars against Volsci and Aequi. On the other hand, we perceive—without being able to prove—that the richest and most powerful members of the aristocracy grabbed a great deal of public land, established successful family alliances with the aristocracies of Latin cities such as Tusculum and Praeneste, and further increased their wealth through usury. From the point of view of social history we can offer only vague generalizations. We suspect that the gap between *patres* and *conscripti* must have widened, and that the *clientela* might become less attractive to the *clientes* in a state of perpetual warfare. If the *clientes* were involved in debts, the barrier separating a *cliens* from a *nexus* might well have become very thin.

Even from the strict legal point of view the situation is not very clear. We are in the habit of assuming that, by the time the Twelve Tables prohibited marriage between patricians and plebeians, the *plebs* included all non-patricians. This may be so. But is it a safe assumption? Are we certain that the Twelve Tables put an absolute prohibition on any marriage of the patricians outside the patrician *gentes*? Are we certain that as a consequence of that law the son of a *pater* could not marry the daughter of a *conscriptus*? I do not know how we can be certain. Our texts simply report the regulation *"ne conubium patribus cum plebe esset"* (Liv. 4. 4. 5; cf. Cic. *de rep.* 2. 37). The Twelve Tables are unlikely to have explained what they meant by *plebs*. The explanation of later jurists, *"plebs est ceteri cives sine senatoribus"* (Gaius *ap. Dig.* 50. 16. 238), is obviously authoritative only for later times.

But the study of the organization of the *plebs* can provide a more convincing explanation of the ultimate success of the plebeians in attracting *conscripti* and *clientes*. We are so used to the organization of the Roman *plebs* that we hardly notice what an extraordinary organization it was. It is difficult to find a parallel in the classical world. The plebeians gave themselves so coherent and efficient an organization that later it became a part of the state itself and contributed to its stability. Within a few decades from the beginning of the Republic the plebeians had organized their own parliament on the basis of the local tribes, had formalized their discussions in the *plebiscita*, and had appointed officials (the ten *tribuni* and the two *aediles*) who were more numerous and possibly more efficient than the city magistrates. The two *aediles* filled a gap in the administration of the city and provided a model for the later *aediles curules*. The tribunician techniques of *auxilium* and *intercessio* became famous both for their efficiency and for their usefulness. Basically, these powers were also at the disposal of ordinary magistrates. But the ordinary magistrate was unwilling to use his own right of veto against a colleague. The tribune of the *plebs* showed himself ready and able to prevent legislative acts and individual actions which he considered unfavorable to the *plebs*. The employment of religious sanctions in political struggles—such as the religious outlawing of the opponents of the *plebs* —appealed to the superstitious and effectively counteracted the authority of the patrician priests and pontiffs. The temple of Ceres was made into a plebeian center with archives which to all appearances were more efficiently organized than anything the patrician families had for their own records. Finally, the Aventine was put aside for the *plebs* (Liv. 3. 31. 1). It might have been conceived as a ghetto, but it proved to be a fortress.

The effectiveness of the plebeian organization becomes more apparent if one considers what the patrician Roman state was like in the fifth century B.C. No doubt the patricians kept the Senate and the *comitia* reasonably under control through their system of clientships. But the weakness of the government began to show even in the first years of the Republic, when a different power structure had to be introduced for cases of emergency. I have shown myself old-fashioned enough to believe that two consuls replaced the king. I conclude, therefore, that the creation of a *dictator* or *magister populi* in a moment of emergency was a confession of weakness. We should probably notice another serious weakness in the Roman organization of the fifth century if we were better informed about the relations between Rome and the Latin League after the so-called *Foedus Cassianum* of about 490 B.C. An obscure text of Festus (276 L.) preserves the otherwise unknown fact that in certain years it fell to the Romans to choose a *praetor*, a military commander, for the Latin League. We do not know how frequently the Romans were supposed to command the federal army. De Sanctis' guess that a Roman led the federal army every second year is as plausible or implausible as Alföldi's contention that Rome was one of the thirty cities to take turns in the federal command. What the fragment of Festus confirms is that, in the fifth century B.C., military command and civil power tended to fall apart in Rome, thus defying the principle of the unity of military and civil command in times of war. In the circumstances the weakening of consular power can be interpreted only as a sign of the difficulties the patricians encountered in exercising power. A further confirmation is to be found in the election of *tribuni militum* with consular powers in the second half of the fifth century. Nobody has yet been able to explain why in certain years—quite irregularly— the *tribuni militum* replaced the consuls as heads of state. But one point is clear. The *tribuni militum* were above all military commanders. Their election with consular powers indicated that the two consuls were inadequate or unable to cope with the perils of a nation at war. It was through the military tribunate with consular powers that plebeians first gained admission to the magistracies.

Lack of evidence is here even more regrettable than elsewhere. The weakness of the consulate, the introduction of dictatorship and of the military tribunate with consular powers, the obligations of Rome in relation to the Latin League, and finally the rise of the plebeian tribunate itself must obviously be closely connected phenomena. But the precise links of the connection escape us almost entirely. What we can perhaps say confidently is that the plebeian organization must soon have become very attractive to anyone outside the *plebs* who was dissatisfied with the patricians. When the tribunes of the *plebs* began to be feared, and the *aediles* began to appear indispensable to the welfare of the city, there must have been many *conscripti* and *clientes* of the patricians who sensed the wind of change. Their prospects of reaching positions of command—or perhaps simply of avoiding humiliation—might seem improved if they joined the *plebs*. There were more places among the *tribuni plebis* than among the consuls. The authority of a tribune compared favorably with that of a consul, at a time when the consul had to obey a dictator or even a Latin praetor. Membership of the *concilia plebis* was a source of strength and elation, absence from them a cause of inferiority and anxiety. To sum up, my contention is that the organization set up by the *plebs* proved so attractive to those living on the periphery of the patrician establishment that they flocked to the *plebs*. Conversely, the patricians had to rely more and more on an inner ring of clients and on their allies in neighboring cities to preserve their power.

The plebeian initiative had a cultural and religious background. As we know, the plebeians had their sanctuary in the temple of Ceres. This temple had been decorated by Greek artists (Plin. *N.H.* 35. 12. 154). In later centuries Greek priestesses from Naples and Velia served in that sanctuary and were given Roman citizenship (Cic. *Pro Balbo* 24. 55; Fest. 268 L.). We do not know when this custom of calling priestesses from Naples and Velia started, but there is no difficulty in stating, against Alföldi, that the custom, like the temple, dates from about 490 B.C. The name of Velia is immediately suggestive. This place had close connections with Massalia, which must have been a friend of Rome even in the fifth century B.C. The golden vessel offered by the Romans to Apollo after the capture of Veii was preserved in Delphi in the treasury of the Massaliotes (Diod. 14. 93. 3; Liv. 5. 25. 10; Plut. *Cam.* 8). It is possible that the special relations of the plebeians with the Phocaeans of Velia was a consequence of the relations of the Romans at large with the Phocaeans of Massalia. Velia itself, the city of Parmenides and Zeno, had a vigorous intellectual and political life from which the Roman plebeians could learn much.

There is another aspect of these curious early relations of the Roman *plebs* with the Greek religious world. According to Dionysius of Halicarnassus (6. 17), the temple of Ceres had been founded after a consultation of the Sibylline Books, which had arrived in Rome from Cumae not many years before. We have, of course, no way of proving or disproving this statement. But two considerations lend it some credibility. It agrees with the Greek character of the temple of Ceres and with the Greek artists who adorned it. Furthermore, we know that, when in 366 B.C. *decemviri* were created to administer the Sibylline Books, plebeians were included in this body (Liv. 6. 37. 12). Here again we have to admit of much obscurity. The *decemviri* had been preceded by *duoviri*, about whom we know nothing. But on the whole one has the impression that the Roman plebeians had a special interest in the Sibylline Books as a part of the Greek religious ideas they were trying to introduce into Rome. Incidentally, long ago Kurt Latte suggested that the *aediles* also were a plebeian imitation of officials of Greek sanctuaries. What makes the introduction of the Sibylline Books particularly interesting is that those who consulted them had to know some Greek.

The traditional patrician ties were with Latium and Etruria. The patrician taste for Athenian vases was an imitation of an Etruscan taste. Even in the fourth century B.C. the Fabii were famous for their knowledge of Etruscan (Liv. 9. 36. 3). They seem to have acquired Greek only in the third century B.C. (Val. Max. 4. 3. 9). But the *plebs* turned toward Magna Graecia and Sicily. The goddess Ceres pointed to the prosperous corn-producing lands of Campania and Sicily. The Roman traders went to these countries to buy corn. They may have come back with something more than bread. It was easy to pick up Greek words like *poiné*—which first appears in the Twelve Tables as *poena*—or to learn that civilized people write down their laws. In the 470's B.C. the prestige of Greek civilization must have been very high along the Tyrrhenian coast. Even if the Romans knew nothing of Salamis, they could not ignore the battles of Himera and Cumae. Wonderful tales about the Dioscuri were coming straight from Locri and spreading through Etruria and Latium. In separating from Etruria, the Roman aristocracy lost the means, or rather the taste, to buy Athenian vases. However, something more important was reaching Rome from Magna Graecia—the notion of written law, the hatred of personal bondage, the ferment of political reform.

For a moment I was tempted to present my considerations on the origins of the Roman Republic under the title "Religion and the Rise of Capitalism in Rome in the Fifth Century B.C." I decided to drop this title, not because it would have been frivolous or misleading, but because it would have exposed my ignorance too readily.

The beginnings of the Roman Republic were contemporary with a multiplication of new temples in Rome. Their dates were preserved and transmitted by the Roman pontiffs. After the temple of Jupiter Capitolinus (509 B.C.), there came the temples of Saturn (497 B.C.), Mercury (495 B.C.), Ceres (493 B.C.), and Castor (484 B.C.). This building activity implies strong religious feelings and available capital. We know something about the social situation which favored the building of the new temples. We may suspect that the patricians were anxious to show their piety and to display their willingness to help the poor by public works. They must also have been anxious to try to canalize and control new religious emotions, such as those of the plebeians toward Ceres and of the knights toward the Dioscuri. But we have no idea of how the temples were paid for. Furthermore, we should like to know whether this boom in temple-building was confined to Rome or whether it extended to other cities of Latium and Etruria. The absence of written records outside Rome makes it hard to answer this question. If we had to rely entirely on archaeological evidence for Rome, we should not know the temple of Mercury—no trace of which, to the best of my knowledge, has yet been found. We should also know much less about the other temples, with the exception of the temple of Jupiter Capitolinus. It is easy to make a list of Latin and Etruscan cities which built or rebuilt temples in the late sixth or early fifth century B.C. A perfunctory perusal of Arvid Andrén, *Architectural Terracottas from Etrusco-Italic Temples* (1940), is enough to provide the foundations of a catalogue. But we know that the study of architectural terra cottas can never lead to exact dates such as we have for the Roman temples. Only complete excavations of sites according to modern methods can provide an adequate substitute for the lack of literary evidence; and these are, so far, very few. The nearest approximation is represented by the exploration of the Portonaccio temple of Veii. Another example is perhaps the Poggio Casetta temple of Volsinii, which also seems to belong to the end of the sixth century B.C. And there are the temples of Ardea, Satricum, Lanuvium. We are only at the beginning of a systematic study of the archaic sanctuaries of Latium and Etruria. The sensational results reached by what one can only call the modest explorations of the area of Sant' Omobono in Rome, of the federal center of Lavinium, and of the Punic center of Pyrgi give an indication of what we may expect from future excavations. The religious and social history of early Latium and Etruria will be written very differently a few years from now.

For the present all we can say is that about 500 B.C. Rome was certainly not behind her neighbors in building temples. If the Greek analogy can be applied, not only sculptors and painters, but architects and masons must have temporarily migrated to Rome to build the temples. Their presence must have put new ideas into the heads of the Roman plebeians. But what matters more is that political and social movements gained impetus from being associated with new temples. The study of the archaic sanctuaries of Latium is bringing us nearer to the spirit of the men who, either as patricians or as plebeians, either as Latins or as Romans, tenaciously fought for their rights in the early fifth century B.C.

BIBLIOGRAPHICAL NOTE

My previous research on this subject is collected mainly in *Terzo contributo alla storia degli studi classici e del mondo antico*, vol. 2 (Rome, 1966), and *Quarto contributo . . .* (in press). *An Interim Report on the Origins of Rome*, which originally appeared in the *Journal of Roman Studies*, 53 (1963), is reprinted in *Terzo contributo*. "Procum patricium," *Journal of Roman Studies*, 56 (1966); the discussion of A. Alföldi's *Early Rome and the Latins*, *Journal of Roman Studies*, 57 (1967); "L'ascesa della plebe nella storia arcaica di Roma," *Rivista storica Italiana*, 79 (1967); "Osservazioni sulla distinzione tra patrizi e plebei," in *Les origines de la république Romaine, Entretiens de la Fondation Hardt* (Vandoeuvres, 1967); "Praetor Maximus e questioni affini," in *Studi in onore di G. Grosso*, vol. 1 (Turin, 1968); and "Il rex sacrorum e l'origine della repubblica," in *Studi in onore di E. Volterra*, vol. 1 (Milan, 1969), are collected in *Quarto contributo*. Among Alföldi's recent research, note "Die Herrschaft der Reiterei in Griechenland und Rom nach dem Sturz der Könige," in *Gestalt und Geschichte: Festschrift Karl Schefold*, vol. 4 of *Antike Kunst* (1967). His arguments, some of which are controverted by D. van Berchem in the same volume, do not explain why the Roman constitutional tradition does not know of the alleged identity of patricians with knights. As for the complexity of the archaeological and literary evidence outside Rome, I should like to refer to the paper "Campanian Cavalry: A Question of Origins" by M. W. Frederiksen, who very kindly allowed me to see it in manuscript. It has now been published in *Dialoghi di Archeologia*, 2 (1968): 3–31.

E. H. GOMBRICH

The Evidence of Images

I. THE VARIABILITY OF VISION

L ATE IN 1967 a book was published in England which is as charming as it must be fascinating to all who are interested in the theory and practice of interpretation.[1] Its principal author is the Dutch naturalist and ethologist Niko Tinbergen, who combined with a friend and artist to photograph the tracks left in the sand of the dunes by a variety of creatures and to reconstruct the stories they reveal in word and in image. The illustration I selected (Figure 1) shows the tracks of

Figure 1. Tracks of an Oyster Catcher

an oyster catcher peacefully walking along over the dunes till something apparently alarmed it, the walk turned into a hop, leaving deeper imprints in the sand, and it took off on its wings. This is not all the naturalists could infer from the configuration of the sand. They know that a bird cannot take off except precisely against the wind. At the time of the event, therefore, the wind

[1] E. A. R. Ennion and N. Tinbergen, *Tracks* (Oxford: Clarendon Press, 1967).

must have blown from the left of the picture. But if you observe the ripples of the sand, they were formed by a wind coming from the direction of the camera. Accordingly, the tracks correctly interpreted reveal another story of the past: there was a change of wind between the formation of the ripples and that of the footprints. Not all of the picture illustrated is a photograph. What the artist has done is to superimpose on it his reconstruction of the oyster catcher taking off. This is how it appears to his mind's eye and how, he is sure, it would have looked to the camera if one had been present at the moment.

I wanted to present at least one of these charming little detective stories because they seemed to me to elucidate much of the theory of interpretation. To interpret a footprint means to match it in our mind with one of the creatures whose shapes and habits we know. The greater the repertoire of our knowledge and experience, the more likely we are to find the perfect fit. Sometimes, as we all know from detective stories, the fit may be literally perfect—a unique foot- or fingerprint may prove the presence of an individual at a certain spot. Sometimes, on the other hand, the fit will be more conjectural if, for instance, the tracks are less distinct or would fit several species. Occasionally, perhaps, the interpreter may be confronted by a track which sets his mind spinning. There is a story by Karel Čapek of the single footprint on a wide virgin plain which is as mysterious as any miracle.[2] Where we cannot reconstruct, where we do not know what is possible, we cannot produce a convincing fit, we cannot interpret.

I do not know whether anyone would call a footprint an image of the foot, but I certainly think it will be helpful if we look at images as traces, natural or artificial ones. After all, a photograph is nothing but such a natural trace, a series of tracks left not in the sand but on the emulsion of the film by the variously distributed lightwaves which produced chemical changes made visible and permanent through further chemical operations. In fact, what the audience of a lecture sees on the screen may be described as the track of a track of a track, all along a chain of mechanical transformations. The screen shows a track or a shadow of the inverted slide in the projector made in a series of operations from the track in printer's ink of the block made from the photograph, which was of course made from a negative which preserved the tonal gradients but not the absolute tones of the developed film or plate. We do not usually think of these intermediate stages, because we rely on their capacity to transmit the original trace, though we know that changes or distortions are possible at every stage. Photographs can be touched up or tampered with or, as in our case, supplemented by

[2] Karel Čapek, "Der Fußstapfen," *Gottesmarter* (Berlin: S. Fischer, 1918); the idea is derived from David Hume.

artificial traces made not by light but by an artist's hand. Unlike the natural trace the artist's trace is made with the intention of being interpretable. It is deliberately clear, rather than blurred, to facilitate the process of reconstruction for those of us who know less about oyster catchers than Niko Tinbergen and his friend.

For knowledge, a well-stocked mind, is clearly the key to the practice of interpretation. Having referred in my title to the evidence of images, I wished to indicate the fact, of which I have already produced evidence, that I would not confine myself to my field, the study of art. The use of images as evidence clearly extends much beyond this field, and I believe that even the student of art can profit from a consideration of the wider problem. Readers of my book *Art and Illusion* may remember that I there confess that my interest in these questions was originally aroused by my wartime work at a listening post where problems of perception and interpretation were thrust upon us in a severely practical context.[3]

I never was concerned with the interpretation of pictures, but of course this constituted one of the most important branches of wartime intelligence. The story of the interpretation of tracks left on the film of a reconnaissance aircraft which flew over the German experimental station of Peenemünde, has now been revealed in a thrilling book by David Irving.[4] It illustrates almost to perfection the role which knowledge and reconstruction play in such a process, both in the failures and in the ultimate success. Our illustration (Figure 2) shows the part of the station where the German long-range rockets and flying-bomb launchers were ultimately located, but it gives no idea of the difficulties with which the British intelligence was confronted. Rumors had reached them early in 1943 that the Germans were working on such weapons, but there was no indication of what they might look like. In fact, it was here that the act of reconstruction first went grievously wrong. The authorities concerned had no official cognizance of any form of rockets fired by liquid fuels, though it turns out *post festum* that they could have had. Now a rocket fueled with cordite would have to be gigantic to achieve an effective range, and accordingly would have to be transported on special trucks and launched from enormous contraptions. It was for these that the intelligence looked and looked in vain. Moreover, it so happens that the officer in charge of the interpretation of these reconnaissance photographs was in his peacetime capacity a classical scholar of some repute whose main interest was in Roman water engineering. It is amusing in retrospect to read that he inter-

[3] E. H. Gombrich, *Art and Illusion: A Study in the Psychology of Pictorial Representation* (New York and London, 1960), chap. VII.

[4] David Irving, *The Mare's Nest* (London: Kimber, 1964).

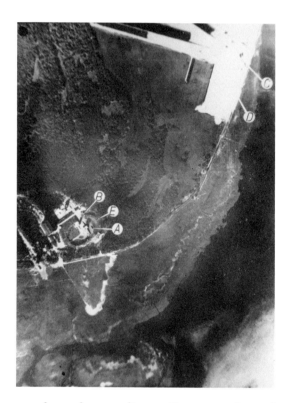

Figure 2. Wartime Reconnaissance Photograph of Peenemünde

preted a rocket standing at Peenemünde in the now familiar position as a "thick vertical column of about 30 ft. height."[5] As to the objects "C" and "D" in the right-hand corner, he plausibly associated them with water engineering and described them as lengths of pipe connected with dredging operations, an hypothesis which impeded their interpretation as launching catapults for many months to come. Only after a further reconnaissance the officer wrote with the true caution of a classical scholar that there was a train in the area which "appears to carry a cylindrical object 38 ft. by 8 ft."[6] It turned out later that the same object had also been visible on the earlier photograph, but nobody had noticed it. "That is hardly surprising," as Irving says, since all there was was "a blur of white on a smudge of grey one and a half millimeters long."[7]

The story now moves to the tangled world of departmental rivalries. A scientist, Dr. R. V. Jones, who was worried by the slow progress of operations,

[5] *Ibid.*, p. 66.
[6] *Ibid.*, p. 60.
[7] *Ibid.*

managed to obtain a private set of these photographs and interpreted the object as a white rocket. He made his interpretation known, and, questioned from above, the classical scholar admitted, still very cautiously, "that the appearance of the object is not incompatible with its being a cylinder tapered at one end and provided with three radial fins at the other."[8] Calling for the earlier photographs, he suddenly saw several such finned objects dotted around the place which he had not seen before. A few weeks later he was even prepared to refer to them as "torpedoes." Fortunately for us, his caution did not win the day. Peenemünde was attacked from the air in a devastating raid, and the German rocket program was set back considerably.

The story of how the true state of affairs was pieced together from stray information and tested against the photographs would take too long to relate. But I cannot withhold the crowning episode. After the raid it had become clear that the Germans had transferred and dispersed much of the production, and the same Dr. Jones was convinced that a site in Poland was now the one to be watched. Once more he obtained photographs and stayed in his office for most of the night till in the early hours of the morning he at last found a blurred white speck of the familiar kind by a railway siding. His reconstruction of the situation was confirmed. But this discovery was too much for the professionals. An official memorandum was sent, pointing out the dangers of amateur interpretation of aerial photographs. What Jones had called a rocket was obviously a locomotive. "Nobody should be allowed to comment on photographs without the proper training."[9] It is a story which should be widely disseminated wherever professionals claim a monopoly of wisdom. For the truth is, of course, that one can learn from the theory of interpretation that interpretation cannot be wholly learned or taught. The reconstruction which fits does not start from the blurred white speck, it ends there. To think of the object that would match it is as much a feat of the creative imagination as of trained observation. There can be no professional stocking of minds with an infinite variety of possibilities. All the professional should learn, and obviously never learns, is the possibility of being mistaken. Without this awareness, without this flexibility, interpretation will easily get stuck on the wrong track, where it will see locomotives which should be there according to the book of rules.

I hope my initial examples will not be found too farfetched, for I believe they present a slow-motion analysis of a process which is much more universal, indeed basic to our understanding of that elusive phenomenon I have called the

[8] *Ibid.*, p. 67.
[9] *Ibid.*, p. 260.

Figure 3. View of Homewood House, The Johns Hopkins University

"variability of vision." To interpret is to construct, and, as I shall try to argue, such construction always underlies our reactions to incoming stimuli. I am not, of course, a psychologist, and so I should like to quote in support of this point of view the book by Ulric Neisser of Cornell University, *Cognitive Psychology*.

> The notion that perception is basically a constructive act rather than a receptive or simply analytic one is quite old. It goes back at least to Brentano's "Act Psychology" and Bergson's "Creative Synthesis," and was eloquently advanced by William James. However it is not put forward here on the basis of its historical credentials ... we shall see *that the mechanisms of visual imagination are continuous with those of visual perception*—a fact which strongly implies that all perceiving is a constructive process.[10]

In *Art and Illusion* I called this constructive process the Beholder's Share, and I argued that, strictly speaking, no two-dimensional image can be interpreted

[10] Ulric Neisser, *Cognitive Psychology* (New York: Appleton-Century-Crofts, 1967), pp. 94–95.

40

as a spatial arrangement without such a constructive contribution of our spatial imagination. This goes for any snapshot no less than for a reconnaissance photograph from the air. The difference is only that as a rule an ordinary snapshot or picture post card shows us familiar classes of objects, people, houses, and trees which superficially, at least, make the work of matching and reconstruction quite easy for us (Figure 3). But the very ease with which we assemble these items from the storehouse of our mind also hides from us the limits of our reconstruction.[11] After all, normally nothing depends for us on finding out from such a picture the exact dimensions of the President's House of Johns Hopkins. Nor have we any reason to feel troubled by the fact that we could not tell the direction of the branches of the trees. We see a tree and leave it at that, unless someone should come with a mind of an intelligence officer and ask us to make a three-dimensional model of those branches when, obviously, an infinite number of solutions would be possible and none provable.

In fact, it is easy to show how readily our constructive process can be tricked into a false reading of an image. Most people will tend to read Figure 4[12] as representing a room seen between some pot plants with a table some distance away in the background, and the picture of the table (Figure 5) will be recon-

Figure 4. A Table behind Plants

Figure 5. The Table

---

[11] E. H. Gombrich, "Zur Psychologie des Bilderlesens," *Röntgen-Blätter*, 20 (February, 1967).

[12] I take this example from the instructive book by Ralph M. Evans, *Eye, Film and Camera in Color Photography* (New York: John Wiley & Sons, 1959), Figs. 2–11 and 8–9.

Figure 6. The Scale of the Table

Figure 7. The Plants behind the Table

structed as a table of normal size. Once the reading has settled they may even for a moment see the woman as a giantess (Figure 6), till they have switched the construction and look at the arrangement from the other side (Figure 7). Now, of course, the original view has to be reconstructed to accommodate the fresh idea of the toy table.

The possibility of such misreadings induced by unfamiliar objects stands in the center of the famous experiments in perception devised by Adelbert Ames, Jr.[13] The most famous of these is a so-called distorted room, a room of unexpected skewy shape which, thanks to the laws of perspective, becomes indistinguishable from a normal square room when seen through a peephole (Figures 8 and 9). Normally, so sure are we of this reading that the people appearing through the windows, which actually lie at different distances, appear unnaturally large or small.

With these demonstrations we have, of course, moved from the problem of interpreting tracks on a photographic plate to a very different problem, the problem of how we perceive the world around us. But is it so different? Could it not be argued that when we see we interpret the tracks left by the lightwaves on the rods and cones of our retina and transmitted from there to the visual cortex? This is indeed the account which was favored by psychology for many

[13] Franklin P. Kilpatrick, ed., *Explorations in Transactional Psychology* (New York: New York University Press, 1961).

42

Figure 8. Monocular Distorted
Room from the Viewing Point

Figure 9. Monocular Distorted
Room from Another Angle

centuries. Its classic formulation is to be found in Berkeley's *New Theory of Vision.* According to this theory, the stimulation of the retina results in a flat image which the mind can interpret as a three-dimensional world only through the experience of touch. There is an all-important difference, according to this account, between the visual sensations, the raw data transmitted to the brain, and the picture of the environment built up by perception. This picture, like the cases here discussed, is a result of knowledge, of experience; it must be distinguished from the stimulus configuration, which is all we really see.[14]

But is it true that we ever really see the uninterpreted sense data? Can we ever experience that uninterpreted vision which the nineteenth century described with the loaded term of the "innocent eye"? In *Art and Illusion* I criticized this notion with the aid of philosophical and psychological arguments. In particular I drew on the methodological views of my friend Sir Karl Popper, who has consistently attacked the positivist account of "sense data" as the ultimate basis of our observations.[15]

Since I published my book the opponents of the sense data theory have received strong reinforcement in the shape of a new book by that great student of vision, Professor J. J. Gibson. Its very title, *The Senses Considered as Perceptual Systems,* is a challenge to the traditional distinction between sensation and per-

[14] Edwin G. Boring, *Sensation and Perception in the History of Experimental Psychology* (New York and London, 1942).

[15] For a recent statement, see K. R. Popper, "Is There an Epistemological Problem of Perception?" in *Problems in the Philosophy of Science,* ed. Imre Lakatos and Alan Musgrave (Amsterdam: North Holland Publishing Co., 1968), pp. 163–64.

ception.[16] Not that Professor Gibson is inclined to deny that our nerve ends come into play in this process; what he denies is merely that it is either possible or useful to try and separate this part of the process from its manifold interactions with others. If I may appeal to a simple experiment to illustrate the artificiality of such a separation, I would ask the reader to join his hands together. He will certainly feel that they touch each other, will feel their warmth and their texture, but, if we ask ourselves how this feeling is derived from individual nerve ends in our right hand and our left hand, we soon discover that the question is absurd. The sense data are something we read about in books; they are not to be analyzed out. Why should they be? Our sensory systems developed in the process of evolution to ensure our survival, to enable us to find our way through the world in search of food or mates and to avoid predators. It is the whole of the organism which reacts to stimulation from the environment, and it is this reaction that matters more than our awareness. Least of all were we endowed with eyes in order to peer through a keyhole and be puzzled by such posers as the ingenuity of Ames has contrived. We have two eyes, and, though introspection would never detect this, it is the disparity of their stimulation which contributes to the resulting perception. There are many other sources of information, such as texture, which are utilized by the sense of sight and which traditional accounts have vastly underrated. But what is really decisive is that visual perception is geared to movement. Granted that the static view of a room through a stationary eye allows of many interpretations, Professor Gibson stresses that as soon as we change our position the transformation of the optic array is what he calls univocal: there is one and only one configuration which fits it (Figure 10).[17] What matters in real life is not that textbook abstraction, the stationary image on one retina, but the succession of stimuli which we experience as we are walking toward a room (Figure 11). We do not need to call in touch or previous knowledge to explain that the structure of the environment can be perceived. Even if we want to think of the mind as solving puzzles transmitted to it by nervous impulses, this particular puzzle allows of only one solution, only one piece of the jigsaw fits into the gap.

The case Professor Gibson makes for this view is so strong that he must indeed ask himself how it is that people ever thought otherwise? His answer is that they were deceived by the very analogy I, too, have drawn, the analogy with the interpretation of pictures. If it were not for the existence of paintings,

[16] James J. Gibson, *The Senses Considered as Perceptual Systems* (Boston: Houghton Mifflin Co., 1966).
[17] *Ibid.*, Ills. and Figs. 10–6, 10–7, 10–10.

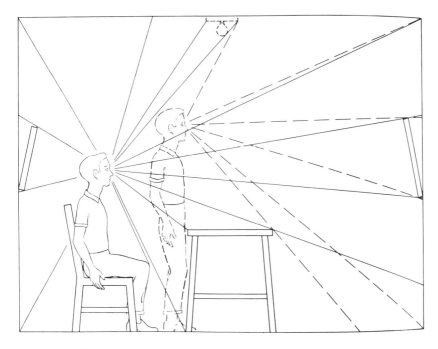

Figure 10. Transformation of the Optic Array

Professor Gibson says, people might never have speculated about sense data and images on the retina. They would not have wanted to reduce the visual world to what he had earlier called the visual field, that flat array of colors which needs interpretation.

When I wrote *Art and Illusion* Professor Gibson had only uttered this suspicion in an aside in the course of a polemic. I am glad I noticed it for I do believe that he has initiated what may be called a Copernican revolution in the study of visual perception. But I would not claim that in my book I fully digested his message, nor, if I may say so without impertinence, am I sure that I want to swallow it whole. For the radical separation between the interpretation of pictures and the perception of the world has some consequences which do not seem to me entirely to square with the facts.[18]

It was a philosopher, my friend and colleague Professor Richard Wollheim, who insisted on this separation in the full knowledge that it would be rather

[18] Julian E. Hochberg, *Perception* (Englewood Cliffs, N.J.: Prentice-Hall, Inc., 1964), who also adopts much of Gibson's point of view, also poses the problem of whether his explanation does not prove a little too much.

45

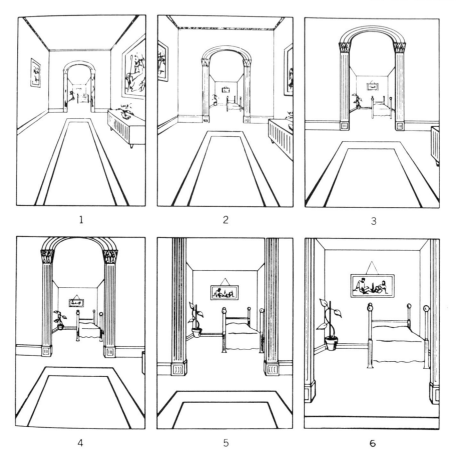

Figure 11. The Optical Transition from One Vista to Another

fatal to the approach I advocated in *Art and Illusion*.[19] For this book rests indeed on the assumption that the illusion which a picture can give us can be explained by the similarity of our reaction to the picture with our reaction to the visible world. Wollheim attacks both sides of that equation. He would admit that we interpret a picture, but he does not think that this interpretation will result in an illusion of reality except in marginal cases where the eye is fooled but the mind left empty.[20] Nor would he admit that it makes sense to speak of interpre-

[19] Richard Wollheim, "Art and Illusion," *British Journal of Aesthetics*, 3, no. 1 (January, 1963): 15–37.

[20] Richard Wollheim, *On Drawing an Object* (London: University College, 1965), an inaugural lecture delivered at University College, London, on December 1, 1964.

46

tation in our commerce with the visible world, for what is it we interpret if we abandon the idea of sense data as he himself is willing to do?

In writing the preface to the second edition of my book I briefly alluded to this disagreement about the term "interpretation" and merely mentioned that I was not wedded to words. Call it something else, I implied, provided it describes what is going on. Now Professor Gibson does indeed call it something else. In his terminology the sensory system picks up and processes the information present in the energy distribution of the environment.

I think and hope I am fully alive to the danger of new words, specially fashionable words, becoming new toys of little cash value. But I do think that this way of putting things may help not only to clarify the point at issue between Professor Wollheim and myself but also to bridge the gulf Professor Gibson has deliberately opened between the world of pictures and the real world.

It certainly was of tremendous importance to stress the amount of information which the organism can utilize in its commerce with the visible world and to contrast it with the relative poverty of information which even a detailed color photograph may contain—though the latest technical wizardry of the holograph reminds us that the ordinary photograph by no means represents the limit of mechanical information storage.[21] But, granted that in walking or driving along a road we would have information of a very different order from what the snapshot gives us, and that we thus could perceive the invariant shape of the road, the houses, and the texture of the road without ambiguity, I am not sure how far our capacity to process this information would ever go. Take the example of trees once more. As we passed them their branches would shift and turn and execute a complex movement which would in theory allow us to reconstruct their shape—but how much of their shape? To how many of the twigs could we attend? And what of the trees farther away? Even as we move, those some distance from us cannot present a univocal picture even for an observer of infinite capacity. The redundancies decrease progressively and increase the need to supplement the information from the store of our imagination. As our eyes scan the distant prospect, uncertainties about the size, shape, color, and meaning of objects surely begin to matter. I should put meaning first, meaning for us. Not that Professor Gibson neglects it. He beautifully describes how in situations of reduced information, at dusk or in mist, for instance, our sensory system goes

[21] Emmet N. Leith and Juris Upatnieks, "Photography by Laser," *Scientific American,* 212 (June, 1965): 24–35; Keith S. Pennington, "Advances in Holography," *Scientific American,* 218 (February, 1968): 40–48.

hunting, as he puts it, to make out what concerns it.[22] Sometimes in such a situation the process runs ahead and we believe we have received information that is not present. We all know that this happens particularly when our emotions are involved through anxiety or desire, which makes us keyed up, as the saying goes, for certain information and allows the slightest partial hint to trigger the relevant reaction. We will attack or run away at the slightest sensory suggestion of danger or the hoped-for prey.

We know that animals can thus react to false or insufficient stimuli, and so can man. But is it not also true that man in such a situation can do what the animal is presumably incapable of doing, turn upon himself and try to learn from the mistake? Would the primitive hunter never have hurled his spear at a shape or rock he had taken for a recumbent bison only to discover on coming closer that he had been deceived? Sometimes, we may surmise, the victim would have blamed a ghost for this mocking apparition, but might he not also have been moved to go back to the place and scrutinize the spot to see how he could have been deceived? And would this self-scrutiny not have forced him to slow down and watch that semi-automatic process that had made him see a bison instead of a few bushes and a stone? Might he not even, to spin out my "Just-So-Story," have asked a mocking companion to come and see for himself how close the resemblance was from that point? Maybe the companion said "I cannot see it," or, maybe, he learned to recognize the resemblance. If he did, he also experienced the variability of vision: the stone began to "look" different.

A trained observer has described this variability so vividly to me that I have asked him for permission to quote his account in this essay. Professor Niko Tinbergen here tells of a perceptual shock he experienced during an expedition to Greenland:

> ... In late autumn, when the land was already covered in snow, but the ocean was still free of polar pack ice, I had climbed a mountain of some 3000 feet. From the top I looked down on the partly frozen fjords, and some ten miles away I saw the ocean.
>
> Looking through my field glasses towards the East—the sun was approximately in the South—I suddenly saw that the surface of the faraway ocean was moving wildly. Having been warned that in that area severe gales may spring up in a matter of ten minutes, I decided to descend quickly. But I had one more good look, and suddenly I realized that what I had thought was violently moving sea, was in fact a cover of pack ice that had arrived from the North.
>
> The ice floes are very thick, and also irregular; they are about four feet above

---

[22] Gibson, *op. cit.*, p. 303.

the water, and of course separated by gullies of that depth. Scattered among the pack ice (which is seawater frozen in the polar basin, covered with several years' snow), one sees icebergs of varying size.

Now the interesting thing was that, at the instant I realized it was not waves, but ice, I saw very vividly how the movement stopped. In one flash the violent motion turned into complete rigidity. I still remember the feeling of shock I had, so vivid had been the impression, the *certainty*, that the ocean surface was in wild motion. I have never since experienced such a striking example of knowledge determining interpretation, and what amazed me was the almost physical blow I received when my interpretation made me see something quite different from what I had seen before. The interesting thing was that the color changed too. I had interpreted the bluish shades in an overall glaringly white surface as the only places where I saw the reflection of the blue sky in the water, and the rest as glitter—half against the sun. Now I suddenly saw a brilliantly white snowscape with irregular shadows.[23]

We need not credit our hypothetical primitive hunters with the power of analytical introspection which marks the great scientist to postulate that the discovery of perceptual mistakes can lead to an increasing awareness of the process of seeing, without the intervention of pictorial devices. Like the intelligence officer of my earlier example, our cave man on the warpath would have begun consciously to match and describe shapes. Only this increased awareness, I would argue, could also lead him ultimately to create artificial tracks and traces, and so to images.

As a student of art I am of course sorry to deprive painting of the central role in man's awareness of himself which Professor Gibson has assigned to it. But I have learned from Sir Karl Popper to assign that central role to man's critical faculties, to his ability to learn from his mistake in a process of trial and error which can be communicated and discussed. This capacity presupposes a certain amount of control over the processing of information, a shift in the threshold of the automatism, but not, if I am right, a total separation between sensation and perception. What I have called in my title "the variability of vision," therefore, is not, in my view, a switch between discontinuous processes, but a shift between what has been called object concentration and stimulus concentration.[24] The fact that stimulus concentration can never come down to the rock-bottom threshold of retinal data seems to me well proved. But I certainly would agree with Professor Gibson that man-made images and symbols provide a

[23] For a parallel account (by G. K. Adams) see my *Art and Illusion*, p. 226.
[24] M. D. Vernon, *A Further Study of Visual Perception* (Cambridge: At the University Press, 1952), p. 145.

most useful testing ground for the exploration of such shifts and the amount of processing that can go on without our becoming aware of it.

The concept of information was developed in the theory of communication and it is here that the point I wish to stress can be most easily demonstrated, particularly if we look at the matter from the angle of the sender rather than that of the recipient of a message. Most of the messages we send out in daily life through gesture, speech, and action depend for their efficacy on the recipient's awareness of the context. They are understood, as the theory of information puts it, because they serve to remove a specific doubt, or, more precisely, because they enable the recipient to choose between alternatives about which he had been in doubt. A nod will suffice to decide between yes and no, a pointing hand will tell the questioner which direction to take at a roadfork. Most message systems employ to some extent what engineers call redundancies, to insure their safe reception. We accompany our gestures with words, and words, if necessary, with written symbols. But the surer the context is given the more we can strip down the redundancies and reduce the actual information to a minimum, relying on the recipient's readiness to supplement it from his own store of knowledge. At least those of us who have a bad handwriting think that we have a perfect right to do so. We cut out the redundancies of the letters and hope the context will make up for them. Up to a point we have a right to believe this. Take the word of Figure 12, which happens to be in the handwriting of

Figure 12

Sir Winston Churchill.[25] Surely there are not enough distinctive features to identify the letters in this wavy line, except that the first letter must be an *s* and the last, to judge by the dot, an *i*. But as soon as we see the context the process becomes almost automatic. The word is a correction made by Churchill on the margin of the draft to the Atlantic Charter suggesting an alternative to the word "because" at the beginning of a sentence (Figure 13). It therefore can only be *since* and it also now begins to look like *since*. In fact, we are hardly bothered now by the contradictory information of the shifted dot.

I have taken the example from reading because reading shows our capacity of information-processing at its most mysterious. In fact, discussing this enigma,

[25] I take the illustration from Winston S. Churchill, *The Second World War* (London: Cassel, 1950), opp. p. 394.

Professor Neisser comes to the paradoxical conclusion that "rapid reading represents an achievement as impossible in theory, as it is commonplace in practice."[26]

But, whether we can fully understand it or not, one thing is clear; the rapidity of the process would not be possible unless it had become almost automatic. We adjust to the message and process the signs obediently even though, in one of Neisser's examples, the *A* and the *H* really have identical form (Figure 14).[27]

I am even more puzzled by the way in which we switch our response together with the language of such messages as *pain et couvert* or *pain and sorrow*. To me, at least, it takes an effort to slow down sufficiently to realize that English pain and French *pain* are composed of the same signs, for my verbal and auditory reactions are too automatic.

The point I wish to make is that in reading we are not aware of the individual letters, nor even of the individual words, but only of the information itself, once it has been processed. You may have read a whole book and yet be unable, on closing it, to specify what font it was printed in. Those of us who have become more or less bilingual by force of circumstance are often unable to tell in which of the two languages we have just spoken or been addressed.[28] Understanding is so automatic that the symbol has become transparent and disappears from awareness; but of course it must first be identified as such a symbol. Where our script is disguised and assimilated to the forms of Indian scripts (Figure 15) we don't make an effort till we discover the deception and adjust to the message.[29]

I believe that if we approach the problem of pictures from this unexpected angle we may be able to sort out the problems that puzzled Professors Gibson and Wollheim. Clearly, almost any picture contains a good deal less information than the object it represents would exhibit. But there are many ways of making up for this deficiency, if we must regard it as such. One is here as always our knowledge of the world, of what Professor Gibson calls the ecology of our sur-

[26] Neisser, *op. cit.*, p. 137.

[27] *Ibid.*; the illustration comes from Fig. 9, p. 47 (after O. G. Selfridge, "Pattern Recognition and Modern Computers," *Proc. West. Joint Computer Conferences* [Los Angeles, Calif., 1955]).

[28] I take this example from a talk given by Professor Abraham Kaplan at Harvard University in 1959 and can confirm it from my own experience.

[29] The dust jacket of R. K. Narayan's *The Sweet-Vendor*, designed by Roy Spencer (London: Bodley Head, 1967).

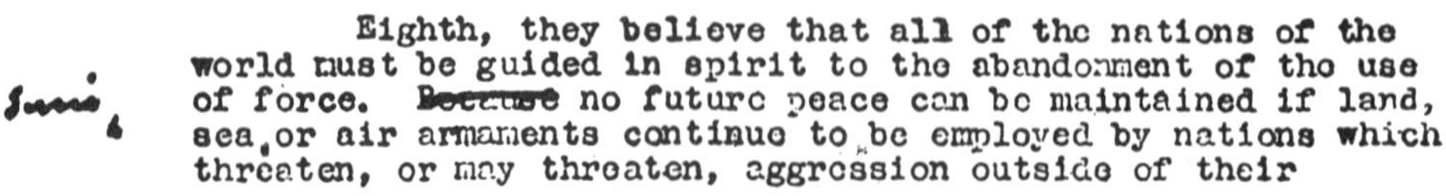

Eighth, they believe that all of the nations of the
world must be guided in spirit to the abandonment of the use
of force. Because no future peace can be maintained if land,
sea, or air armaments continue to be employed by nations which
threaten, or may threaten, aggression outside of their

Figure 13. Extract from the Draft of the Atlantic Charter

THE CAT

Figure 14

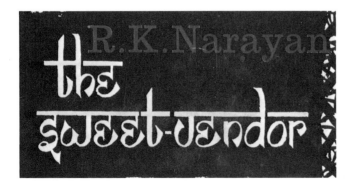

Figure 15. Detail of a Book Jacket Designed by Roy Spencer

rounding. It is such knowledge that enables us effortlessly to adjust to M. C. Escher's print of trees reflected in a pool of water (Figure 16), though when you come to think of it the operation required is rather a complex one, separating the construction of trees with straight branches from the action of the water on the

Figure 16. M. C. Escher, "Rippled Surface," linocut 1950

image. Another print by Escher, called "Three Worlds" (Figure 17), carries this operation even further without causing us any difficulty in matching his forms from our experience.

The objective similarity between the prints and the situation they represent is small if you think in terms of elements. But it is strong if you think in terms of systems of relationships. It is to such systems, with all their effort-saving redundancies, that our processing is obviously geared. The variability of vision includes the capacity to adjust to fresh systems, provided we can learn their rules of transformation and invariance. Hence our construction can soon make allowance for any kind of systematic distortion, like the distortion of the water surface. That there is more to this adjustment than mere inference is shown by experiments with distorting, inverting, or colored spectacles which wearers gradually cease to notice, only to have to relearn the processing of undistorted in-

Figure 17. M. C. Escher, "Three Worlds," lithograph 1955

formation when returning to normal vision. Once more Escher shows us in another print (Figure 18) how even arrested distortion remains legible, since our knowledge of what is possible or probable in the visible world will guide us to a correct construction.

As long as we talk in terms of information, moreover, we need not be particular about the form in which the information reaches us. The whole wretched question of how many of the means of art are conventional and how many natural is reduced to its proper proportion. Language is conventional and yet transparent, and even the minimal information of a picture can become so transparent if context or description adds the required information.

I have alluded before to the game invented by the Carracci and recently christened "Droodles," the abbreviated joke picture which only a caption makes us see.[30] Figure 19 is called by its author, Roger Price, "Ship Arriving Too Late to Save Drowning Witch." Even such an absurd caption tends to settle on the

[30] Gombrich, *Art and Illusion*, chap. VII; Roger Price, *Droodles* (London: W. H. Allen, 1954), Plate 56.

Figure 18. M. C. Escher, "Balcony," lithograph 1945

Figure 19. "Ship Arriving Too Late to Save Drowning Witch"

configuration. I find it hard at least not to see the horizontal as the ocean separating the water from the sky. I can easily turn the witch's hat into the sugar-loaf mountain and see it recede into the distance. I find it less easy to eliminate the ship and the surface of the sea, for it is hard to think of alternative objects. Try to make it part of a runway (Figure 20) seen by a landing pilot through a rectangular window—an operation which involves a switch between figure and ground.

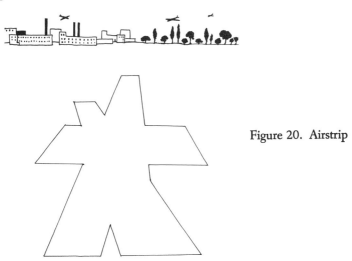

Figure 20. Airstrip

I believe that the training of art historians and art critics should include such exercises, not because the joke is all that good, but because it demonstrates one aspect of the variability of vision which must especially concern him, its obedience to suggestion. The word "evidence," of course, derives from *video* and implies that what lies in front of our eyes cannot and need not be questioned any further. But the point is here, as always, that visual evidence never comes neat, as it were, unmixed with imagination. The processing of visual information is impossible without this ingredient. Whether we are students of man-made images, of tracks left in the sand, or of intelligence photographs, we must scan the configuration for its message, for its meaning. In doing so we make ready to construct the answer from the elements of possible solutions we have stored. We are always trying for a fit, and this process can never be completely halted so long as our mind remains active. The perception of meaning can more easily be triggered than it can be eradicated, because it is automatic.

Take one of the most basic systems of visual information, that of facial expression, which conveys the moods and intentions of our fellow creatures. Surely it is these moods we perceive without being aware of the individual elements that contribute to our perception. On the contrary, awareness hardly succeeds in breaking the automatism of response. I have in mind the effects of one of the oldest forms of visual art, the art of makeup. We may know and even watch the transforming strokes of a lipstick or an actor's grease paint, but we shall still not be able to separate in our own reactions what we see from what we know. The information put into the face affects us willy nilly.

I believe, indeed, that this kind of automatism in the processing of information goes much further in the visual arts than I may have indicated in my book. Take the experience of Greek sculpture, which became so adept in conveying the feeling of the existence of a living body beneath the drapery (Figure 21). I would maintain that it is truer to our experience to say that we perceive the body underneath the garment than to say that what we really see is only the variously buckled surface of a block of marble.

When we approach the problem of illusion from this angle, the distinction between the picture surface and the objects represented upon it, which has been so much discussed, becomes the distinction between the symbol and the information it conveys. While we scan a picture for such information the surface is irrelevant to our processing and disappears from our awareness. Once more we can leave the problem of illusion on one side and still say that the painting surface has become somewhat transparent to our mind, as transparent, at least, as has the written or the spoken word while we attend to its meaning.

We are all familiar with this experience—if not with the painted pictures, then with the images on the cinema or the television screen. When watching an exciting film we surely attend to the information rather than to the screen. The movie is altogether a good example of what I called automatic processing. We process the successive frames of the film as information about movement, and in this case we are quite unable to halt the automatism, which is partly physiological. We see movement, not a succession of stills, and similarly, I would maintain, we also see a man coming toward us rather than a configuration of shapes getting larger. The dark, of course, which blots out the screen helps to suppress the contradictory information presented by the surround; you can do the same with any painted picture if you screen off the frame and the wall with your hands or look at it through a tube. The distance of the painting surface will then be hard to establish and this will enhance the experience of depth.

Figure 21. Statue of Sophocles

Since I wrote my book I have learned an excellent term with which painters sometimes describe this experience which can even occur in normal conditions. They call it "losing the surface," a feeling they do not necessarily welcome. The so-called illusionistic picture easily makes us lose the surface. Once more sculpture provides an interesting confirmation of this process. The pictorial relief presents a three-dimensional scene on a shallow but equally three-dimensional stage (Figure 22). Nobody, in looking at such a relief, will claim that it looks

Figure 22. Benedetto da Majano, "The Confirmation of the Franciscan Rule"

like reality, but if we ask ourselves whether we could draw the ground plan of the relief rather than of the intended stage we would soon find that this is hard. Our normal processing of information has been directed at the representation, and the actual shape of the relief has been lost from our full awareness.

The most dramatic device for losing the surface is of course the stereoscope. The stereoscopic picture provides the same kind of information as we derive from binocular vision. The disparity of the two images permits us to plot the objects of a certain zone in depth. Once more the automatic nature of this processing is apparent in the stereoscope: we don't know how we do it but we are compelled to perceive the objects with almost unpleasant solidity. I am interested in this experience because it easily illustrates the difference between an illusion and a delusion—we don't believe we see a solid object but we have the illusion of solidity.

Moreover, the stereoscope demonstrates that there is no qualitative difference between this experience and that of looking at a monocular picture. There are at least two arguments in favor of this assertion. One rests on the introspective account of what happens when you close one eye in looking at a stereoscope. Something of the feeling of solidity will inevitably disappear, but there is no dramatic difference between the one-eyed and the two-eyed vision, since most of the information you process remains of course the same. But, apart from this introspective feeling of similarity between the two-eyed and the one-eyed picture, there is also a logical argument in favor of the continuity between the processing of stereoscopic information and that of monocular information. Binocular disparity after all only provides effective spatial information about the foreground. The disparity dwindles with the distance and becomes imperceptible. Accordingly the two images of a landscape produced by a double-lensed stereoscopic camera differ only in their foreground features, and it is these features only which can really be said to be perceived stereoscopically, that is, in three dimensions, when the two images are made to fuse in the stereoscopic viewer. Yet it would surely be untrue to experience to say that in this situation we can distinguish between those objects which are seen in "3-D" and those parts of the image which are flat. Here, as in real life, the gradual thinning out of information does not result in any discontinuity—the distance, too, appears to extend in depth. But since pictures of distant prospects produced by the stereoscopic camera are indistinguishable from those made by an ordinary monocular camera there cannot be a difference in principle between the way we see the resulting images.

We can thus return to the problems posed by Professors Gibson and Wollheim with some assurance that the divorce between the perception of pictures and that of reality which they advocated can never be carried out completely.

In particular it seems to me that Professor Wollheim's objections to the application of the term "interpretation" to our perception of the world and of the term "illusion" to our perception of pictures cannot really be upheld without running into difficulties. For what I have called the processing of information seems to me indistinguishable in many cases from what is usually known as interpretation. Surely there is no discontinuity between the intelligence officer's work as he is bent over his photograph and that of the airman on a reconnaissance flight. Both try to "make out" what they see, even if the airman has more chance of succeeding because he has additional information, which, by the way, can also be recorded through films and stereoscopic cameras. What both of them try to do is perhaps best explained by looking at the efforts to prevent a correct interpretation —they try to identify objects. It is this, of course, which the camouflage artist attempts to counteract by breaking up the contours of objects and making them merge with the ground. To be more exact, camouflage is intended to prevent the identification of particular objects. The enemy should see only familiar, innocuous sights—trees, ponds, rocks—and should reconstruct these normal things so automatically that his attention is not arrested by what is to be concealed.

Now the formulation that the interpretation of reality and that of pictures are both concerned with the identification and reconstruction of objects may at first sight look almost embarrassingly obvious. But what looks obvious is not necessarily simple. It is by no means easy to specify how we identify objects in our surrounding, though the psychology of perception is making great strides in this direction. All I need for my purpose is the hypothesis that the isolation and reconstruction of an object is an operation in time which for all its rapidity is certainly complex.

It seems to me demonstrable that this operation also comes into play when we look at representations of objects on a flat surface.

There are several arguments in favor of this assertion. One of them is the puzzling effect of those configurations known as "impossible figures" which we also owe to M. C. Escher (Figure 23). The very discomfort they cause us, I

Figure 23. "Impossible Figure"

would contend, is due to the compulsion to read them in terms of a three-dimensional object which, as we soon discover, leads us into contradictions.[31]

[31] See E. H. Gombrich, "Illusion and Visual Deadlock," *Meditations on a Hobby Horse* (London: Phaidon, 1963), and Gibson, *op. cit.*, p. 248, Fig. 11–8.

It looks indeed as if the description of such an experience in terms of the processing of information will get us further than other descriptions.[32] We start somewhere along the contour and make certain assumptions which are proving invalid; we start again and are stumped once more. Some of the discomfort disappears if we shorten the process and allow the eye to take in more of the configuration at one glance (Figure 24). We then discover quickly where the

 Figure 24. "Impossible Figure" Redrawn

inconsistent switch is located; apparently the difficulty of matching successive fixations was at the root of the original difficulty. There may be other variables as well. I believe that if we keep the distance but vary the length of the individual rods (Figure 25) we are a little less easily taken in. It looks as if the similarity of the apparent rod endings tricked us into accepting the three as alike alto-

[32] It is admittedly tricky to discuss this operation without being pushed into the discredited distinction between the raw sense data on the one hand and their product in perception on the other. It is understandable, therefore, that the desire to avoid such a distinction has tempted both philosophers and psychologists into the opposite position, which asserts that we do not "infer" the world, we simply perceive it. Such phenomena as the "constancies," which intrigued earlier psychologists because they presented an unexpected deviation from the data of sensations, become on this view the normal condition of perception, which is directed toward the invariant features of our environment. According to this view, a man in the distance does not "appear to be small"; he looks his size, and only a derivative "pictorial attitude" discovers the change in his "apparent size."

In a recent discussion of my book *Art and Illusion* at Cornell University in September, 1967, Professor Gibson rightly and gracefully pointed out that I had talked about Pygmalion's power but had omitted the experience of Narcissus, the discovery of the virtual or "apparent" image which fostered what he calls the "pictorial attitude." I gladly accept this challenge, for, as I tried to hint in the text of this essay (p. 52), the viewing of a reflection indeed offers an excellent example of what I mean by a perceptual operation. We can separate the distortions due to ripples from the object we contemplate: we look across the appearance at a reality. But is it true that such an awareness of the difference between appearance and reality occurs only in such exceptional circumstances? I remember from my childhood days how puzzled I was to find that the courtyard into which we looked from the sixth floor of our apartment looked much smaller from the ground floor than from the bird's-eye view. The change of appearance intrigued me before I had ever learned the pictorial attitude. But, even if this kind of evidence is disregarded, there are, after all, features in our visual world

gether. But, whatever the analysis of the experience may add, one thing is clear: if the apparent solidity of the figure did not trigger automatic processing, we would feel no puzzlement. We cannot so easily see the configuration in the plane. In fact, I find it even hard to copy it.

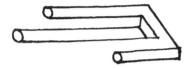

Figure 25. Another Version of the "Impossible Figure"

What this experience suggests is that the reading of a picture is indeed a reaction in time which involves certain specified operations.[33]

The question we have to answer is really whether or not these operations are at least analogous to certain equally automatic operations which are connected with our perception of the visible world. This was the point I took for granted in writing *Art and Illusion*, and it is a position I still want to defend.

which cannot be perceived "as they are"—the moon for instance. Yet we all know that the moon looks larger close to the horizon than it does high in the sky. The most likely explanation of that much-discussed illusion is surely the one which connects the apparent size with its apparent distance—paradoxically, the moon looks larger when it appears to be farther away because the same object when farther away would have to be larger to subtend an identical visual angle. It is this kind of automatic processing which I have in mind when I speak of a perceptual "operation." The estimate of distance reacts on the estimate of size, both in reality and in the viewing of pictures. What is "given" in reality is only the visual angle; what appears in our awareness is the product of this analysis, which splits up the "given" (of which we know nothing) into an object and its modification through its relation to us. There is a parallel operation performed in the separation of color and illumination. The light reflected from an object is treated as the product of its invariant or so-called local color and the color of the light. I have argued in a lecture I gave at Cornell on the occasion mentioned above that the same applies to our interpretation of facial expression, where we must separate the invariant form from the expressive movement. Perhaps Chomsky's distinction between "surface structure" and "deep structure" in the perception and understanding of language points to a similar two-step process in our reconstructive activity. Unless I misunderstand the situation, this two-step process is built into the very fabric of perceiving and reaches down to near-physiological levels. The Land experiments on color perception at least appear to suggest that in favorable conditions our perceptual system can establish a median against which the distribution of light frequencies is plotted, regardless of the objective color of the light that stimulates the retina. Heterogeneous as the phenomena here enumerated may seem, they all point to the role of interpretation at the heart of the perceptual operation and are therefore relevant to the topic of this paper.

[33] Herbert A. Simon, "An Information-Processing Explanation of Some Perceptual Phenomena," *British Journal of Psychology*, 58 (May, 1967): 1–12.

I must apologize if I here return to an example I have discussed elsewhere (Figure 26); it is a little experiment I owe to a book by Ralph Evans.[34] I think I have learned more from this simple trick photograph than from many a book on perception. It is a demonstration of the so-called constancy phenomenon, the observation that we underrate the effect of distance on size and see a row of posts or houses relatively of the same size despite perspective diminution. Now the con-

Figure 26. Ralph M. Evans: A Demonstration of Size Constancy

stancy phenomenon itself has become much less surprising since Professor Gibson's analysis of our perceptual world. If the lampposts or posts are of the same size, we have enough information about them also to perceive them as identical. Remember that the information present in the optic array really is generally sufficient to allow us to perceive what is there. But that this also holds good in a picture which cuts down this information to a fraction seems to me much less obvious. And yet Evans has proved it by a simple trick. He has transferred the

[34] Ralph M. Evans, *An Introduction to Color* (New York: John Wiley & Sons, 1948), p. 149. I have used this example in "Visual Discovery through Art," *Arts Magazine*, November, 1965.

lamppost also to the front and placed a replica of the last post next to the first. We cannot believe our eyes and have to resort to measurement to convince ourselves that on the picture plane the two are really identical.

I think this little experiment proves indeed that we feed the information from the picture plane into the same kind of mill into which we also feed the information from the optic array. And because it is a mill, a process, an operation, it is not easy to halt. I would not say and never did say that we could not halt it up to a point, and view the picture plane as such. What I doubted and continue to doubt is that we can do both at the same time. We cannot, for the same reason that we cannot speak or write two different words at the same time.

But does not this demonstration prove too much? Is it not a fact that we are not under the illusion that we see a road extending into the background? Are we not always aware of sitting or standing in front of a picture? Of course we are. The illusions caused by this operation are again not delusions. And yet I would admit that there is a problem here which I should like again to illustrate with a print by M. C. Escher, whose work presents so many interesting comments on the puzzles of representation (Figure 27).[35] He shows us the boy in the print gallery both outside and inside the picture of a harbor. He never quite loses the awareness of where he is, but he is still engrossed in what he sees. While he reads the print, and insofar as he reads it he must construct and make out, he must give the processes of matching from experience free rein, and I doubt if he can do that while concentrating fully on the surface arrangement. We cannot perform two different operations simultaneously with the same message. This does not mean, however, that we cannot process different messages at the same time. Of course we can. We can all listen and look; if we could not, we could not give illustrated lectures. We can also process different types of visual information at the same time, pictures and captions or galleries and paintings. There are indeed situations in which our responses to various sets of visual information must be kept marvelously distinct.

The driver of a motorcar has no difficulty in distinguishing between the information that reaches him through the mirror and the other that he picks up across the windshield. More surprisingly still, because more closely linked to motor reactions, the dentist learns to adjust his movement to the reverse picture he sees in the mirror and to the surround he sees normally. Here, as always, the plasticity of our processing capacity is astounding.

But let us remember again that such feats of perceptual skill would not be possible if the information which reaches us from both sources would not exhibit

---

[35] "Illusion and Visual Deadlock"; see note 31 above.

Figure 27. M. C. Escher, "Print Gallery," lithograph 1956

the same kind of systematic redundancies which mark all efficient systems of information. It is these redundancies we learn to disregard in our search for meaning, thus freeing our conscious capacity for the resolution of doubts. In hearing, this selective attention is called listening, in seeing, looking. Looking means focusing, physically and mentally, and this capacity must in the nature of things be limited. How limited we are in the simultaneous processing of visual information is a question which the student of art must hand over to the experimental psychologist. He would need his co-operation badly, for it lies in the

66

nature of art that it presses against the limits of our mental capacities—both in the direction of increasing refinement and discrimination and in that of richness and complexity. Thus the visual arts have taken on the role of exercises in the variability of vision. The artist, at least the modern artist, is engaged in a constant fight against the automatisms of perception. He certainly does not want us to look through his representation at what is represented: he does not want his picture to trigger responses which belong to reality.[36] I believe in fact that the resistance against any assertion of the kind I have been making is due to the wish that things were different. I have more or less refrained from discussing works of art precisely because the artist wants us to attend to his art. Neither does the poet want his words to become transparent for us so that we disregard their sound for the sake of the message. All art needs an awareness of form.

It is the discovery of this need which has increasingly been used by aestheticians and philosophers to decry those processes of everyday perception which bypass our conscious awareness. We are told to get out of this bad and lazy habit and to learn to see. I think we owe a special debt of gratitude to psychologists, such as Gibson, who have taught us to marvel at the subtlety and richness of the senses as perceptual systems. To abolish their operations for the sake of a pretended innocence and self-awareness would result at best in the paralysis of the proverbial centipede who was asked to take care which of its hundred legs it moved every time. Of course, you can throw a spanner into the marvelous works by paralyzing some of the operations—which is, I believe, the main effect of those dangerous drugs which a foolish philosophy has described as opening the doors of perception. Maybe they sometimes slow down the automatism and therefore change the appearance of the world, breaking down the constancies and enhancing the awareness of color and shapes.[37] We can get that more cheaply and innocuously by looking at a landscape with head down between our legs.

[36] Gombrich, *Art and Illusion*, chap. VI; *idem*, "Psycho-Analysis and the History of Art," *Meditations on a Hobby Horse*. It is at this point, perhaps, that this paper links up with my lecture to the American Psychological Society, "The Use of Art for the Study of Symbols," *American Psychologist*, January, 1965, where I discuss the traditional problems of "form" and "content" from the point of view of simultaneous information processing.

[37] I have never taken hallucigenic drugs and do not intend to do so, but some of the descriptions I have read and heard of what are experienced as "heightened" perceptions fit in well with the hypothesis that the integrative actions of the process are impeded. Instead of achieving a perception of invariants, the person under drugs may see the same variations due to illumination and distance which interest the artist. He may even fail to keep the world stable through "feedback" when moving his eyes and thus see swinging patterns streaking past. The interpretation that such experiences tear the veil from reality and restore some mystic immediacy is understandable but also sadly naïve.

The way to art does not lie through mechanical tampering with our brain or our senses. It is true that the artist may be in need of slowing down and observing the process of vision, but he can do so, I believe, only through the discovery of fresh interpretations, fresh meanings. We are so made that we can instruct and retool our perception to the finest points which interest us. If that were not so, neither the perception of language nor the miracle of reading would be possible. Both, I believe, use the mechanism that may have enabled the primitive hunter to discover and follow those tracks with which I began my paper. The interests of the civilized human being are perhaps less intense, but they are manifold, and so his vision is more variable. Of course, we all see the same world, but we learn to attend to different aspects. With luck I may have performed such an experiment, at least I hope that some of us, when next we take a walk, will suddenly see trees with different eyes. We may ask ourselves how much of their shape we could reconstruct, and as we pass them we may watch the intricate dance of their branches and twigs revealing their direction at least partially to the attentive eye. Maybe we will be reminded of mobiles and other forms of kinetic art which may indeed have enhanced our capacity to code and construct these complexities by presenting us with simpler models. So far I should certainly like to go along with Professor Gibson's tribute to the powers of art. And if my experiment succeeds it should also suggest the reason why the variability of vision is purchased at the price of exclusiveness. Sometimes, as the proverb says, we cannot see the wood for the trees, sometimes the wood replaces the trees. The richness of the optic array allows of an infinite number of interpretations as we scan this world of ours for meaning, whether we are naturalists or intelligence officers, students of vision or students of art.

II. THE PRIORITY OF CONTEXT OVER EXPRESSION

In the first part of my discussion of the theory and practice of interpretation, I had inevitably to concentrate on the psychological theory of the use of pictures as evidence. In turning to the practice of my particular field, the history of art, I hope that it may throw some light on the general theory. But here, as always, I think, this "feedback" can come into play only if we are ready to consider both successes and failures. Indeed, it is in the nature of things that the failures are more instructive than the successes, for we can learn most from the mistakes that were made by intelligent practitioners. If, therefore, I refer here to proved or possible mistakes made by other scholars, I hope the reader will not attribute this to a sense of superiority. I shall also stick out my own neck, though naturally I hope that it will be safe.

Once upon a time a great German museum acquired a little statuette of Hercules swinging his club, his left hand resting on a curious zigzag contraption (Figure 28). The distinguished art historian who published the work attributed it to the Nürnberg sculptor Peter Vischer the Elder and dated it from the first decades of the sixteenth century.[38] He knew that this attribution would not at first sound convincing, but he was captivated by the mixture of awkwardness and strength in the statuette, which he explained by the hypothesis that the artist had been brought up in a Gothic idiom and learned the language of classicism only relatively late in life. The impression of quality and profundity the statuette gave him was reinforced in his mind by the enigmatic attribute to which I have drawn attention, the zigzag implement, which was obviously a symbol. It could be only a ladder or steps. Ladders or steps, he argued, would lead either up or down, and this would not be a bad attribute with which to characterize Hercules, who had experienced his ups and downs. Moreover, he consulted one of the old tomes expounding the meaning of Christian symbols, the *Speculum imaginum* by the seventeenth-century Jesuit Jacob Massen, and found under *scala* a reference to Jacob's ladder which included impressive quotations from Philo of Alexandria in which that ladder is interpreted as the Ladder of Virtue. After all, Hercules, too, was virtuous—at least sometimes. The symbol seemed intended to say that he would attain the heights of Olympus, and that he was here identified with a Christian Knight, an association for which other learned parallels could be found. The only item that puzzled the scholar somewhat was what he took to be a "Phrygian cap" on top of the ladder. It is to his credit, I think, that he did not argue that the Phrygian cap was a symbol of liberty and that Hercules after all achieved freedom from bondage.

Actually it was this detail which was the undoing of the Christian Knight. That great connoisseur of Renaissance bronzes Leo Planiscig noticed that the so-called Phrygian cap was really a Venetian doge's hat. Since he had surely never accepted the attribution of the statuette to a Nürnberg Renaissance sculptor anyhow, he had no difficulty in following up this cue. He remembered that the steps were the coat of arms of the Venetian family of the Gradenigo, representing a pun on their name (*grado* meaning steps), or what is known as a "canting device." The family had a right to display the doge's hat, having three times held that great office. And to clinch the matter he reproduced in his article that came out in the subsequent year a pair of similar statuettes from the Museo

---

[38] *Münchner Jahrbuch der bildenden Kunst, n.s.,* 8 (1931): 133–55.

Figure 28. Statuette of "Hercules"

70

Civico Correr in Venice (Figure 29).[39] The alleged Peter Vischer was obviously part of a set of armorial bearers which came, in all likelihood, from a seventeenth-century piece of furniture made for the Gradenigos.

I have told the story not in order to gloat over the mistakes of a colleague who is no longer alive but to illustrate what I have called the priority of context over expression in the theory and practice of interpretation. In a way the little incident also illustrates how rarely theory can help the interpreter and how much is and will always remain practice. The theoretical lesson, on one level, is really what I stressed in my discussion of intelligence work: the interpreter should have a very well-stocked mind, but even then he also has to have luck, as Planiscig had in remembering the clinching evidence. But on another level our story yields perhaps a little more. It shows what I have called the variability of vision in action. For if we read the article by the art historian who saw the statuette as of a masterpiece by Peter Vischer we will soon become aware of how much this initial mistake in context colored his very perception. This is how he described the facial expression of the figure he took to embody a deep spiritual conception of Hercules as a Christian Knight (Figure 30):

> The eyes gaze into the distance, they stand in a face that bears the marks of hard experiences. This man is no longer a wild adventurer, he is sensitive to the sufferings destiny has laid upon him; it is with sorrow that he awaits the next test, though he is sure that he will win through in the end.[40]

So taken was our author by this idea of a reluctant Hercules that he placed his find far above the mere muscleman, such as the *Hercules Farnese*, as far as its profound psychological penetration was concerned. True, the German master was still struggling with formal problems, but in depth of expression he was a match to them all.

Would he have said the same, no, would he have *seen* the same had he known the statuette for what it is, one of a decorative set of armorial bearers on a wardrobe? Surely not. He had fallen victim to that formidable foe whom the beloved late Professor Panofsky so beautifully described as the Boa Constructor. But the true methodological problem, as I see it, is that we cannot ever do without the Boa Constructor. It may present a danger sometimes, indeed often, but it is also an indispensable friend and helpmate. As I argued in the first part of my paper, perception is a constructive process, not a passive one. Anything is

[39] Leo Planiscig, "Die Wappenhalter der Familie Gradenigo," *Jahrbuch der preussischen Kunstsammlungen,* 53 (1932): 16–18.

[40] *Ibid.,* p. 149.

Figure 29. Armorial Bearers

grist to the mill of this constructive process which takes its materials from past experience as much as from incoming stimuli. The old division between "seeing and knowing" is a bit crude precisely because the separation of any of these and other elements is never possible. Our guesses, our anticipations, and our knowledge all enter into this structure, and once it is formed it is not easily dissolved or erased. Without what I have called the beholder's share the picture could never be understood. Where it is reconstructed correctly we are not usually bothered by the need to allocate an exact share of the resulting experience to the artist and to the beholder. In fact we want the beholder to contribute his share, to bring the picture to life.

There was a time, for instance, when it was still generally understood that a large class of religious and mythological paintings are narrative in content and

Figure 30. Detail of Figure 28

context. In looking at such a painting and responding to it the beholder would enter into the story and would reconstruct the event in his own terms. His imagination might sometimes run ahead and he would think he saw what he only fancied.

Vasari is a case in point. When he described a painting he admired, he always added from his own store of imagination. Thus, in writing about Masaccio's tribute money in the *Carmine*, he says, as he usually does, that "the figures really appear to live."

> And most of all St. Peter, who is working so hard at cutting the money out of the belly of the fish that his face has become flushed from bending down....[41]

It would seem to me not only pointless but misleading to ask in such a case whether Vasari has seen correctly, or laboriously to compare the color of St. Peter's face with that of other faces in the fresco to find out whether he has possibly imagined things. Of course he imagined things, but this is what he was expected to do. In responding to the biblical narrative he added something of his own. Would we not all do this if we were asked to read the narrative aloud? We must interpret the text or it would be dead; the actor, even more than the reader, adds inflection, gesture, and expression to the lines he is asked to speak, just as the musician interprets the score by filling it with life and meaning without

[41] G. Vasari, *Le Vite*, ed. G. Milanesi (Florence, 1878–85), 2: 298. For Vasari's general approach see also E. H. Gombrich, "The Leaven of Criticism in Renaissance Art," in Charles S. Singleton, ed., *Art, Science, and History in the Renaissance* (Baltimore: The Johns Hopkins Press, 1968).

Figure 31. Jerome Bosch, "Epiphany"

doing violence to what is there. In that sense Vasari deserves good marks for entering into the action and identifying with the figures, for I am convinced that this unfashionable way of interpreting a narrative painting is the intended one.

But the same tendency to run ahead and to fill a configuration with meaning clearly can become an embarrassment, as we have seen, if the initial assumptions turn out to have been mistaken. I know that this conclusion has become an offense in the eyes of those who wish us to respond to a work of art without the intellectual intervention of historical and scholarly lore. I have much sympathy for this desire, for I, too, like to look at works of art from regions and cultures of which I know nothing, and I should like to think that I am not merely indulging in self-communion. But I would not be interested in the theory and practice of interpretation if I had not become convinced of the bearing which our interpretation may have on the way we actually see and experience a picture.

I did not want to discuss this problem without contributing at least one example of my own, giving hostages to fortune, and so I must ask the reader's patience with a rather complicated story, complicated because it concerns perhaps the most enigmatic and puzzling of painters in the history of art: I mean Jerome Bosch.

The painting I have selected is the famous triptych of "The Epiphany" in the Prado (Figure 31), which has recently been the subject of the most divergent interpretations.[42] Some of it is normal enough. The three Magi are appearing with their gifts before the Christ child at Bethlehem: the old one, Caspar, the younger, Melchior, and the Moor Balthazar. The embroideries on their cloaks show that Bosch knew of the typological tradition which sees in Old Testament scenes prefigurations of the Gospel story. The cope of the middle one shows the visit of the Queen of Sheba to Solomon; the golden container carried by the Moor in all probability is Abner's homage to David.[43] The goldsmithery deposited at the feet of the Virgin shows the group of Abraham sacrificing Isaac; it rests on horrible toads, presumably evil things crushed by that symbol of redemption.

So far the picture is no more odd than we have come to expect of Bosch's weird imagination, but who is the figure in the doorway (Figure 32)? An interesting discussion has sprung up, particularly during the last fifteen years, around

[42] For the bibliography see Charles de Tolnay, *Hieronymus Bosch* (New York: Reynal & Co., 1966), pp. 371–73.

[43] These, at least, are the subjects normally associated with the Adoration of the Magi in the various editions of the *Biblia Pauperum*.

Figure 32. Detail of Figure 31

the problem of how this figure is to be interpreted after the publication in the *Art Bulletin* of an immensely learned article by Lotte Brand Philip.[44] It would take too long to reproduce her very intricate arguments in full, supported as they are by extensive footnotes, but briefly she sees in that figure a picture of the Jewish Messiah, who, according to her, can be identified "with certainty" by two of the attributes which point to two different legends well known in Jewish scriptures.

The first of these is the golden chain, by which, as she says, "the arms of the figure are fettered." This, she thinks, is an allusion to the moving Jewish legend according to which the Messiah lives in Paradise as a beautiful young king and is so anxious to help the Jewish people that he has to be restrained by means of a golden chain, a legend which apparently is told in full only by Heinrich Heine,

[44] Lotte Brand Philip, "The Prado 'Epiphany' by Jerome Bosch," *Art Bulletin*, 35 (1953): 267–93.

though there are allusions to it in earlier Jewish sources. The second attribute by which she identifies the figure is his characterization as a leper by the white color of his skin "and by a large sore on his leg visible through a fancy gold-framed transparent bandage which resembles the crystal tube in a metal setting familiar in reliquaries."

We all remember from Handel's *Messiah* the prophecy of Isaiah applied to the figure:

> He is despised and rejected of men; a man of sorrows and acquainted with
> grief (Isa. 53: 3).

A Jewish legend in the Babylonian Talmud has elaborated this prophecy and tells of the Messiah as a leper never untying more than one of his sores at a time lest he be called. The authoress thinks that Bosch knew of both stories from oral tradition and fused them into one figure, although the two legends are not really compatible. But she still has to explain the presence of the Jewish Messiah in a picture of the Magi. He represents to her an obvious symbol of the synagogue, which is also symbolized by the ruined hut. The ass's head seen without the customary companion of the ox[45] reminds her of the interpretation of the donkey as the old law and of the rumor that Jews worshiped asses' heads. But this is not all, for these assembled symbols of the synagogue are in her view a representation of evil as such. For the Jewish Messiah becomes in Christian lore the Antichrist who was sometimes identified with the devil himself or with the son of Satan. In Bosch's painting, we read, the figure is not only designated as the Jewish Messiah but also characterized as a Jew by his long dark beard. What characterizes him as the Antichrist is most of all the crown of thorns, which alludes to his feigning the life of Christ, while among other things the little bell between his legs characterizes him as the bad shepherd. I must leave it to those interested in the technique of interpretation to look up the article and to marvel at the ingenuity with which every detail is made to fit. Thus the strange instrument he holds is thought to represent among other things the funnel of hell as pictured by Dante.

Moreover, since the Antichrist is also connected with the end of the world, Mrs. Brand Philip at the end of her long article also suggests that the three armies visible in the background represent the approach of Armageddon. In the

---

[45] Ludwig von Baldass, *Bosch* (New York: Harry N. Abrams, Inc., 1960), p. 242, noticed correctly that the head of the ox is still faintly visible behind that of the ass.

main her erudition has convinced many authors on Bosch, including Ludwig Baldass and, to some extent, even the great Panofsky.[46]

Meanwhile, however, the most formidable and most controversial of Bosch's interpreters had worked out a rival theory. I refer to Wilhelm Fraenger, who had caused a sensation some years before with his suggestion that Bosch's so-called "Garden of Delights" must have been intended as an altar painting of a heretical sect of Adamites who practiced their nudist orgies in a secret conventicle at s'Hertogenbosch.[47] Given this context it is perhaps not surprising that Fraenger interpreted our figure as Adam and, given his fabulous erudition, it is not surprising either that he could cram his article with the most out-of-the-way references to support this hypothesis.[48] It would take more space than I have to recount and dissect all his evidence; suffice it to say that Fraenger tries to establish this link by quoting an Ethiopian legend about the three Magi according to which their gifts to the Christ child derived from Paradise. These three gifts of gold, frankincense, and myrrh are interpreted in that source as referring to the three roles of the Savior: gold for the king, myrrh for the physician, and frankincense for the priest. Now, there is a Jewish tradition according to which the same three roles have been assigned to Adam, and the headgear held by the figure could be interpreted as a triple crown signifying the threefold office. This identification with Adam, according to Fraenger, does not exclude the identification with the Jewish Messiah as well. For Fraenger, too, knows of the legend of the Messiah as a leper. Given this identification, Fraenger sees in the altar an esoteric allusion to a heretical Judeo-Christian sect which did not accept the orthodox contrast between the sinful "old Adam" and the second Adam, who is Christ. On the contrary, Bosch's Adam is Christ's equal. In handing over to the newborn child the insignia of his threefold office he testifies to a union between Jewish and Christian ideas which would have been repugnant to the Roman church but acceptable at that very moment to the man whose spiritual pilgrimage Fraenger saw reflected in most of Bosch's paintings, one Jakob van Almaengien, a man we know to have been a Jew who was baptized in Bosch's home town in 1496 and who later reverted to his earlier faith. Clearly I cannot follow these

[46] Erwin Panofsky, *Early Netherlandish Painting: Its Origins and Character*, 2 vols. (Cambridge, Mass.: Harvard University Press, 1954), 1: 358, n. 7.

[47] Wilhelm Fraenger, *Das Tausendjährige Reich* (Coburg, 1947), translated into English as *The Millennium of Hieronymus Bosch* (London: Faber and Faber, 1952).

[48] Wilhelm Fraenger, "Der vierte König des Madrider Epiphanias Altars von Hieronymus Bosch," *Deutsches Jahrbuch für Volkskunde*, 3 (1957): 169–346, where also all Fraenger's earlier studies and the previous interpretations of the painting (excepting Brand Philip's) are conveniently quoted.

and other ramifications of Fraenger's system. What is more relevant to my topic is the effect which this context had on the way he saw the figure. He described his impression as one of enthusiastic rejoicing and spoke of "the joyful animation of his step."

> His delicately wrought hands are imbued with an expression of love and awe in the way they embrace the door frame and gently stroke it. The transfigured radiance of his countenance and the manner in which his impatient longing for the divine child are expressed in his hands and his feet make him into the most fascinating figure of the whole picture.[49]

The latest interpreter of that figure, Professor Charles de Tolnay, has not accepted Fraenger's hypothesis about Bosch's heretical associations. He consequently does not accept the reading of the figure as Adam, but he appears to agree with Fraenger that the figure's expression is friendly and joyful. He therefore rejects Mrs. Brand Philip's interpretation insofar as it relates to the Antichrist and the presence of evil in the world, yet he also thinks it represents the Messiah as described by Isaiah, but, as such, the figure "must be thought of as a prefiguration of Christ and His Passion." Since the real Christ is actually depicted in our picture sitting on the lap of His mother, this does not seem to me a very likely interpretation, but Professor Tolnay suggests that the golden chains allude to the seizure of Christ, the wound on his leg "wrapped up like a relic" to the entire story of the Passion, as does the crown of thorns. The little bell is the Christmas bell that heralds the coming of Christ; the gentle way in which he touches the wooden doorposts is probably an allusion to the wood of Christ's cross. The ruined hut is not necessarily the symbol of the synagogue, but an expression of the humility and poverty of the Holy Family. The man's young bearded face anticipates the face of Christ. Moreover, he observes the child Jesus "with lively interest." "Because of the ambiguity of the elements presented in Bosch's painting," concludes Professor de Tolnay, "the surest guide to a proper understanding of his spiritual intentions is the expressive value of his forms. If we neglect them, it is unavoidable that they will be related to traditions and texts with which they have no connexion."

---

[49] "Der vierte König," p. 178: "... das enthusiastische Frohlocken seiner Miene und die freudige Beschwingtheit seines Schrittes. ... Auch seine feingliedrigen Hände beseelt ein Ausdruck inniger Ergriffenheit, wie sie den Türpfosten umarmen und behutsam streicheln. Gerade das verzückte Leuchten seines Angesichts und sein in Hand und Fuss sich ungeduldig äußerndes Verlangen nach dem Gotteskind machen den Türhüter zur faszinierendsten Gestalt des Bildes."

It was this last sentence, I confess, enjoining us to start from the expressive values of the forms, which I regarded as a challenge.[50] For my own position is that we must know the context before we can interpret the expression, particularly, I would say, in the case of an artist as enigmatic and ambiguous as Bosch. I recalled the words with which Fritz Saxl used to react to a puzzle that troubled him: "Surely it must be possible to find that out." I also recalled the letter my friend and colleague Otto Kurz once wrote in his capacity as librarian of the Warburg Institute, when he was asked for the best book on Christian symbolism. "Dear Sir," he replied, "the best book on Christian Symbolism is the Bible."

Now what does the Bible tell about the story of the Magi? We read in the second chapter of the Gospel of St. Matthew that

> ... when Jesus was born in Bethlehem of Judaea in the days of Herod the king, behold there came wise men from the east to Jerusalem. Saying, Where is he that is born King of the Jews? for we have seen his star in the east, and are come to worship him. When Herod the king had heard these things, he was troubled, and all Jerusalem with him. And when he had gathered all the chief priests and scribes of the people together, he demanded of them where Christ should be born. And they said unto him, In Bethlehem of Judaea: for thus it is written by the prophet.... Then Herod, when he had privily called the wise men, inquired of them diligently what time the star appeared. And he sent them to Bethlehem, and said, Go and search diligently for the young child; and when ye have found him, bring me word again, that I may come and worship him also. When they had heard the king, they departed; and, lo, the star, which they saw in the east, went before them, till it came and stood over where the young child was.... And being warned of God in a dream that they should not return to Herod, they departed into their own country another way.
>
> . . . .
>
> Then Herod, when he saw that he was mocked of the wise men, was exceeding wroth, and sent forth, and slew all the children that were in Bethlehem.

We also read, of course, of the flight to Egypt, and that the Holy family did not return before the death of King Herod. This, as many commentators have pointed out, presents chronological difficulties because, according to our chronology, King Herod actually died four years before the beginning of our era. But this difficulty has come to the fore only with the new criticism and need not concern us at all. For, if you take the biblical narrative at face value, there clearly

[50] I referred to this discrepancy in a review of Professor de Tolnay's book in the *New York Review of Books*, February 23, 1967.

was one person besides the Magi who had an interest in the newborn child, and that was King Herod. It was his "chief priests and scribes" who had sent the Wise Men to Bethlehem and he had every reason for wanting to know where this reputed King of the Jews was to be found. Might not Lionel Cust have been right, who suggested forty years ago that this mysterious figure is one of the King's priests, scribes, or spies?[51] Or could he perhaps be Herod himself watching and plotting murder?

But what did Herod look like? We have plenty of pictures of the Massacre of the Innocents, where he appears as an evil king (Figure 33), but I know of no painting of the Adoration of the Magi where he appears, least of all as a victim of sores.

Figure 33. Master P. M., "The Massacre of the Innocents," engraving

On the other hand, history and legend do so describe him, not only in general terms, but in repulsive detail worthy of Bosch's "Chamber of Horrors." It was Josephus Flavius who originally recorded these symptoms of Herod's disease, and his account was embodied in a text which was almost better known in the Middle Ages than the Bible itself, the *Historia Scholastica* by the twelfth-century

[51] L. Cust, "The Adoration of the Kings by H. Bosch," *Apollo*, 8 (1928): 551.

theologian Petrus Comestor. There need be no doubt that Bosch could have had access to this book. No less than eight editions appeared in his lifetime,[52] and, as luck will have it, the copy of the 1485 printing in the Paris Bibliothèque Nationale comes from the Chartreuse of Bois le Duc, Bosch's home town.

We read that in the last year of King Herod's cruel reign he executed Jewish patriots who had hurled the Roman eagle from the roof of the temple. As a punishment he was visited by a disgusting skin disease which is described with clinical detail by Josephus and his translator. King Herod suffered from fever and an intolerable itch all over the body's surface, he had a chronic torturing pain in the neck, the legs were swollen through a sore in the skin, and his festering testicles bred worms.[53]

Considering the case history of this picture one must of course hesitate to use the word "certain" in proposing a fresh interpretation. In fact, I know that I cannot expect those for whom one of the earlier readings has by now firmly settled on the picture to see it all at once in the light of this text. But it might not be easy for anyone who wishes to challenge it to find another personage entitled to wear royal attire, and described as having a sore on his leg (*intercutaneum vitium*), who figures in the story of the Magi.

Herod was indeed the central figure of that story when it came to be enacted in the mystery plays at the Feast of Epiphany.[54] I could not hope to describe this

---

[52] The catalogue of the Paris Bibliothèque Nationale lists so many separate printings between 1473 and 1503.

[53] Petrus Comestor: *"De Magnitudine Morbi Herodis*: Dehinc variis affligabatur languoribus. Nam febris non mediocris erat, prurigo intolerabilis in omni corporis superfice, assiduis vexabatur colle tormentis, pedes intercutaneo vitio tumuerant, putredo testiculorum vermes generabat, creber anhalitus et interrupta suspira, quae ad vindictam Dei ab omnibus referebantur" (Migne, *Patrologia Latina*, 198, 1546).

[54] For the Latin and French plays see in particular Isaac Sondheimer, *Die Herodes-Partien im Lateinischen Liturgischen Drama und in den Französischen Mysterien* (Beiträge zur Geschichte der Romanischen Sprachen und Literaturen, no. 3) (Halle, 1912).

For the English plays see Warren E. Tomlinson, *Der Herodes-Charakter im englischen Drama* (Palaestra 195) (Leipzig, 1934).

Much of the German material is referred to in Georges Duriez, *Les Apocryphes dans le Drame Réligieux en Allemagne au Moyen Age* (Mémoires et Traveaux publiés par des Professeurs des Facultés Catholiques de Lille, no. 10) (Lille, 1914).

I know of no monograph on the subject in the Netherlands, but there is some material in such standard works as Wilhelm Creizenach, *Geschichte des neueren Dramas* (Halle, 1911); see also note 66 below. I should like here to thank the members of my audience at Johns Hopkins, and in particular Professor George Boas and Dr. William M. C. Randall, for drawing my attention to the plays and helping with references.

development more graphically and more succinctly than did Grace Frank, of The Johns Hopkins University, in her book *The Medieval French Drama*:

> As soon as Herod himself appeared in the plays further opportunities for dramatic development became obvious and liturgical authors soon made effective use of his presence. They could now introduce not only a more complicated plot, with an element of suspense, but also portray a villain whose speech and actions, costume and accessories might be used to suggest his vicious character. The Three Kings had been slightly individualized in dress, perhaps in deportment, but Herod's was the first role capable of giving us a real person and not a type. The contrast between the cruel, powerful, worldly monarch on his richly decorated throne, surrounded by ornately costumed courtiers, and the innocent child in the manger, as well as Herod's angry action in brandishing his sword and his fierce words uttered in loud tones, all contained new emotional possibilities, so that the incidents concerned with Herod regularly came to be added to the simpler Magi plays.[55]

The author's conclusion, as she evokes these spectacles to her mind's eye, reads almost like a description of our painting: ". . . the splendid costumes of oriental potentates must have glowed brilliantly beside the tunics of the shepherds and the white robes of the angels; Herod's pride and arrogance would be accentuated by the humility of the worshipers before the *praesepe* of the Holy Child. . . ."[56]

Even the story of Herod's illness figures in many of the plays, though not always in the same clinical detail. It is usually presented there—as it is in Bede's *Martyrology*[57] and in the *Legenda Aurea*[58]—as a punishment for the Massacre of the Innocents, and usually leads to the villain's suicide. "For the grim pantomime," writes Karl Young in his description of this final scene in the Benediktbeuren play, "the playwright was supplied with ample details. His own contribution was merely the courage necessary in putting so offensive an incident onto the stage."[59]

Nobody would doubt that Bosch had plenty of this courage. But, alas, we must ask whether the public of those days regarded such repulsive afflictions in the same light as we do, or at least did before the vogue of sick humor. The suffering of the wicked was often regarded as comic,[60] and Herod was certainly

[55] (Oxford, 1954), pp. 34–35.
[56] *Ibid.*, p. 39.
[57] Migne, *Patrologia Latina*, 94, 1144.
[58] Jacobus de Varagine, *Legenda Aurea*, ed. Th. Graesse (Bratislava, 1890), 10: 65ff.
[59] Karl Young, *The Drama of the Medieval Church* (Oxford, 1933), 2: 194–95.
[60] Rainer Hess, *Das Romanische Geistliche Schauspiel als Profane und Religiöse Komödie* (Freiburger Schriften zur romanischen Philologie, no. 4) (Munich, 1965), has a chapter "Defektenkomik," pp. 80–89.

represented as a comic villain, both in his impotent ravings and in his undignified end.[61]

Of course, it may be argued that the sources quoted still give no warrant for my identification of the afflicted figure with Herod, for in the scene represented by Bosch the Massacre still lies in the future. Actually, there is at least one text of a play which might be used to counter this particular objection, for in Arnoul Greban's famous *Mystère de la Passion* of 1452 the King's illness, which breaks out so virulently after the Massacre, is explicitly said to be of long standing, having first appeared as a punishment for the murder of his sons.[62] But it is hardly necessary to invoke this text, since Bosch would have used the sores simply as the attributes of the wicked King to mark him off from the Magi.

For all this, there is no denying the difficulty which must come immediately to mind, that if Herod had been present at the Adoration and had managed to see the child he would not have had to plot the massacre of all the children of Bethlehem, since he would have known his rival. Strangely enough there is another play which somewhat disregards the logic of this argument, at least insofar as Herod there asks the soldiers to bring him the body or at least a limb of the slain Christ child (forgetting that if that were possible the other children could be spared).[63] Even so, it remains true that neither the Bible nor any play known to me makes Herod accompany the Magi to Bethlehem. What he says in the Gospel and what is embroidered in the plays is merely that he desires to go there and worship the child. The importance of this remark as a symptom of Herod's wickedness was not lost on the early commentators of the Scriptures. The *glossa ordinaria* says: "Herod promises devotion, but sharpens his sword; covering up the malice of his heart with the colour of humility. He feigns in words and means to worship Him Whom he secretly intends to kill. His person is represented by the hypocrites who pretend to seek God and never desire to find Him."[64]

It would clearly be beyond the means of painting to illustrate this feature of Herod's character—of promising to worship and planning to kill—while stick-

---

[61] For Herod's antics see in particular Young, *op. cit.*, 2: 100. In fifteenth-century Bourges a clerk on horseback rode through the streets dressed up as Herod, stopping at every crossroad to represent the different episodes in the life of the King of the Jews "au milieu des lazzi des jongleurs" (Jean Mellot, "A propos du théâtre liturgique de Bourges," *Mélanges . . . offerts à Gustave Cohen* [Nizet, 1950], p. 194).

[62] Arnoul Greban, *Le Mystère de la Passion*, ed. Gaston Paris and Gaston Raynant (Paris, 1878), vv. 7898f.; cf. Sondheimer, *op. cit.*, p. 146.

[63] *Le Geu des trois Roys*; cf. Sondheimer, *op. cit.*, p. 103.

[64] Migne, *Patrologia Latina* 114. 74.

ing closely to the sequence of events. If the meaning of the text was to be brought out, it could be done only by some such method as Bosch adopted. Moreover, it may be that the inconsistency of the King watching the Adoration was a little less obvious to those who had attended Epiphany plays than it would be to us. For it is well known that these plays were not acted on a picture stage but on simultaneous settings. "Instead of the succession of scenes to which we are used," writes Creizenach in his standard work on the subject, "there was simultaneity. From the very beginning Herod was found on his throne, the midwife by the manger and the shepherds again at a different place."[65] Memling's Munich painting, "The Seven Joys of the Virgin" (Figure 34), is often

Figure 34. Memling, "The Seven Joys of the Virgin," detail

[65] *Op. cit.*, p. 58.

Figure 35. The Magi at the Court of Herod, detail of Figure 34

quoted as a translation of this convention into a pictorial narrative. Here, for instance, we see the Magi arriving at the court of Herod (Figure 35), and we also see Herod nearby consulting the scribes in the temple, while the foreground is filled with the pageant of the actual Adoration. One might well imagine that in some performance, inside or outside the church, Herod would have remained at his court, dismissing the Magi and waiting in vain for their return; but being the boisterous figure he was he might well have continued to mime and even to participate in the action while the Adoration was being enacted in the neighboring structure or on an appropriate float. It has been suspected that it was in particular the antics of Herod which brought the Epiphany plays into disfavor with the Church and occasionally even led to the banning of the plays.[66]

Admittedly, these are *ad hoc* explanations which may well betray the influence, nefarious or benign, of the "Boa Constructor." Even so, it is reassuring to know that the account books of the Confraternity of Our Lady of s'Hertogen-

[66] *Ibid.*

86

bosch, of which Bosch was a member, contain frequent entries throughout the fifteenth century referring to expenditure on Epiphany shows and processions.[67] In one of them a painter who was Bosch's uncle is actually paid for painting one of the king's garments.[68] The influence of these and similar shows on pictorial iconography has of course been much debated. Here, as elsewhere, it must remain hypothetical.[69]

What is no mere hypothesis, however, is the fact that the figure I propose to call Herod is represented by Bosch as an actual participant of the scene rather than as a symbolic bystander. The painter has indicated this by a narrative detail which strangely has escaped the attention of commentators and has caused much unnecessary speculation—I mean the object the figure holds in his hands. It is the tiara of the middle king. Here I would venture the dangerous words that "there can be no doubt," for, though photographs may not reveal this connection very clearly, an inspection of the original shows that Bosch has taken great care to indicate that the tiara matches the king's collar in tone and also in decoration, and that the row of jewels in the center of the tiara corresponds exactly to the row encircling the king's neck.

As to the decoration of this tiara, it seems to me likely that it also matches, in spirit, the fantastic design on the kings' gifts and on the garment of the third king. This shows human-headed birds, fabulous monsters which, in the imagination of the Middle Ages, peopled the distant regions whence the Magi came;[70] the motif of the tiara might well reflect a similar feature of the second king's remote homeland, the fight between Pygmies and cranes which belongs to the same stock of exotic travelers' tales.[71] In some of the mystery plays the foreign character of the kings was emphasized by making them speak a strange gib-

[67] C. R. Hermans, *Bijdragen tot de Geschiedenis . . . der Provincie Noord-Braband*, vol. 1 (s'Hertogenbosch, 1845). The kings are mentioned in the accounts of 1396–97, 1399–1400, 1423–24, 1426–27, 1441–42, 1446–47, 1464–65, 1493–94, 1495–96, 1501–2.

[68] Jan Mosmans, *Jheronymus . . . Bosch* (s'Hertogenbosch, 1947), shows that Goesse de Maelre, who was paid in 1441–42 for the service, was Bosch's uncle. For the frequency of such participation by artists in the mystery plays, see Leopold Schmidt, "Maler-Regisseure des Mittelalters," *Maske und Kothurn*, 4 (1958): 1.

[69] Leopold Schmidt, *loc. cit.*, offers a detailed bibliography of this debate. A more recent contribution is M. D. Anderson, *Drama and Imagery in English Medieval Churches* (Cambridge: At the University Press, 1963). In our context it is interesting that she convincingly traces the roof bosses of Norwich Cathedral, which include representations of Herod's illness and death, to mystery plays.

[70] Rudolf Wittkower, "Marvels of the East," *Journal of the Warburg and Courtauld Institutes*, 5 (1942).

[71] *Ibid.*, p. 160.

berish.[72] Bosch's decoration of their garments may present the visual equivalent of this device.

That the tiara is really the king's is confirmed by the fact that, if we refused to assign it to him, he alone would be without a headgear, which would be quite out of character. As to Herod's own strange head covering, I feel that not too much need be read into its fantastic shape. It is definitely not a crown of thorns but rather a kind of turban surrounded by plaited twigs issuing in a flower. One of the tormentors of Christ on the ruined outer wing of the Bruges triptych wears a similar headgear. The Lisbon "Temptation of St. Anthony" also shows a female figure with a rather similar headcovering made of flowering twigs, and the winged demon on top of "The Hay-Wain" is similarly attired.[73] These parallels fit in quite well with Herod's evil nature, and so does his garment, decorated (on the ribbon with the bell) with toadlike creatures very similar to those Bosch liked to represent on the shield of Christ's tormentors.

The bell may correspond to the leper's rattle, but it may also be a fanciful decoration of the royal garb. The same applies to the chains, which certainly do not look like fetters. The King is simply festooned with golden chains, for his costume must suggest pomp and vainglory. For Herod in the plays is not only the villain; he is the Oriental despot who swears by Mohammed and boasts of his "gorgeous array."

> Behold my contenance and my colur,
> Bryghtur then in the sun in the meddis of the dey.
> Where can you haue a more grettur succur
> Then to behold my person that ys soo gaye?
> My fawcun and fassion with my gorgis araye,—[74]

It is Herod, therefore, who, in my interpretation, stands in the shadows of the stables in the midst of his scribes and tries to spy out the Christ child. To avoid suspicion he has picked up the king's tiara as if he were a page.

Such a representation, it is true, would be unique in the history of Christian painting,[75] but so are many other of Bosch's inventions. It is his disregard of tra-

---

[72] Grace Frank, *op. cit.*, p. 37.

[73] Cf. plates 188, 129, and 149 in Tolnay, *op. cit.*

[74] I quote this passage from the Coventry plays after Tomlinson, *op. cit.*, p. 17; he gives further references to similar descriptions on p. 27.

[75] Mrs. Jamison, *Legends of the Madonna* (London, 1857), p. 20, thought she spotted Herod watching the Adoration from a balcony in a painting by Lucas van Leyden, but I have not been able to identify this composition. Bosch's picture belongs to his most frequently copied works (the copies are listed in M. J. Friedländer, *Die altniederländische Malerei*, vol. 5 [Leiden, 1934]). But the most characteristic attributes

ditional iconographic conventions, rather than any proved reliance on esoteric texts or ideas, which confronts the interpreter with such difficulties.

But, whether or not the interpretation here proposed will ultimately be found acceptable, it can certainly serve to demonstrate the truth of what I have called "the priority of context over expression." If we see the figure as the Herod of the mystery plays, its bearing and expression begin to look very different from the way it looked to previous interpreters. For me, at any rate, his attitude is one of stealth, and his expression is strained and furious, the bulging eyes betraying Herod's eagerness to spy out the secret of his dreaded rival. Thus I find in this representation the same mixture of villainy and horseplay that marked the role of Herod in medieval drama. Nor does this reading conflict with my general conception of Bosch's art. I have pointed out elsewhere that his inventions were not seen in the same portentous light as that in which they appear to many modern critics. He certainly did not find the rendering of evil at all incompatible with comic effects.[76]

But it is time to take stock and to ask what this exercise in hermeneutics may have contributed to the general theory of interpretation. It is, I am afraid, the disappointing truth that, contrary to our wish, pictures don't tell their own story. In the first part of this discussion, I felt compelled to throw some doubt on the importance of painting in the history of man's awareness of perception, which Professor Gibson had postulated so persuasively. It is a little sad for me again to have to qualify the importance of the evidence of pictures for the historian, but my insistence on the priority of context really comes down to this. Unaided, we cannot infer from the pictures by Bosch that there were Adamite sects in s'Hertogenbosch at his time, which are nowhere recorded in documents; we cannot infer from them either that Jewish legends were passed on in his environment by word of mouth, which only Heinrich Heine finally wrote down. Pictures, in other words, can be an aid to the historian, but they cannot often serve him as the only source.

I am not only referring to the interpretation of subject matter, as in the case of Bosch's Epiphany. I am also thinking of the use of images as evidence for more general trends and opinions. Let me give an example which may offer some

---

of Herod, notably the skin wound on the leg, are not always shown, and the figure is gradually turned into a conventional bystander. It survives as such in the large compositions of the Adoration attributed to Jan Breughel (versions in Vienna and at the National Gallery in London).

[76] Cf. my note "The Earliest Description of Bosch's Garden of Delight," *Journal of the Warburg and Courtauld Institutes*, 30 (1967).

Figure 36. Dürer, "Epiphany"

light relief, though it has its sad aspects. I take it from a communist East German journal for school teachers, though I must add in fairness that it dates back to the worst Stalinist period. It also concerns a painting of the Adoration of the Magi, this time by Dürer (Figure 36). According to the communist teacher:

> ... the special feature of that picture lies in the fact that the center of the painting is taken up by gigantic glittering silver vessels. It is toward these that the Christ child stretches out its little hands. The three wise men look neither at Christ nor at the Madonna. Their eyes are glued to the vessels they brought and one can read in their expression their immeasurable regret at having to part with these treasures. The Madonna also looks only at the presents and her gaze betrays an immeasurable greed and undisguised delight.

90

One simply could not imagine a bolder and, from the standpoint of the Church a more blasphemous painting. The artist selected this apparently innocent theme from the Bible in order boldly to hurl into the face of the Church the accusation of avarice and greed for profit.[77]

I don't want to make too much of this grotesque example, for I have no proof that the poor hack who wrote this really believed what he wrote. Maybe he even had his tongue in his cheek. Here is another problem of interpretation which I do not propose to pursue, the problem of a writer's sincerity.

But, though this interpretation represents a caricature, it only shows in monstrous magnification to what extent the reading of the historical context itself can influence the way the pictorial evidence is seen. In fact, the literature on Dürer is particularly rich in such examples. Not that anyone else took the Uffizi painting to be an illustration of the *Communist Manifesto*, but it is a little different with the woodcuts to the "Apocalypse." A few years ago a detailed iconological study of that woodcut series was published in Czechoslovakia by Rudolf Chadraba, a study which presents a detailed and learned interpretation of this work as a manifesto by the rising bourgeoisie against the Church of Rome.[78] The pivot of the book is the identification of the great whore of Babylon with the pope, an interpretation which became indeed commonplace in Protestant propaganda (including Luther's Bible) and which can also be documented from earlier polemics against the Church. Since the text actually says that the seven heads of the beast "are seven mountains on which the woman sitteth," this exegetic twist was almost inescapable for those who wanted to turn against Rome. But the City of Seven Hills referred to in the Revelation is of course pagan Rome, and clearly the Church would not have accepted the Apocalypse into the Bible nor disseminated illustrations throughout the Middle Ages if that original reference had not been understood.

Even so, it must be admitted that Chadraba's interpretation is not simply the product of Marxist historiography. The tendency to see in Dürer's tremendous cycle a portent of the coming Reformation can be traced back to the nineteenth century.[79] Nationalism may originally have contributed to this. Dürer, the quintessential German artist, was seen as a kind of Luther who used images

---

[77] A. D. Epstein, "Weltanschauung und Kultur der Renaissance," Sonderheft der Zeitschrift *Geschichte in der Schule* (Berlin: Volk und Wissen, Volkseigener Verlag, 1952), p. 23.

[78] Rudolf Chadraba, *Dürers Apokalypse: Eine Ikonologische Deutung* (Prague, 1964).

[79] M. Thausing, *Albrecht Dürer* (Leipzig, 1876).

instead of words in his assertion of German independence. I confess I was surprised to see to what extent this reading colored even the lecture which Max Dvořák gave on the Apocalypse in 1922.[80] In fact, it is this lecture to which our Czech author appeals as his authority. Dvořák, too, had taken it for granted that Dürer's woodcut of the whore of Babylon (Figure 37) was aimed at papal Rome. In Dürer, he writes, as distinct from the biblical text, the woman on the beast does not appear to St. John, but to a crowd of men and women in contemporary costume (Figure 38).

> Only one of them seems to admire her, a little monk with wide open eyes and pursed lips, sinks to his knees, to adore her. The faces of the others reflect timid horror or opposition. The peasant looks at her with stolid contemptuous defiance. The figure in the center in which we might surmise a portrait of Dürer himself stands with his feet firmly planted on the ground in an unyielding attitude, the hands on his hips and scrutinises the whore with a critical gaze.[81]

But, before we allow this suggestive description to settle on the picture, we must really inquire what we are asked to accept: no more, but no less, I would contend, than that Dürer published and signed a series of woodcuts which would have brought him to the stake if it had been seen by his contemporaries in the light of an open challenge to the Church. If that is true, we have to take it as a secret, underhand satire intelligible to initiates only.[82] Is that likely? Was not Wilhelm Waetzoldt more probably right when he reminded us that popes, emperors, and clerics appeared quite frequently among the damned in medieval imagery without anybody taking these pictures to be an attack against the institution of the Church itself?[83] But do we have to see the monk as worshiping the scarlet woman? Here, as always, a glance at the literature about a given work of art brings it home to us to what an extent any description of what is represented is in reality an interpretation. It was Wölfflin, I believe, who set the key for Dvořák's reading when he described the monk as "the only one who has immediately sunk to his knees at the appearance of the whore."[84] Half a century before him A. von Eye had regarded the figure in a different light: "It is only the monk," he writes, "... who sees further this time. He collapses and folds his

---

[80] Max Dvořák, *Kunstgeschichte als Geistesgeschichte* (Munich: R. Piper, 1923), pp. 193–202.

[81] *Ibid.*, p. 200.

[82] According to Chadraba, *op. cit.*, pp. 47–48, who speaks of a "hidden" tendency.

[83] Wilhelm Waetzoldt, *Dürer und seine Zeit* (Vienna: Phaidon Verlag, 1935), p. 69.

[84] Heinrich Wölfflin, *Die Kunst Albrecht Dürers* (Munich, 1926), p. 71.

Figure 37. Dürer, woodcut from the "Apocalypse"

Figure 38. Detail of Figure 37

94

hands in prayer while fear and terror mark his countenance. For while below the Babylonian woman still struts about, the Angel of the Lord is already hovering above her. . . ."[85]

Indeed, if further proof were needed that we do not have to describe the monk as subservient to evil, there are two recent books which offer rather startling alternatives. Franz Juraschek interprets the whole cycle of woodcuts not as an anticipation of Luther's Reformation but rather as an elaborate presentation of the philosophy of Nicolaus Cusanus.[86] He sees in our monk a portrait of the theologian, "the exegete," whom he postulates as the author of that surprising program which Dürer could not have invented. The second book puts forward the even more startling theory that the monk is a portrait of, and monument to, Savonarola, who is shown "looking with wide-open rapturous eye at the fire that will destroy Babylon,"[87] while the group of men evokes for that interpreter "the upright citizens of Florence," who followed the *frate*.

We need not take this seriously, but so much may be true, I believe, that there is no reason why the monk should be read together with the whore of Babylon. Does he not really rather look up to the angel "who came down from heaven with great power"?

As for the expression of the crowd, would it not square best with another verse of the Apocalypse, which reads that "they that dwell on earth shall wonder, whose names were not written in the book of life from the foundation of the world, when they behold the beast that was, and is not, and yet is"?[88]

Dvořák obviously ignored the tenuous character of the visual evidence on which the interpretation of the sequence as a pictorial counterpart to Luther's Reformation was based. He was convinced that the spirit of the age spoke more directly from such works of art. Steeped, as he was, in a Hegelian evolutionist conception of cultural history, he had no doubt of the fact that by 1498 the *Zeitgeist* was already pregnant with the Reformation. Accordingly, he looked for a method to plot the position of Dürer's early work in that sequence of evolving

---

[85] A. von Eye, *Leben und Wirken Albrecht Dürers* (Nördlingen: Beck, 1860), p. 155.

[86] Franz Juraschek, *Das Rätsel in Dürers Gottesschau: Die Holzschnitt-Apokalypse und Nikolaus Cusanus* (Salzburg: Otto Müller Verlag, 1955), esp. chap. IV, n. 130, and chap. VIII, n. 27.

[87] Antonie Leinz von Dessauer, *Savonarola und Albrecht Dürer* (Munich and Zurich, 1961), p. 24; also printed in *Das Münster*, 14 (1961).

[88] See also Juraschek, *op. cit.*, pp. 43–44. Admittedly, the Koberger Bible which was Dürer's iconographic model shows the mighty of this earth worshiping the whore, but it may be that he wanted to avoid a repetition of the group worshiping the beast and therefore selected another verse for illustration.

world views in which Luther's break with the church was such a decisive point of reference.

What marks Dürer's "Apocalypse" in Dvořák's eyes is its high degree of "subjectivism." In the Middle Ages, Dvořák says, the theological explanation of the world had been too universally compelling for man to develop a personal point of view. The fifteenth century witnessed the weakening of its hold. In Italy and in the Netherlands man's relation to the world was placed on a new footing by means of observation and experiment. In these two countries, then, the cultivation of the senses led to the imitation of nature in art and the recognition of natural laws in science. Germany, however, pursued the same aim by means of an enrichment of the inner life through spiritual edification and self-education. Hence, we learn, the role of art in Germany was very different from what it was elsewhere. In this sense "Dürer's Apocalypse is the first great German work of art of the Modern Age . . . a sermon of an eloquence and profundity equal to Luther's before Luther. . . ."[89]

The woodcut sequence, then, was born out of a feeling of responsibility toward the main problems of man's spiritual life, problems which transcend those of art.

> This attitude still recalls the Middle Ages, while the personal note of the confession anticipates the tendencies through which Michelangelo, a few decades later, shattered the impersonal artistic ideals of the Renaissance and which subsequently conquered the whole of European art. Thus the Apocalypse stands between two worlds, rounding off one and introducing the other, providing a link between the state of things before the Renaissance and the one that was to come after it.[90]

I have paraphrased and translated so much of this interpretation because I feel that little more than quotation is needed to show up its limitations in the light of what I have said before. For Dvořák the context was given: the year 1498 suggested both the end of the Middle Ages and the dawn of the century that would witness Luther's Reformation. Is it unfair to suggest that he read as much into the work as he read out of it?

I do not think it is, since I have emphasized that without this activity of our imagination we would never get any interpretation at all. But here, as always, the problem is rather how we can look critically at this indispensable activity, how we can slow down the process of automatism which triggers the association

[89] Dvořák, *op. cit.*, p. 197.
[90] *Ibid.*, p. 201.

96

with Luther as soon as Dürer's period comes into view. What we would have to ask the author is what other evidence he has for his interpretation that the Reformation was already potentially present in the mind of Dürer twenty years before Luther nailed his theses to the church door of Wittenberg. It is no use talking of *Zeitgeist* and *Zeitstimmung* to account for a work of art unless we can specify a little more clearly what we mean in terms of people, of movements, and of reactions. I am not a historian of the period, but I believe it is correct to say that the criticism of the clergy and of the monastic orders—which certainly was voiced in Germany, as it was voiced elsewhere in the later Middle Ages—was not aiming at a new world view; above all, it had nothing to do with either the observation of nature manifested in Netherlandish art or the discovery of natural laws for which the fifteenth century was not, in any case, very conspicuous. I must not, at this point, ride off on my anti-Hegelian hobbyhorse, having given it free rein elsewhere.[91] But I do not think we can discuss the evidence of images without pointing to this short cut in the interpretation of art. Not that there cannot be any links between the age and the art it produces; this would be a ridiculous assertion. But, to establish this link, we have first to specify the context much more precisely than was generally done by the school of *Geistesgeschichte*. The temptation to think that the landmarks which interest the historian today loomed equally large in the lives of the people of the past is anyhow hard to resist. Hence I would make it a methodological rule to subject any such link to a particularly careful scrutiny.

That scrutiny is particularly needed in a field such as ours, which deals not with statements but with images. For it is in the nature of things that images need much more of a context to be unambiguous than do statements. Language can form propositions, pictures cannot. It seems strange to me how little this obvious fact has been stressed in the methodology of art history. We speak of the expression of Weltanschauung, of the world view of the artist, but we would look in vain for the illustration of even the most central philosophical proposition, such as *Universalia sunt ante rem* or *entia non sunt multiplicanda praeter necessitatem*. The means of visual art cannot match the statement function of language. Art can present and juxtapose images, even relatively unambiguous images, but it cannot specify their relationship.[92]

It so happens that this important truth can also be illustrated from the

[91] E. H. Gombrich, *In Search of Cultural History*, The Philip Maurice Deneke Lecture (Oxford: Clarendon Press, 1969).

[92] See my review of Charles Morris, "Signs, Language and Behavior," *Art Bulletin*, 31 (1949): 70ff., and *Art and Illusion*, chap. II.

œuvre of Albrecht Dürer. His famous engraving which he called "The Horseman" is now known under the title "Knight, Death and Devil" (Figure 39). Though dated 1513, four years before Luther's Reformation, it, too, has called forth the conditioned reflex of Lutheranism.[93] Earlier interpretations saw in it an ideal portrait of the Humanist Franz von Sickingen, but the usual reaction is to see in the knight an image of heroic defiance of death and of the devil, an anticipation of Luther's hymn with its rousing lines "and if the world were full of devils and threatened to devour us, we shall not be too much afraid, we shall yet win through."

So much has this interpretation fused with the image that the print has become the symbol of heroic defiance as such in the minds of many Germans from Nietzsche onward.[94] I believe Göring chose it as his bookplate, and I certainly remember from my wartime listening how often the symbol was invoked by Goebbels and his tools in their desperate appeals to the German people to stand united "against death and the devil."

I believe that even the most learned interpretations are not quite uninfluenced by this reading which sees the knight as defying death and the devil. The text that is most often quoted is the pamphlet by Erasmus of Rotterdam on the Christian Knight, who fights the good fight fearless of spooks and threats.[95]

But I believe that, if we slow down our automatic reaction, we are entitled to ask whether it is really true that a good Christian should not be afraid of the devil? I do not think it is true. Fear of hell is as important in orthodox teaching

---

[93] It is interesting to see that as early as 1860 A. von Eye (*op. cit.*, p. 355) was aware of the problematic character of this interpretation and yet finally succumbed to it: "People have wanted to call this print ... 'The Knight of the Reformation' without considering that it was made several years before the beginning of the Reformation. And yet this title suggests itself so easily and appears to be so fitting that it tempts us to overlook the anticipation in chronology. For in truth the German people at that time were about to tread this path. . . ."

[94] Ernst Bertram, *Nietzsche: Versuch einer Mythologie* (Berlin, 1918), pp. 42–63.

[95] The identification of this parallel is due to Hermann Grimm. For a detailed discussion of this and other literary texts see Paul Weber, *Beiträge zu Dürers Weltanschauung* (Studien zur deutschen Kunstgeschichte, no. 23) (Strasbourg, 1900), who criticizes the exclusive association with Erasmus and stresses the connection with devotional imagery and traditions, though he, too, speaks (p. 15) of "the fearless and contemptuous way the Knight strides past the empty bogeys. . . ." Erwin Panofsky, *Albrecht Dürer* (Princeton: Princeton University Press, 1943), returns to Erasmus as a source, and also writes that the specter of death "tries in vain to frighten the Knight." Friedrich Winkler, *Albrecht Dürer* (Berlin: Mann, 1957), p. 239, also speaks of "the Christian Knight's fearless fight against Death and the Devil."

Figure 39. Dürer, "Knight, Death and Devil," engraving

Kein ding hilfft für den zeitlichen Todt/
Darumb dienent Gott frü vnd spott.

1510

Das mög wir all wol erspehen
Das bald vns ein mensch ist geschehen
Daṅ so wir heut ein mensch haben
Vileicht wirt er morgenvergraßen
Darumb O menschlich hertikeit
Warumb sind dir nit dein sünd leyd
So du doch wol bist vernemen
Das Gott all böß würt beschemen
In ewikeit durch sein streng ge richt

Do entfleucht keyner dem Richter nit
Durch allein du fürchtest hie Gott
Dardurch entrinst dem ewigen tod
Drumb heß an nach Christo zuleben
Der kan dir ewiges leben geben
Des halß kain zeytlichs ding an sich
Aber noch künfftigem richt dich
Vnd thu stets noch gnaden werben
Als soltestu all stund sterben

Spar dein beßrung nicht biß auff morn
Dann vngwiß ding ist bald verlorn

Gots gnad auff erden ehe er starb
Welcher die welt thut auffgeben

Figure 40. Dürer, "Death and the Landsknecht"

—including, of course, Lutheran teaching—as is hope of heaven. It is different with death, death of the body, that is. Of death the Christian will not be afraid, because he hopes to have so lived as to escape the grasp of the devil.

Seen in this context, which admittedly I have now set up, the Knight perhaps does not ride forward regardless of *Tod und Teufel*; he listens to the warnings of Death, who shows him the hourglass. And that Dürer could see the relation of Death and a warrior in precisely these terms we know from a print for which we have his own interpretations in propositional language, that is, in a long and rather prosy poem.[96]

I refer to the woodcut "Death and the Landsknecht" (Figure 40), which Dürer published in 1510, three years before our print, accompanied by a poem of seventy-eight lines. The woodcut, it is true, is a thoroughly unmemorable image; indeed, Dürer himself may have thought so, or else he would not have supported its message by means of words. But the words, though not eloquent, are unambiguous.

> Nothing avails against the death of the body,
> Hence worship God all the time
> For we can easily see
> That man is soon done for,
> Anyone who is among us today
> May be buried tomorrow.
> Therefore, you hardened hearts
> Why do you not repent your sins? . . .
> Only if you fear God here beneath
> Will you escape eternal death
> Hence begin to live in the spirit of Christ
> Who can secure life eternal for you . . .
> Always seek for grace
> As if you might die any moment . . .
> He whose conscience is clear
> Does not need to fear death at any time
> And does not ask how long a span
> God will grant him here on earth;
> It is very rare indeed in a long life
> That people get better,
> Rather they augment their sins,
> Wish God I could lead a short, but good life,

---

[96] Hans Rupprich, ed., *Dürers schriftlicher Nachlass* (Berlin, 1956), pp. 137–38. Weber, *loc. cit.*, refers to the poem but does not stress the parallel.

However fearsome it may be to die
Long life does not always secure
Divine Grace and Blessing
But increases the torments of hell . . .
Hence he who leads a just life
Will be seized by strong courage
And is glad in the hour of death
When he will know bliss. . . .

This may suffice to show the tenor of this rhymed sermon. It could be argued that Dürer himself felt the inadequacy of his equipment as a poet, and that he therefore turned to his own art, the art of engraving, to embody this message which was so important to him. If I am right, we must slightly adjust the emphasis. It is Death who speaks to the horseman, it is he who warns the Knight that he might move athwart his path at any moment, and that in that hour the devil will be ready to grab him unless he is ready all the time. I do not know if the reader is willing with me to perform a switch in the reading of the expressions of both protagonists; but I am persuaded that the physiognomy of the Knight is compatible with a soldier in need of the sermon, and that the message of the print is one not of proud defiance but of the need for contrition.[97] Like some of Dante's sinners and Shakespeare's Shylock, Milton's Satan or Mozart's Don Giovanni, Dürer's Knight has been taken out of the context which its creator took for granted and has been turned into a romantic image of Nietzschean individualism.

There are critics who think that such shifts are inevitable, that the greatness of an artistic creation lies in its richness, ambiguity, and interpretability, and that it is both futile and somehow wrong to search for the correct interpretation, the one which the author intended. I do not hold this view. I do not believe that

---

[97] It is at this point that I should like to take up the argument used by Panofsky and others in favor of the identification of the horseman with Erasmus' image of the Christian knight. It is the famous entry in Dürer's diary during the journey to the Netherlands (May 17, 1521) in which he appealed to Erasmus to save Luther. "O Erasme Rotterdame, where are you? Behold what unjust tyranny of the worldly powers can do and how great is the might of Darkness. Heark thou, Knight of Christ, ride forward by the side of our Lord Christ, protect Truth and gain the martyr's crown. . . ." It is not to be excluded that in writing these lines Dürer thought of his own print of 1513, but I see no compelling reason to think so, even if he had then or later read the pamphlet by Erasmus. Moreover, the appeal tells the scholar to remember that he will die in any case ("you are anyhow an old man"), and is thus quite in tune with Dürer's meditations on death.

102

any interpretation is sure and infallible, any more than any other hypothesis can be. But I do think that we can try as historians to restore the original context in which these works were intended to function, and that it is always worth-while to venture upon this perilous path, accompanied by a tame "Boa Constructor."

SOURCES OF FIGURES

1. From E. A. R. Ennion and N. Tinbergen, *Tracks* (Oxford: The Clarendon Press, 1967). By permission of authors and publisher.
2. From David Irving, *The Mare's Nest* (London: William Kimber & Co., 1964). By permission of the publisher and the Imperial War Museum, London.
3. Photo by Blakeslee Lane Inc.
4. From Ralph M. Evans, *Eye, Film, and Camera in Color Photography* (New York: John Wiley & Sons, 1959). By permission of author and publisher.
5. Source and permission as for Figure 4.
6. Source and permission as for Figure 4.
7. Source and permission as for Figure 4.
8. From William Ittelson, *The Ames Demonstrations in Perception* (Princeton: Princeton University Press, 1952). By permission of Hafner Publishing Co.
9. Source and permission as for Figure 8.
10. From J. J. Gibson, *The Senses Considered as Perceptual Systems* (Boston: Houghton Mifflin Co., 1966). By permission of the publisher.
11. Source and permission as for Figure 10.
12. From Winston S. Churchill, *The Second World War*, vol. 3 (London: Cassell & Co., 1950). By permission of the publishers; Crown copyright.
13. Source and permission as for Figure 12.
14. From Ulric Neisser, *Cognitive Psychology* (New York: Appleton-Century-Crofts, 1967), after Selfridge, "Pattern Recognition and Modern Computers," Proc. West. Joint Computer Conference, Los Angeles, Calif., 1955. By permission.
15. From the jacket of R. K. Narayan, *The Sweet-Vendor*, designed by Roy Spencer (London: The Bodley Head Ltd., 1967). By permission.
16. By permission of N. V. Koninklijke Drukkerij en Uitgeverij Erven J. J. Tijil, Zwolle.
17. Permission as for Figure 16.
18. Permisson as for Figure 16.
19. From Roger Price, *Droodles* (London: W. H. Allen & Co. Ltd., 1954). Copyright © 1953 by Roger Price. Reprinted by permission of Simon and Schuster Inc.
20. Copyright © 1968 by Joan Forsdyke.
21. Courtesy of The Lateran Museums, Rome. Photo by Alinari.
22. Courtesy of the Victoria & Albert Museum, London.
23. Source and permission as for Figure 10.
24. Diagram by Joan Forsdyke.
25. Diagram by Joan Forsdyke.
26. From Ralph M. Evans, *An Introduction to Color* (New York: John Wiley & Sons, 1948). By permission of author and publisher.
27. Permission as for Figure 16.
28. Courtesy of the Bayerisches Nationalmuseum, Munich.
29. Courtesy of the Museo Civico Correr, Venice.

30. As for Figure 28.
31. Courtesy of the Museo del Prado, Madrid.
32. As for Figure 31.
33. Courtesy of The British Museum, London. Copyright © 1968 by The Warburg Institute, University of London.
34. Courtesy of the Álte Pinakothek, Munich.
35. As for Figure 34.
36. Courtesy of the Uffizi, Florence.
37. B. 73. Courtesy of The British Museum, London.
38. As for Figure 37.
39. B. 98. Courtesy of The British Museum, London.
40. B. 132. Courtesy of The British Museum, London.

3 JEAN-PIERRE VERNANT

Tensions and Ambiguities
in Greek Tragedy

WHAT can sociology and psychology contribute to the interpretation of Greek
tragedy? Obviously they cannot replace the traditional philological and historical
methods of analysis. On the contrary, they must depend on the scholarly work
begun long ago by the specialists. They do, however, add a new dimension to
Greek studies. In trying to situate exactly the phenomenon of tragedy in Greek
social life and in marking its place in the psychological history of Western man,
these sciences clearly illuminate some problems that Hellenists have encountered
only incidentally and that they have dealt with only indirectly.

I would like to call attention to a few of these problems. Tragedy appears in
Greece at the end of the sixth century B.C. Before even a century has passed,
the tragic vein has exhausted itself; and when, in the fourth century, Aristotle
tries to establish its theory in the *Poetics,* he no longer understands the tragic
hero, who, we might say, has become a stranger to him. In the wake of the epic
and of lyric poetry, waning while philosophy triumphs, tragedy as a literary
genre appears as the expression of a particular type of human experience, tied
to definite social and psychological conditions. This aspect of a historic moment,
very precisely situated in space and time, imposes certain rules of method in the
interpretation of tragic works. Each play constitutes a message, borne in a text,
inscribed in the structures of a discourse, which must be dealt with, on every
level, by appropriate philological, stylistic, and literary analyses. But this text can
be fully understood only by taking into account a context. It is by means of this
context that communication is established between the author and his fifth-
century public, and that the work can recover, for the contemporary reader, its
full authenticity and weight of meaning.

But what do we mean by context? On what level of reality shall we situate
it? How shall we understand its relation to the text? In my opinion, it is a question of a mental context, of a human universe of meanings, consequently homologous to the very text to which it is referred: verbal and intellectual tools, categories of thought, types of reasoning, a system of representations, of beliefs, of

Professor Vernant's essay was translated from French for publication in this volume.

values, forms of sensibility, modalities of action and of agency. In this respect, one could speak of an intellectual and spiritual world peculiar to the fifth-century Greeks, if the formula did not carry with it a serious risk of error. In fact, it would allow one to suppose that there existed somewhere an already constituted intellectual and spiritual domain which tragedy would simply reflect in its own way. However, there is no spiritual universe existing in itself, outside of the various practices which man constantly elaborates and renews in the course of social life and cultural creation. Each type of institution, each category of work, possesses its own particular intellectual and spiritual universe that it has had to elaborate in order to become an autonomous discipline, a specialized activity, corresponding to a particular domain of human experience.

Thus the spiritual universe of religion is entirely embodied in rites, myths, and figurative representations of the divine. When law develops in the Greek world, it simultaneously assumes the aspect of social institutions and forms of human behavior as well as of mental categories which define, by opposition to other forms of thought (religious thought in particular), the legal spirit. With the city also, a system of institutions, modes of conduct, and a way of thinking, all of which are peculiarly political, develop as a social entity. Here again there is a striking contrast with the ancient arcane forms of power and social action which the *polis* has replaced, along with the practices and mentality peculiar to them. It is the same for tragedy: it could not reflect a reality in any way extraneous to it. It projects its own intellectual and spiritual world. Just so, there can be no plastic vision or plastic object except in or through painting. The tragic consciousness, also, is born and develops along with tragedy itself. It is through expression in the form of an original literary genre that tragic thought, the tragic world, and tragic man are constituted.

To use a spatial comparison, we could say, then, that the context, in the sense meant here, is not situated *beside* these works, on the margin of tragedy; it is not so much in juxtaposition with the text as subjacent to it. Even more than a context, it constitutes a *sub-text* that an informed reading must decipher from *within* the density of the work by a double movement, a procedure of alternate detour and return. First, it is necessary to situate the work, by enlarging the field of inquiry to the whole of the social and mental conditions that were responsible for the appearance of the tragic consciousness. But then it is necessary to concentrate the inquiry exclusively on those things which make up the tragic vocation: the forms, the object, the specific problems of tragedy. In fact, no reference to the other domains of social life—religion, law, politics, ethics— could be pertinent unless it is also demonstrated, in assimilating and integrating

106

the borrowed element into its own perspective, that tragedy makes it undergo a real transmutation. Let us take an example: the almost obsessive presence in the tragedian's language of a technical legal vocabulary, the predilection for themes of blood crimes rising from the competence of this or that tribunal, the very form of judgment given to certain plays, require the literary historian, if he wants to ascertain the exact values of terms and all the implications of the drama, to leave his speciality and become a historian of Greek law. But he will find in legal thought no light capable of illuminating directly the tragic text, as if the latter were no more than a carbon copy. For the interpreter it can be a question of no more than a preface which must finally lead him back to the tragedy and to the world that is peculiar to it, in order to explore certain of its dimensions which, without this excursus into law, would have remained hidden in the density of the work. In fact, no tragedy is a legal debate any more than the law entails, in itself, anything tragic. Poets use words, notions, and schemes of thought quite differently from orators or tribunals. Outside of their technical context, they change their function in some way. Under the pen of the tragic playwrights they have become, combined with and opposed to other words and ideas, the elements of a general confrontation of values, of a questioning of all norms, in view of an inquiry which no longer has anything to do with the law and which bears on man himself. What is this being that tragedy terms *deinos*, an incomprehensible and disconcerting monster, simultaneously agent and acted upon, guilty and innocent, lucid and blind, mastering all nature by his industrious mind but incapable of governing himself? What are the relationships between this man and the actions which one sees him deliberate on the stage, for which one sees him take the initiative and carry the responsibility, but whose real sense lies beyond him and escapes him, so that it is not so much the agent who explains the action, but rather the action which, revealing its authentic significance after the event, redefines the agent, discloses what he is and what he has really accomplished without knowing it? What, finally, is the place of this man in a universe that is ambiguous on all levels and shot through with contradictions, where no rule appears definitely established, where one god struggles against another, one law against another, where justice, even while the action is taking place, shifts, turns, and transforms itself into its opposite?

*　　*　　*

The performance of tragedy is not only an art form, it is a social institution to which the city, by founding the tragic competitions, gives status along with its political and legal instruments. By establishing, under the authority of the *archon eponymos* in the same civic arena and following the same institutional norms as the assemblies or the popular tribunals, a performance open to all citizens, directed, played, and judged by qualified representatives of the various tribes, the city makes itself into a theater;[1] in a way it becomes an object of representation and plays itself before the public. But if tragedy, therefore, appears to be, more than any other literary genre, rooted in social reality, that does not mean that it is its reflection. It does not reflect reality; it expresses the entire problematics of this reality. In presenting society as torn and divided against itself, tragedy makes it profoundly questionable. The drama brings on stage an ancient legend of heroes. This legendary world constitutes the city's past—a past distant enough so that the new forms of legal and political thought in fifth-century Athens are clearly defined, but a past also close enough so that value conflicts are still painfully felt and there is still a real confrontation. Tragedy, as W. Nestle correctly observes, is born when myth is seen with the citizen's eye. But it is not only the mythical universe which loses its consistency and dissolves under this gaze. The world of the city also finds itself in question, and the debate contests its fundamental values. Even in the most optimistic of the tragedians, Aeschylus, the exaltation of the civic ideal and the affirmation of its victory over all the forces of the past has less the nature of a testament of tranquil assurance than of a hope and of an appeal where anguish is always present, even in the joy of the final apotheoses.[2] Once the questions are asked, there is no

[1] Only men can be qualified representatives of the city; women are alien to political life. That is why the members of the chorus (not to speak of the actors) are always and exclusively males. Even when the chorus is supposed to represent a group of girls or women, which is the case in a whole series of plays, it is men, in disguise, who make up the chorus.

[2] At the end of the *Oresteia* of Aeschylus, the founding of the human tribunal and the integration of the Erinyes into the new order of the city do not entirely dispense with the contradictions between the old and the new gods, the heroic past of the noble *genè* and the present of fifth-century Athenian democracy. An equilibrium is established, but it is based on tensions. In the background there continues to be conflict between opposing forces. In this sense, tragic ambiguity is not resolved; ambivalence remains. To demonstrate, it will suffice to recall that the majority of human judges spoke against Orestes, for it is Athena who ties the voting (cf. line 735 and scholium at line 746). That it is necessary to take the *psèphos* of line 735 in the sense of voting token, vote placed in the urn, is confirmed by the relationship between line 751, "one more vote raises a house again," and Orestes' remark after the announcement of the voting in line 754: "Oh Pallas, you who have just saved my house...." The same is true of Euripides' *Iphigenia in Tauris* 1469. This equality of the voices for and against avoids condemnation of the matricide in vengeance of the father; it absolves legally, by a procedural convention, the crime of murder, but it does not justify it or absolve it

longer any answer which can fully satisfy the tragic consciousness and conclude its interrogation.

This debate with a still-living past opens up in the heart of each tragic work an initial perspective which the interpreter must take into account. This perspective is expressed in the form of the drama by the tension between the two elements which occupy the tragic stage: on one side the chorus, a collective and anonymous character, incarnated by an official body of citizens whose role is to express in its fears, hopes, interrogations, and judgments the sentiments of the spectators who compose the civic community; on the other side, played by a professional actor, the individualized character whose action forms the center of the drama and who represents the hero of another age, always more or less alien to

---

of guilt (cf. 741 and 752; on the significance of this rule of procedure, see Aristotle *Problemata* XXIX. 13). It implies a sort of equilibrium maintained between the ancient *dikè* of the Erinyes (cf. 476, 511, 514, 539, 550, 554, 564) and the opposing *dikè* of the new gods like Apollo (615–619). Athena is therefore correct in telling the daughters of Night: "You are not defeated; it is only an uncertain judgment that has come from the urn" (*isopsèphos dikè*, 794–95). Recalling their lot in the world of the gods at the beginning of the play, the Erinyes observed that, in spite of living underground in a darkness closed off from the sun, they nonetheless had their *timè*, their share of honor (*oud'atimias curô*, 394). It is these honors that Athena recognizes after the verdict of the tribunal: "You are not humiliated" (*ouk' est' atimoi*, 824), these same honors that she proclaims incessantly, with an extraordinary insistence, until the end of the tragedy (796, 807, 833, 868, 884, 891, 894, 917, 1029). In fact, it is to be noted that in establishing Areopagos, that is, in founding the city governed by law, Athena affirms the necessity of giving the sinister forces incarnated by the Erinyes their rightful place in the human collectivity. *Philia*, mutual friendship, and *peitho*, persuasion by reason, do not suffice to unite the citizens in a harmonious community. The city expects the intervention of powers of another nature, which act not by sweetness and reason but by constraint and terror. "These are cases, proclaimed the Erinyes, where Dread (*to deinon*) is useful, and must sit permanently as a vigilant guardian of hearts" (516ff.). When she establishes the Council of Judges on the Areopagos, Athena repeats this theme, word for word: "On this mountain henceforth Respect and Fear (*Phobos*), her sister, will keep the citizens far from crime.... Dread (*to deinon*) especially must not be chased from the walls of my city; if there is nothing to fear, what mortal does as he should?" (690–99). Neither anarchy nor despotism, insisted the Erinyes (525); neither anarchy nor despotism, echoes Athena as she founds the tribunal. In establishing this rule as the imperative which her city must obey, the goddess emphasizes that the good is situated between two extremes, the city being based on a difficult accord between opposing powers which must find an equilibrium without destroying each other. Opposite the god of speech, *Zeus agoraios* (974), and sweet *Peitho*, who has guided Athena's tongue, are seen the august Erinyes, propagating respect, fear, and dread. And this power of terror, which emanates from the Erinyes and which the Areopagos represents on the level of human institutions, will have a beneficent effect on the citizens by preventing them from committing

the daily life of the citizen.[3] There is a duality in the language of tragedy which corresponds to this division between the chorus and the tragic hero. But here we already note the aspect of ambiguity which seems to me to characterize the tragic genre. It is the language of the chorus, in the parts that are sung, which continues the lyric tradition of a poetry celebrating the exemplary virtues of ancient heroes. The meter of the dialogue parts spoken by the protagonists of the drama is, on the contrary, close to prose. At the same time that the character is magnified by stage effects and the use of masks to the dimensions of one of those exceptional beings to whom the city pays homage, he is also, through the language he uses, brought closer to the ordinary man.[4] And this rapprochement makes him, in his legendary adventure, somehow contemporary with the public, so that inside each protagonist is found again the tension that I have noted between the past and the present, the mythical universe and the world of the city. The same tragic character seems to be sometimes projected into a distant mythical past, the hero of another age, full of a formidable religious power, incarnating all the excessiveness of ancient kings of legend—sometimes talking, thinking, and living in the present age of the city, like a "bourgeois" of Athens in the midst of his fellow citizens.

It is also stating the problem falsely to question, along with certain modern

---

crimes against one another. Athena can therefore say (989–90), in speaking of the monstrous aspect of the goddesses who have just agreed to reside in Attica: "I see a great advantage for the City coming from these terrifying faces." At the end of the tragedy it is Athena herself who celebrates the power of the ancient goddesses among the immortals, as among the gods of the underworld (950–51), and who reminds the guardians of the city that these uncompromising divinities have the power "to determine everything among men" (930), to give "some songs, others tears" (954–55). Moreover, it is necessary to recall that in very closely associating the Erinyes-Eumenides with the founding of the Areopagos, in placing this council, whose nocturnal and secret character (cf. 692, 705–6) is twice underlined, under the sign not of the religious powers which reign at the agora, like *Peitho*, persuasive speech, but of those who inspire *Sebas* and *Phobos*, Respect and Fear, Aeschylus is in no way innovating. He is conforming to a mythical and cultural tradition that all the Athenians recognize; see Pausanias 1. 28. 5–6 (sanctuary of the Semnai-Erinyes in the Areopagos), to which is to be compared the indications of Diogenes Laertes concerning the purification of Athens by Epimenides: it is from the Areopagos that the purifier drives out the black and white lambs whose sacrifice is supposed to erase the city's taints; it is to the Eumenides that he dedicates a sanctuary.

[3] See Aristotle *Problemata* 19. 48: "On the stage, the actors imitate heroes because, among the Ancients, only heroes were chiefs and kings; the people were ordinary men, who make up the chorus."

[4] Aristotle *Poetics* 1449. 24–28: "Of all the meters, the iambic trimeter is the most conversational; one indication of this is that we use a great number of iambic trimeter when we speak, but rarely any hexameters, and only when we move away from a conversational tone."

interpreters, the greater or lesser unity of character of tragic figures. According to Wilamowitz, the character of Eteocles, in the *Seven Against Thebes*, does not appear to be drawn with a very firm hand: his behavior at the end of the play is scarcely compatible with the portrait painted earlier. For Mazon, on the contrary, this same Eteocles counts among the most beautiful figures in Greek theater; he incarnates with perfect coherence the type of the cursed hero.

This debate is meaningless save in the perspective of a modern drama constructed on the psychological unity of the protagonists. But the tragedy of Aeschylus is not centered on a single character, in the complexity of his interior life. The real character of the *Seven* is the city: that is, the values, the modes of thought, and the attitudes that it governs. As the head of Thebes, Eteocles represents these values and attitudes as long as the name of his brother is not pronounced before him. For he has only to hear the name of Polynices to revert from the sphere of the *polis* to another universe: he finds himself once again the legendary Labdacidanean, the man of the noble *genè*, the great royal families of the past, on whom weigh ancestral defilement and curses. He who, in the face of the emotional religiosity of the women of Thebes and of the warlike impiety of the men of Argos, incarnated those virtues of moderation, reflection, and self-control which make the political man, suddenly, by abandoning himself to the fraternal hatred by which he is entirely "possessed," rushes headlong into catastrophe. The murderous insanity which will henceforth define his character, his *ethos*, is not merely a human sentiment but a demoniac power which overwhelms Eteocles from all sides. It envelops him in the dark cloud of the *atè*; it penetrates him—like a god taking possession, from the inside, of a man whose ruin he has already determined—in the form of a *mania*, a *lyssa*, of a delirium engendering criminal acts of *hybris*. While present within him, Eteocles' madness appears also as an alien and exterior reality: it is identified with the pernicious power of a taint which, arising from ancient misdeeds, is transmitted from generation to generation through the whole line of the house of Laius. The destructive furor which seizes the chief of Thebes is none other than the never-purified *miasma*, the *Erinys* of the race, now installed in him by the effect of the *ara*, the curse uttered by Oedipus against his sons. *Mania, lyssa, atè, ara, miasma, Erinys*—all these names ultimately overlay a single mythical reality, a sinister *numen* manifesting itself at various moments through multiple forms both in the soul of the hero and outside him; it is a power of misfortune which embraces, in addition to the criminal, the crime itself, its most distant antecedents, its psychological motivations, its consequences, the taint that it carries with it, and the punishment that it prepares for the guilty one and all his descendants. There is a term in Greek that designates this type of unparticularized divine power, acting most often in a baleful way and under multiple forms, at the heart of human life: it is *daimôn*. Euripides is faithful to the tragic spirit of Aeschylus when he uses the verb *daimonan* to characterize the psychological state of the sons of Oedipus, pledged to fratricide by their father's curse: they are, in the correct sense, possessed by a *daimôn*, an evil spirit.[5]

We see in what measure and from what point of view we have the right to speak of a transformation of Eteocles' character. It is not a question of the unity or discontinuity of the person, in the sense in which we understand it today. As Aristotle observes, tragedy does not unfold in conformity with the requirements of a character; on the contrary, it is the character which must bend to the requirements of the action (*muthos*) of the story, of which the tragedy is precisely the imitation.[6] At the beginning of the play the *ethos* of Eteocles corresponds to a psychological model, that of the *homo politicus*, as the fifth-century Greeks conceived him. What we call a change *in the character* of Eteocles would more correctly be called a passage to another psychological model, the gradual shift *within the tragedy* from a political psychology to a mythical psychology, implied in the legend of the house of Laius by the episode of the reciprocal murder of the two brothers. One could even add that it is the successive reference to these two models, the confrontation within the same character of two opposite types of behavior, of two forms of psychology implying different categories of action and agent, which essentially constitutes, in the *Seven Against Thebes*, the tragic effect. As long as tragedy remains living, this duality or tension in the psychology of characters will not weaken. The sentiments, the conversation, and the actions of the tragic hero are ascribable to his character (*ethos*), which the poets analyze as subtly and interpret as practically as, for example, would the orators or a historian such as Thucydides.[7] But these sentiments, conversations, and actions simultaneously appear as the expression of a religious power, of a *daimôn* acting through them. In fact, great tragic art will consist in rendering simultaneously what in Aeschylus' Eteocles is still successive. At every moment the life of the hero will unfold as if on two planes, of which each, taken in itself, would suffice to explain the episodes of the drama, but which in fact the tragedy aims at presenting as inseparable: each action appears in the line and the logic of a character, of an *ethos*, at the same time that it reveals itself as the manifestation of a power from beyond, of a *daimôn*.

[5] Euripides *Phoenicians* 888.

[6] Aristotle *Poetics* 1449b 24, 31, 36; 1450a 15–23; 1450a 23–25, 38–39; 1450b 2–3.

[7] On this aspect of the tragic work and on the heroic nature of Sophocles' characters, see B. Knox, *The Heroic Temper: Studies in Sophoclean Tragedy* (Berkeley and Los Angeles, 1964).

Ethos-daimôn—it is within this interval that the tragic figure takes shape. If either of the two terms is suppressed, this figure disappears. To paraphrase R. P. Winnington-Ingram's pertinent remark,[8] one could say that tragedy is based on a double reading of Heraclitus' famous formula ἦθος ἀνθρώπῳ δαίμων. Only as long as it can be read in one sense equally as clearly as in the other (as the symmetrical syntax allows) does the formula retain its enigmatic character and its ambiguity. And only as long as this is true is there a tragic consciousness; for, in order that the tragedy may exist, it must be possible for the text to mean simultaneously: (1) man's character is what is called a demon; and, inversely, (2) what is called man's character is really a demon.

For our mentality today (and already, in a large measure, for Aristotle's) these two interpretations are mutually exclusive. But the logic of tragedy consists in sliding from one meaning to the other, being, of course, conscious of their opposition but without ever renouncing either of them. An ambiguous logic, one might say. But it is no longer, as it was in the myth, a naïve ambiguity which does not yet question itself. On the contrary, when tragedy passes from one plane to another, it emphasizes the distances and underlines the contradictions. However, even with Aeschylus, it never reaches a solution that would make the conflicts disappear, either by conciliation or by transcending the oppositions. And this tension, which is never entirely accepted nor entirely suppressed, makes of tragedy a questioning which has no answer. In the tragic perspective, man and human action are drawn, not as realities that might be defined or described, but as problems. They are presented as enigmas whose double sense can never be fixed or exhausted.

*   *   *

Beyond character there is another domain where the interpreter must locate aspects of tension and ambiguity. We have noted that the tragedians willingly turn to technical legal terms. But, when they use this vocabulary, it is almost always to play on its uncertainties, its hesitations, its incompleteness: imprecision of terms, variability of meaning, incoherences, and oppositions which reveal (at the heart of a body of legal thought whose form is not, as it was in Rome, that of an elaborate system) discordances and internal tensions. They also use it to express the conflicts between legal values, on the one hand, and, on the other, a more ancient religious tradition as well as a budding moral reflection from which the law is already distinguishable, although its domain is not clearly marked off from theirs. In fact, the Greeks do not conceive of an absolute law

---

[8] "Tragedy and Greek Archaic Thought," *Classical Drama and Its Influence: Essays Presented to H. D. F. Kitto,* ed. M. J. Anderson (London, 1965), pp. 31–50.

based on principles and organized in a coherent whole. For them, there are various degrees of laws superimposed on one another, some of which blend and overlap. At one pole, the law sanctions existing authority: it relies on constraint, of which it is, in a sense, only the extension. At the opposite pole, it touches the religious: it questions sacred powers, the order of the world, the justice of Zeus. It also asks moral questions concerning the degree of responsibility of human agents. From this point of view, divine justice, which often makes sons pay for the crimes of their fathers, can appear as opaque and arbitrary as the violence of a tyrant. Thus in *The Suppliants* we see the notion of *cratos* oscillate between two contrary meanings without settling on either one. On the lips of King Pelasgos, *cratos*, associated with *curos*, designates a legitimate authority, the influence which the tutor rightfully exerts on whoever is legally dependent on his power; on the lips of the Danaides, the same word, drawn into the semantic field of *bia*, designates brutal force, the constraint of violence in the aspect most opposed to justice and law.[9] This tension between two contrary meanings is expressed in a particularly striking way in the formula of line 315, whose ambiguity has been fully demonstrated by E. W. Whittle.[10] The word ῥύσιος, which also belongs to legal language and which is here applied to the influence exerted on Io by the touch of Zeus, means simultaneously and contradictorily the brutal violence of a grasp and the sweet gentleness of a deliverance. This effect of ambiguity is not

[9] In 387ff., the king asks the Danaides if the sons of Aegyptos have, by the law of their country, power over them as their closest relations (Εἴ τοι κρατοῦσι). The legal value of this *cratos* is defined in the following lines. The king observes that, if it were thus, nobody could stand in the way of the pretensions of the Aegyptiades over their cousins; it would therefore be necessary for the latter to plead, inversely, that, following the laws of their country, their cousins do not in reality have this power of guardianship (κῦρος) over them. The response of the Danaides is entirely beside the point. They see only the other aspect of *cratos*, and the word, on their lips, takes an opposite meaning from that which Pelasgos gives it: it no longer designates the legal power of guardianship which their cousins might claim over them, but rather pure violence, the brutal force of the male, masculine domination to which women can only submit: "Ah, may I never be submitted to the power of males" (ὑποχείρος κάρτεσιν ἀρσένων, 392–93). For this aspect of violence, cf. 820, 831, 863. To the *cratos* of man (951), the Danaides want to oppose the *cratos* of women (1069). If the sons of Aegyptos are wrong in trying to impose marriage on them, convincing them not by persuasion but by violence (940–41, 943), the Danaides are no less at fault: in their hatred of the other sex they will go as far as murder. King Pelasgos could reproach the Aegyptiades for wanting to unite themselves to the girls against their will, without the agreement of their father, and outside *Peitho*. But the daughters of Danaos also refuse to recognize *Peitho*: they reject Aphrodite, who is everywhere accompanied by *Peitho*; they do not let themselves be charmed or appeased by the seduction of *Peitho* (1941, 1956).

[10] "An Ambiguity in Aeschylus," *Classica et Mediaevalia*, 25, no. 1–2 (1964): 1–7.

gratuitous. It is intended by the poet, and it introduces us into the heart of a work, one of whose major themes consists precisely of an interrogation on the true nature of *cratos*. What is authority—that of man over woman, of husband over wife, of the chief of state over its citizens, of the city over the stranger and the alien, of the gods over mortals? Is *cratos* based on law, that is to say on mutual accord, on sweet persuasion, *peitho*? Or is it, on the contrary, based on domination, pure force, brutal violence, *bia*? The wordplay to which the supposedly precise legal vocabulary lends itself permits expression enigmatically of the problematic character of the foundations of power exercised over others.

What is true of legal language is no less true of religious language. The tragedians do not content themselves with opposing one god to another, Zeus to Prometheus, Artemis to Aphrodite, Apollo, and Athena to the Erinyes. More profoundly, the divine universe is presented as being wholly dominated by conflict. The powers which compose it appear grouped in sharply contrasting categories, among which agreement is difficult or impossible because they are not all on the same level: the ancient divinities belong to a different religious world from the "new" gods, as the Olympians are alien to the Chthonians. This duality can appear within a single divine figure. To the Zeus on high, whom the Danaides invoke at first to persuade Pelasgos to respect his duties toward the suppliants, is opposed the "other" Zeus, the one here below, to whom they turn in despair to constrain the king to yield.[11] In the same way, the *dikè* of the dead is opposed to the celestial *dikè*: Antigone comes into bitter conflict with the power of the latter because she had been willing to recognize only that of the former.[12]

But it is especially on the level of human experience of the divine that these oppositions are drawn. One finds in tragedy no single unique category of religion but, rather, various forms of religious life which appear contradictory and mutually exclusive. The chorus of Thebans in the *Seven*, with its anguished appeals to a divine presence, its frantic distraction and tumultuous cries, its zealous attachment to the oldest idols (the *archaia bretè*)—not in the temples consecrated to the gods, but in the center of town in the public square—this chorus embodies a feminine religion which is categorically condemned by Eteocles in the name of another religious spirit at once virile and civic. For the chief of state the emotional fervor of the women means not only disorder, cowardliness (191–92 and 236–38), and savagery (280); it also has an element of impiety. True piety supposes wisdom and discipline, *sôphrosunè* (186) and *peitharchia* (224); it recognizes the distance of the gods to whom it appeals, instead of trying, like

[11] Aeschylus, *The Suppliants* 154–61 and 231.
[12] Sophocles, *Antigone* 23ff., 451, 538–42, on one hand, 853ff. on the other.

the women's religion, to overcome it. The only contribution that Eteocles accepts from the feminine element to add to the public and political cult, which respects this aloof character of the gods without pretending to mingle the human and the divine, is the *ololuge*; this is the "yoo-yoo," termed *hieros* (268) because the city has integrated it into its own religion and recognizes it as the ritual cry accompanying the fall of the victim in the great blood-sacrifice.

An analogous antinomy underlies the conflict between Antigone and Creon. This is an opposition not of religion, represented by a girl, to irreligion, represented by Creon, or of a religious spirit and a political spirit, but of two different types of religion: one a family religion, purely private, limited to a narrow circle of close relatives (*philoi*) and centered around the household and the cult of the dead; the other a public religion in which the tutelary gods of the city tend finally to become indistinguishable from the supreme values of the state. Between these two domains of religious life there is a constant tension which in certain cases (the very ones that tragedy records) can lead to an insoluble conflict. As the *coryphaeus* observes in 872–75: it is pious to honor piously one's dead, but the supreme magistrate of the city must insist on respect for his *cratos* and the law which he has decreed. After all, the Socrates of the *Crito* will assert that piety, like justice, commands one to obey the laws of one's country, even though they be unjust and even though this injustice turn against one and condemn one to death. For the city—that is, its *nomoi*—is more venerable, more sacred, than a mother, a father, or all one's ancestors together.[13] Of the two religious attitudes that the *Antigone* sets in conflict, neither in itself could be the right one without granting the other one its place, without recognizing that which limits it and contests it. In this respect it is very significant that the only divinities to which the chorus refers are Dionysos and Eros. As gods who are nocturnal, mysterious, elusive, close to women, and alien to politics, they primarily condemn the pseudo religion of Creon, the chief of state, who measures the divine by the cubit of his own poor common sense, trying to make the gods endorse his hates and personal ambitions. But they also turn against Antigone, closed in her *philia* of family, willingly pledged to Hades; for these two gods express, even in their connection with death, the powers of life and of renewal. Antigone has not been able to hear the appeal to detach herself from "her own" and from the familial *philia* in order to open herself to the other, to receive Eros, and in union with a "stranger" to transmit, in her turn, life.

*   *   *

[13] Plato, *Crito* 51a–c.

This presence in the language of the tragedians of a multiplicity of levels, more or less distant from each other—the same word relating to different semantic fields, depending on whether it belongs to a religious, legal, political, or quotidian vocabulary, or to a particular level of one of these vocabularies—gives the text a particular depth and makes it necessary to read on several levels at once. Between the dialogue as it is exchanged and lived by the protagonists and as it is interpreted and commented on by the chorus or received and understood by the spectators, there is a shift in meaning which constitutes an essential element of the tragic effect. On stage the heroes of the drama all use, in their discussions, the same words, but with opposing meanings.[14] The term *nomos* means for Antigone the opposite of what, in all conviction, Creon calls *nomos*; and one could, with Charles-Paul Segal, expose the same ambiguity in other terms which have a major place in the structure of the work: *philos* and *philia*, *kerdos*, *sebas*, *timè*, *tolma*, *orgè*, *deinos*, etc.[15] The words exchanged on stage function less to establish communication between the various characters than to mark the blocks, the barriers, the imperviousness of minds, to emphasize the points of conflict. For each protagonist, closed in his own particular universe, the vocabulary used remains largely opaque; it has one and only one meaning. The limited understanding of one individual clashes violently with that of another. Tragic irony can consist in showing how, in the course of the drama, the hero finds himself literally "taken at his word"—a word which turns against him and brings him the bitter experience of that meaning which he obstinately refused to recognize. Most often, the chorus hesitates and wavers, cast from one meaning to the other, or sometimes obscurely senses a still-secret meaning, or unknowingly formulates it through a play of words, an expression with a double meaning.[16]

Only for the spectator can the language of the text be clear at all of its levels, in its polyvalence and in its ambiguities. From the author to the spectator, language therefore recovers this full function of communication which it had lost on stage between the characters of the drama. But what the tragic message communicates, when it is understood, is precisely that there exist, in the words exchanged by men, zones of opacity and incommunicability. While seeing the

[14] See Euripides *Phoenicians* 409ff.: "If the same thing were equally beautiful and wise for all, human beings would no longer know the controversy of quarrels. But for mortals nothing is same or equal except in words; reality is all different."

[15] "Sophocles' Praise of Man and the Conflicts of the *Antigone*," *Arion*, 3, no. 2 (1964): 46–60.

[16] On the place and role of ambiguity in the tragedians, see W. B. Stanford, *Ambiguity in Greek Literature: Studies in Theory and Practice* (Oxford, 1939), chaps. X–XII.

protagonists adhere exclusively to one meaning and, thus blinded, become distracted or lost, the spectator must understand that there are really at least two possible meanings, or even more. Language becomes clear to him, and the tragic message communicable, only to the degree that he discovers the ambiguity of words, of values, and of man himself, to the degree that he recognizes the universe as conflict-ridden, and that, abandoning his old certainties and opening himself to a problematic vision of the world, he becomes, through the performance, himself a tragic consciousness.

*   *   *

A distance between the heroic past and the city's present, a tension between the myth and legal and political forms of thought, conflicts in man, in the world of values, and in the universe of the gods, an ambiguous and equivocal character of language—all these traits strongly mark Greek tragedy. But what perhaps defines it essentially is that the drama unfolds simultaneously on the level of everyday existence, in a human temporality that is opaque and composed of successive and limited present moments, and also in a realm beyond earthly life, in a divine temporality that is omnipresent, embracing at every instant the totality of events, sometimes to hide them, sometimes to reveal them, so that nothing ever escapes or is forgotten. By means of this constant union and confrontation throughout the plot of human and divine temporalities, the drama brings about a striking revelation of the divine in the course of human actions.

Tragedy, notes Aristotle, is the imitation of an action, *mimèsis praxeôs*. It presents characters in the process of acting, *prattontes*. And the word *drama* derives from the Doric *dran*, corresponding to the Attic *prattein*, to act. In fact, contrary to the epic and to lyric poetry, which never depict action nor project man as an agent, tragedy presents individuals in the attitude of action; it places them at the crossroads of a choice which involves them totally; it shows them questioning themselves, on the threshold of a decision, concerning the best course of action. Πυλάδη, τί δράσω ("Pylades, what must I do?"), cries Orestes in *The Choephoroe* (899), and Pelasgos says, at the beginning of *The Suppliants* (379–80), "I don't know what to do; anguish grips my heart, should I act or not?" However, the king adds at once a formula which, in its connection with the preceding, underlines the polarity of tragic action: "To act or not to act; and to tempt fate?" Τε καὶ τύχην ἑλεῖν. To tempt fate: for the tragedians, human action in itself does not have enough strength to make do without the gods, not enough autonomy to conceive itself fully independently of them. Without their presence and their support, it is nothing; it miscarries or bears fruits quite different from those expected. Human action is therefore a sort of wager, on the future, on fate, and on oneself—in the last analysis, a wager on the gods, who, one hopes, are on one's side. In this gambling, of which he is not the master, man always risks being caught in the trap of his own decisions. The gods are incomprehensible to him. If he takes the precaution of questioning them before acting and if they are willing to speak, their answer is just as equivocal and ambiguous as the situation about which their advice was solicited.

In the tragic perspective, therefore, action involves a double nature: one aspect is to take council with oneself, to weigh the pro and the con, and to foresee the priority of means and ends; the other aspect is to wager on the unknown and the incomprehensible, to hazard oneself in an inscrutable situation, to enter into the play of supernatural forces, which may, in entering the game with you, be preparing your success or your ruin. The most thoroughly considered action of the most far-sighted man retains the nature of a hazardous appeal thrown to the gods, the worth and meaning of which one will learn only by their response and most often to one's undoing. It is at the end of the drama that actions reveal their true significance and that the agents discover, through what they have really accomplished without knowing it, their true identity. Until the final consummation, human affairs remain enigmas, all the more obscure because the actors feel more assured of what they are doing and what they are. Cast in his character of a decipherer of enigmas and a justice-dispensing king, convinced that he is inspired by the gods, proclaiming himself the son of *Tychè*, of Good Fortune, how could Oedipus understand that he is, himself, the enigma, whose meaning he will guess only by discovering himself to be the opposite of what he thought he was: not the son of *Tychè* but her victim, not the dispenser of justice but the criminal, not the savior of his city, but the vile taint from which it is perishing? And, at the very moment when he sees that he is responsible for having forged his misfortune with his own hands, he will be able to accuse the gods of having plotted it all in advance, of having played him from the beginning to the end of the drama in such a way as better to bring about his ruin.[17]

As tragic character is formed in the range between *daimôn* and *ethos*, so is tragic guilt established between the ancient religious conception of the criminal taint, of the ἁμαρτία, a mental or spiritual illness, a divinely caused insanity which necessarily engenders crime, and the new conception according to which

---

[17] See R. P. Winnington-Ingram, *loc. cit.*; and, concerning the same problem in Aeschylus, see A. Lesky, "Decision and Responsibility in the Tragedy of Aeschylus," *Journal of Hellenic Studies*, 86 (1966): 78–85. As Lesky notes, "Freedom and compulsion are united in a genuinely tragic way" because one of the major traits of the tragedy of Aeschylus is precisely "the close union of necessity imposed by the Gods and the personal decision to act."

the guilty one, ἁμαρτών and especially ἀδικῶν, is defined as one who, without being constrained, has deliberately chosen to offend against the law.[18] In endeavoring to distinguish the categories of murder belonging to different tribunals —φόνος δίκαιος, ἀκούσιος, ἑκούσιος—even if it still does so in a clumsy and hesitant way—the law is emphasizing the notions of intention and responsibility; it is raising the problem of the degrees of involvement of the agent in his actions. On the other hand, in the framework of a city where the affairs of state are directed by citizens through public discussions of a secular character, man begins to have a sense of himself as an agent, more or less autonomous from the religious forces which dominate the universe, more or less master of his actions, having more or less assumed by his *gnômè*, his *phronèsis*, responsibility for his own political and personal destiny. This experience, still vacillating and undecided, of what is destined to be in the psychological history of Western man the category of the will (we know that there is in ancient Greece no real vocabulary of the will), is expressed in tragedy in the form of an anxious questioning of the agent's relation to his actions: in what measure is man really the source of his own actions? Even when he consciously deliberates his actions, when he takes the initiative and assumes the responsibility for them, do they not have their real source outside him? Does not the meaning of actions remain unclear to the one who commits them? Do not actions draw their reality not from the intentions of the agent but from the general order of the world, over which only the gods preside?

In order for there to be tragic action, the notion of a human nature, having its own characteristics, must have already evolved, so that the human and divine realms are already distinct enough to be in opposition; but, at the same time, they must not cease to appear inseparable. The tragic sense of responsibility appears when human action makes room in the interior debate for intention and premeditation but before it acquires enough firmness or autonomy to be entirely self-sufficient. The proper domain of tragedy is situated at that frontier zone where human actions are joined with the divine powers, where they take their true meaning, unknown to the agent, in becoming an integral part of an order which

---

[18] In the formula that Aeschylus puts on the lips of the *coryphaeus* (*Agamemnon*, 1337–38) the two conceptions are to some extent superimposed or confused in the same words. In fact, in its ambiguity the phrase lends itself to a double interpretation: Νῦν δ'εἰ προτέρων ἁιμ' ἀποτείσει could mean "And now if he must pay for the blood that his ancestors have spilled," but it could also mean "And now if he must pay for the blood that he has spilled in the past." In the first case, Agamemnon is the victim of an ancestral curse: he pays for faults that he has not committed. In the second, he expiates the crimes for which he is responsible.

goes beyond man and escapes him. For Thucydides, human nature, ἀνθρωπίνη φύσις, defines itself in absolute contrast to the religious power that is τύχη. They are two radically different orders of reality. In tragedy they constitute, rather, two aspects, opposed but complementary, two faces, of an identical ambiguous reality.

Every tragedy, therefore, necessarily plays on two levels. Its function as an inquiry of man the responsible agent has value only as counterpoint to the central theme. It would be a mistake, then, to focus all the light on the psychological element. In the famous carpet scene in *Agamemnon*, the sovereign's fatal decision is perhaps a result of his pitiful human vanity, also of his guilty conscience as a husband—all the more inclined to give in to the wishes of his wife since he is bringing Cassandra back to the house as a concubine. But that is not the essential thing. The peculiarly tragic effect comes from the intimate connection and, at the same time, the extraordinary distance between the banal act of walking on a purple carpet, with its too human motivations, and the religious forces which are inexorably released by this action.

As soon as Agamemnon has placed his foot on the carpet, the drama is consummated. And, although the play goes on for a while longer, it cannot, from now on, produce anything which is not already ordained. Past, present, and future merge in a single and same significance, revealed and condensed in the symbolism of this act of impious *hybris*. Now we know what the sacrifice of Iphigenia really was: less the obedience to the orders of Artemis, less the hard duty of a king who does not want to wrong his allies (cf. 213), than the guilty weakness of an ambitious man whose passion, in conspiracy with the divine *Tychè* (cf. 187: ἐμπαίοις τύχαισι συμπνέων),[19] has driven him to sacrifice his own daughter. We know what the taking of Troy really was: less the triumph of justice and the punishment of the guilty than the sacrilegious destruction of a whole city with its temples. And in this double impiety the more ancient crimes of the Atrides live again, and all those which will ensue are here foretold: the blow which strikes Agamemnon and which will finally reach Clytemnestra through Orestes. At this culminating point of the tragedy, where everything is tied together, divine temporality appears on the stage and becomes visible in human temporality.[20]

[19] For this line see the commentary of Ed. Fraenkel, *Aeschylus: Agamemnon* (Oxford, 1950), 2: 115; with reference to l. 219, see pp. 127–28.

[20] On the relationships between the two orders of temporality, refer to the study of P. Vidal-Naquet, "Temps des dieux et temps des hommes," *Revue de l'Histoire des Religions*, January-March, 1960, pp. 55–80.

4 EZIO RAIMONDI

I Promessi Sposi: *Genesis and Structure of a "Catholic" Novel*

> *"I do not think your anonymous manuscript is the*
> *work of a seventeenth-century writer, but of Pascal*
> *who had Shakespeare write it out for him."*
> —Ermes Visconti

I

In many writers of the last generation of eighteenth-century Europe, the awareness of the crisis, which, whether accepted or rejected, strikes at the roots of the poetic system of the Western tradition and its world of values, after the Jacobin revolution, is expressed as a conviction that objective classical mythology is in decline. This awareness becomes a search for a new and more complex mythical dimension.

Right at the beginning of the century, in the midst of an experiment already under way, Friedrich Schlegel, with the acumen of a prophet deciphering from the past the hieroglyphs of future history, declared programmatically:

Our poetry, I say, lacks a center, which mythology provided for that of the ancients, and the essential reason why modern poetry lags behind that of the ancients may be expressed in the statement that we have no mythology. However, I would add, we are near to acquiring one, or rather, the moment is at hand when we must co-operate in the creation of one. For, it will come to us by a completely different path from that of ancient mythology, which was everywhere the first flowering of youthful fantasy, fastening on, and drawing its inspiration directly from, whatever in the world of the senses was closest and most living. The new mythology however must be drawn from the remotest depths of the spirit.

And shortly afterward, in the magniloquent *Génie du Christianisme*, Chateaubriand put forward the same alternative, again in the form of a Catholicism rich in images and pathos, prepared to take its place in Napoleonic society:

Professor Raimondi's essay was translated from Italian for publication in this volume. Most of the quotations from Alessandro Manzoni's I Promessi Sposi *are taken from the English translation by Archibald Colquhoun,* The Betrothed *(New York: Dutton, 1951).*

123

... la mythologie peuplant l'univers d'élégants phantômes, ôtait à la création sa gravité, sa grandeur et sa solitude. Il a fallu que le christianisme vint chasser ce peuple de faunes, de satyres et de nymphes, pour rendre aux grottes leur silence, et aux bois leur rêverie. . . . Le spectacle de l'univers ne pouvait faire sentir aux Grecs et aux Romains les émotions qu'il porte à notre âme. Au lieu de ce soleil couchant dont le rayon allongé tantôt illumine une forêt, tantôt forme une tangente d'or sur l'arc roulant des mers; au lieu de ces accidents de lumière qui nous retracent chaque matin le miracle de la création, les anciens ne voyaient partout qu'une uniforme machine d'opéra.

Certainly, even if such a work as *René* was later to spring from it, in Chateaubriand all this remained descriptive aestheticism, a scenography of fashionable formulas and contrasts. With a poet of Coleridge's quality, this did not occur when, two years after the second edition of the *Lyrical Ballads*, he sketched a modern hypothesis for the lyrical experience, tracing it back with the most intimate logic of poetic creation to the dialectic of the imagery itself, associating the example of Shakespeare with the Bible in a way that Chateaubriand would never have done: "All natural objects were dead, mere hollow statues, but there was a Godkin or Goddessling included in each. . . . At best it is but fancy, or the aggregating faculty of the mind, not imagination or the modifying and coadunating faculty. This the Hebrew poets appear to me to have possessed beyond all others, and next to them the English. In the Hebrew poets each thing has a life of its own, and yet they are all our life."

A prospective of this kind, especially in Coleridge's terms, seems necessary in connection with Manzoni and his poetic development also. Perhaps only in this way will it assume a truly European stature, with its lucid, consistent, fearless research, which then draws on discretion, modesty, and irony to silence the anxieties, conflicts, and ruptures that prepare for and accompany the great inner choices in the face of the "chaos of possibilities." Furthermore, his "solitary and dispassionate" history (the adjectives are Manzoni's) cannot be understood until it be recognized that, to the composure and homogeneity that distinguish it like an innate grace corresponds, behind the order of the finished page, an often dramatic dialectic of experiments, challenges, and "impasses." And in this dialectic, the struggle toward a new language, destined to demolish the whole hierarchy of traditional "genres," precisely along the lines of Coleridge's hypothesis, identifies itself with the awareness of one in whom, in the words of Drieu la Rochelle, the spectacle of the years from 1789 to 1815 had raised doubts as to the efficacy of reason, but who, like a man of the eighteenth century, being inclined to put his faith in it, ends up not renouncing it but clinging to it desperately.

It takes Manzoni a decade to reach the crucial point of his poetical career. During this period, spent partly in Milan, partly in Paris, he tries out the themes and forms of neoclassical literature, from Alfieri to Monti, from Parini almost up to Foscolo, in a series of highly promising exercises already rich in personal notes. They are transposed into a key of moral meditation in which not only Parini's example but the stoic wisdom of the *Idéologie*, filtered through the splendid, affectionate intelligence of Fauriel, seems to play a decisive part. Manzoni very soon distinguishes between truth and the cult of the "self" in, one might say, his taste for ideological "debunking," in which he is confirmed, above all, by his exchange of ideas with his French friend. However, the young writer's enthusiasm still operates within the limits of a crystallized poetic diction and upholds its decorative structures and its mythical functions; this is in perfect agreement with Fauriel, the reformer of the *Réflexions Préliminaires,* of the *Parthénéide,* that, if, on the one hand, "les objects et les phénomènes de la nature inanimée n'ont et ne peuvent avoir de caractère et d'intérêt poétique, qu'autant qu'ils ont quelque rapport, quelque convenance avec nos sentiments intimes," then, on the other, "la mythologie grecque n'est autre chose qu'une personification ingénieuse et brillante des phénomènes généraux les plus évidents de la nature physique et morale," insofar as "les êtres dont elle peuple l'univers ne sont qu'une des manières diverses dont l'homme peut envisager les forces et mouvements de la nature, quand il cède à la tentation ou au besoin de s'en faire une idée fixe et absolue: ce sont des fantômes; mais des fantômes qui ont dans l'imagination humaine une raison d'exister."

However this may be, the balance amounts only to a compromise, which is destroyed the moment his return to Catholicism—the outcome of the austere drama of a spirit that suddenly finds itself on the brink of Pascal's abyss—compels Manzoni to make a radical choice, with regard to poetry as well—not, indeed, in the rather facile sense of a writer like Chateaubriand, for whom, as Sainte-Beuve was later to observe, a Catholic imagination sufficed, but in the far more difficult and strenuous sense of a Christian sensibility to be lived to the full in a period which appears continually to reject it. It cannot be overemphasized that the *Inni Sacri* mark a turning point in Manzoni's career, where his whole future as a romantic is already in play. Just when the author is becoming aware of his truest, deepest self, the poetry of the "I" disappears. It now becomes the poetry of the "we," by virtue of a reduction or sublimating mortification of his personal experience. Along with its stubborn distrust of all subjective hyperbole, this poetry of the "we" postulates a mysterious order, a bond of communion between men and things, which permanently excludes mythology from the possibility of serving as mediator. In the *Inni Sacri* there is no longer a place for the imagery of mythological classicism. There is a radical change in the inner form of the lyrical discourse, which now derives its innovating force from the language of the Bible, rediscovered in the manner of Pascal, "*en un sens dans lequel tous les passages s'accordent*," as a revelation of an inner dynamic tension, as the presence of a vital rhythm which, in its dialectic, comes to comprehend even the void and the "anguish" of the modern neurosis. Manzoni, in addition to the victorious tones of fulgurating poetry composed of choral pronouncements and intense meditative sequences ("He is arisen: now, how was this prey snatched from death?"), tries out a biblical type of poetic logic built upon a well-founded relationship, an organic correspondence between the physical world and the inner universe. And he does so without fear of the unevenness and approximations consequent upon it, and at the cost also of producing an excess of Christian, patristic, and baroque oratory. Now, as Professor Northrop Frye has shown, a "framework of images," although always connected with a "belief," is simply a way of organizing images and pursuing metaphors, rather than an expression of faith.

Anyone who examines this "framework" in the *Inni Sacri* will find that in the end it revolves around the themes of barrenness, reawakening, light, and inmost breath, in an area of existential analogies which is quite close, moreover, to that which, according to Professor Abrams, encompasses the English romantic lyric at the archetypal level. One has only to think of "Pentecost," even though this is the noblest, maturest example of Manzoni's *Inni Sacri*, with "The sun that causes the flower to blossom from the lazy seed; then, slowly to die ungathered on the humble grass," with "We beseech thee! O pleasing breath, consoling breeze, descend into the languid thoughts of the unhappy man: descend, O storm . . . ," and, above all, with the new kind of simile, functioning through a prodigious yet tranquil synesthesia, "like as the rapid light that rains from thing to thing and kindles the different hues wherever it comes to rest, so the voice of the Spirit resounded in all its variety." Madame de Staël also, in a page of *De l'Allemagne* which Manzoni must certainly have remembered since it deals with "*sujets historiques*" and the "*plus d'imagination*" that they require, had resorted to a very similar analogy: "La poesie fidèle fait ressortir la vérité comme le rayon du soleil les couleurs, et donne aux événements qu'elle retrace l'éclat que les ténèbres du temps leur avaient ravi." But it is clear that, for the author of the poem "Pentecost," the relation between the two terms of the simile has become dynamic and, as it were, bilateral, which makes the coincidence, whether accidental or otherwise, valuable. The phenomenon of light, seen in terms of its radiating power, associates the commemorated event with the very tension of nature, and the miracle of the "manifold voice" projects itself into the physical reality with that wholly intellectual power of a spirituality bursting forth victoriously.

According to an American critic, there is a kindred process also in the structure of the romantic metaphor, although it is accompanied by a taste for the irrational or the unformed, which seems foreign to Manzoni's diction, with its need for an order that will give it a foundation and certainty. More than one critic has observed that in Manzoni's linguistic practice and theory the metaphor loses the decorative function assigned to it by the sensationalists, in whose view it *"doit toujours former une image qu'on puisse peindre,"* so as to take on the evocative and epistemological function of an illumination within the real, since *"on ne peut faire de la poésie sans idées."* Much later on, when an old man, the author was to declare that the "metaphor, by revealing an analogy between two objects, gives a glimpse of a law to which both are subject, an order to which both appertain." But this is a principle already inherent in the *Inni Sacri* and in their aesthetic of the harmonies of nature, as Di Breme, another Italian romantic, would have said: an aesthetic which in fact sanctions the passage in a poet's career from the mimetic conception of the word as "mirror" to the cognitive conception of the word as "lamp," to adopt Abrams' terms. This, however, does not in any way prevent old habits from continuing to mingle with the new in the text, or neoclassical fictions from re-emerging, possibly in the form of eclectic allegories. It is not without reason that on several occasions, in the drafts of the *Inni Sacri* and elsewhere, we get the impression of a conflict between the writer and his memory, and of a far from easy, far from assured attempt to rise to a sense of the real, from which also stems a dramatic conception of man's life on this earth.

What opens up before Manzoni as a result of his great experiment with Christian poetry is, in the end, a system of analogies which, by mediating between nature and time, restores to poetry the sense of history, outside the neoclassical or Ossianic framework recognized, for example, by Monti, in the tradition of a biblical inwardness which does not pass through Chateaubriand or De Maistre, but which gains strength from Bossuet (in a wholly Augustinian key) and even more from Pascal or Nicole. We may imagine the Manzoni of those stormy years—barely out of the "antiheroic" school of the *Idéologues* and still on close terms with the Fauriel of *Les Derniers Jours du Consulat*—reading the Bible. The sacred text, even in the mysterious light of a vertical dimension, reveals a historical reality at the roots of responsibility and guilt, which grows increasingly complex and ambiguous the more it penetrates the secret world of man. For an immediate confirmation of this, one has only to open Manzoni's

Osservazioni sulla Morale Cattolica to a page in the introductory section. (Although there is an interval of a few years, no anachronism is involved in this case.) Here, already, we find early intimations of the voice of Federigo in its broad and passionate eloquence:

> That which is, and that which should be, poverty and greed, and the ever-living idea of perfection and order which dwell side by side in us, good and evil; the words of divine wisdom, and the various discourses of men, the vigilant joy of the just, the sufferings and consolations of the penitent, the dread and imperturbability of the wicked, the triumphs of justice and those of iniquity; the designs of men accomplished in the face of a thousand obstacles, or overthrown by an unforeseen obstacle, the faith that awaits its reward, and feels the vanity of what is transient, disbelief itself; all is explained in the New Testament, everything confirms the New Testament: the revelation of a past whose sad testimony man carries in his heart, without possessing the tradition, or the key to it, and the revelation of a future, of which only a confused idea of dread and desire remained, are what illuminate the present which is before our eyes.

In the light of these premises it is hardly surprising that Manzoni immediately recognizes himself in a dramatic system for which *"tout est tragédie dans les événements qui intéressent les nations,"* when, ever the solitary reader, he becomes acquainted with Madame de Staël's *De l'Allemagne*, Schlegel's *Cours de littérature dramatique*, or Sismondi's *Littérature du Midi*—texts, that is, which convey the official critical paradigms of the new romantic literary conscience in a halo of Christian spiritualism. Nor is it surprising that, following upon an inner struggle, of which there remain only a few echoes in the letters to Fauriel, a change in his "ideas" is approaching maturity within him. Departing more and more from the principles of classicism, he ends by rediscovering Shakespeare and proposing a type of drama which must be, in the words of his oft-repeated formula, "a history of the human heart." In the play of convergent influences and stresses, of which the whole of Manzoni's work avails itself, Shakespeare seems to intervene at the right moment to focus the poetical theory of true sentiment announced by the *Inni Sacri* on a more fervent secular material, and to bring out the historical matrix, with the addition of the passions and anxiety of the political problem. He also enables the writer to reconcile the engagement of the moralist with the contemplative observer's interest in the theater of existence ("Shakespeare stands above all others because he is more moral. The deeper one goes into the heart, the more one discovers the eternal principles of virtue.") insofar as the action and plot are transferred into the introspective analysis or the inner truth of the character, who is revealed to himself through the waverings of his heart. As Manzoni says in a justly famous fragment of his *Materiali Estetici*, "There is a type of tragedy which sets out to arouse a lively interest by presenting the passions of men, and their inner being, as developed by a succession of circumstances and events; which aims to depict human nature and create the interest that is aroused in man when he sees represented the errors, passions, virtues, enthusiasms, and dejection into which men are led in the gravest situations of life, when he considers, in the representation of others, the mystery of himself."

This Shakespeare "naturaliter" Christian is largely the Shakespeare of the romantic sensibility, where the emphasis is on the monologues, the great meditations of the heroes in crisis, on the discovery of the deepest layer of the "ego," which attains to self-realization almost by denying itself. One is actually reminded of Guizot's *Vie de Shakespeare*, one of the few texts that bears comparison with the *Lettre à M. Chauvet*. Guizot observes, on the one hand, that the heart of man is *"la scène où viennent jouer leur rôle les événements de ce monde,"* and, on the other, that *"le monde offre maintenant au poète des esprits pareils à celui d'Hamlet, profonds dans l'observation de ces combats intérieurs."* When he speaks of modern Hamlets, Guizot is certainly thinking of a state of mind whose political implications can be immediately extended to the complicated liberalism of Manzoni. There is no doubt that Manzoni projects his utopian and irresolute intellectual's disposition into the characters of his dramas, recording, page by page, the enthusiasm or bewilderment of his conscience at a still ambiguous present which lies just beyond the text, and halts, then, at the antinomy between power and morality, force and justice, to examine in it the drama of man, which is also the perennial drama of history. What for Schiller's Wallenstein still remains a difficult, desperate starting point from which the politician cannot escape ("Ich muss Gewalt ausüben oder leiden . . . da herrscht der Streit, und nur die Stärke siegt . . . dem bösen Geist gehört die Erde. . . .") becomes for Adelchi a final truth, henceforth on the fringe of the action: "nothing remains but to do wrong, or suffer it. A fierce power possesses the earth."

But, precisely because the conflict always turns into an inner experience which the character absorbs at the origins of its being, in the darkness of a vital force which is wearing itself out and, as it were, withering away, the language of Manzoni's anti-Aristotelian drama takes up again and deepens the technique of dynamic analogy with a new and active grafting of biblical lyricism into the imagery of the tragedy. An example of this, in its tone of greatest density, is Marco's soliloquy in *Carmagnola*: "O all-discerning Lord, reveal my heart to me; so that I may at last see into what abyss I am fallen, whether I was the more foolish, or cowardly, or unfortunate ... the guilty fear which he caused to fall, drop by drop on my soul. . . . I am but on the brink of the precipice; I see it, and may yet draw back. . . ." Or it is Adelchi's confession: "My heart aches, Anfrido; it commands me to perform high, noble deeds; and fortune condemns me to perform unrighteous ones; and I drag myself along a road not chosen by me, dark, without a goal; and my heart grows barren as the seed which falls on evil ground and is swept away by the wind." Or, lastly, it is Ermengarda's great elegy: "As the dew to the withered tuft of grass makes life flow again, fresh in the dried-up blades, so that they rise green once more in the temperate dawn, so to the mind, which the impious virtue of love wearies, descends the refreshing coolness of a friendly word ... But as the sun which climbs the fiery steep with its diligent flames sets the motionless air ablaze, barely have they revived when the frail stems are burnt again to the ground; so, quickly, drowsy love returns immortal from its fragile forgetfulness, and assails the fearful soul, recalling the straying images to the familiar grief."

If history invites the man who contemplates it to descend into the mystery of himself, the poet of the Shakespearean romantic system is, in fact, called upon to reconstruct the inner man which the past lets sink beneath the events, to *"pénétrer dans les profondeurs de l'histoire,"* to *"deviner tout ce que la volonté humaine a de fort ou de mystérieux, le malheur de réligieux et de profond."* In short, he must seize the *"dedans,"* the inner countenance of historical truth. And this is the thesis, as the quotations already announce, of Manzoni's *Lettre à M. Chauvet,* a thesis which justifies, within Manzoni's open system, the presence of a modern historiographic reasoning which the writer cannot renounce. However, at the same time, this thesis, where the relationship between man and society grows so complex as to cause even feelings to be included in the dialectic of prejudices, of collective phenomena, ends up by putting in question the dramatic hypothesis itself of *Carmagnola* and *Adelchi.* For it is open to the suspicion of having that same "romanesque" character already imputed to the classical genre and its artificial order. Meanwhile, it is necessary to get accustomed to the image of a Manzoni in a state of dynamic equilibrium in a network of exigencies that do not always harmonize, under the pressure of a meditation that easily turns into irony and that never settles into provisional conclusions; even the poet is able to wait. This does not mean that his experience as a writer proceeds by inevitable and univocal integrations along a single track of segments that gradually accumulate. Trials, stagnation, and bypaths exist for him too. Thus the crisis of the concept of tragedy, which it would be superficial to interpret in psychological terms as the surmounting of pessimism, and which is the outcome, rather, of the spread of sociological "debunking" (paradoxically, both Christian and illuministic), is brought about by the recognition of Shakespeare's comic realism and by the rejection of the tragic character who serves as spokesman for the author himself; at the same time, the project of *Spartaco* exhausts itself in a brief spell of experiments, and what remains of Manzoni's enthusiasm for the problematic figure of a modern hero burns itself out in the dirge for Napoleon. But traces of this crisis survive even in the novel, in a blend of powerful, picturesque impastos which may even please.

In any event, amid the sadness of those early months in 1821, which destroy so many illusions and summon the intellectuals to a bitter self-examination, the idea of the novel immediately becomes clear in Manzoni's mind. However amazing the letters to Fauriel may be, it is even better to read the much less famous one written by Visconti to Cousin and dated April of that year. It is an exact transcription of the conversations between the apprentice novelist and his friend about the still almost blank manuscript of *Fermo e Lucia*. The plan which is outlined there (and which Manzoni was later to call his *"projet"*) is even more striking in its completeness.

La tragédie d'Adelgive ne sera pas achevée dans cette année; car Alexandre a été entraîné par la lecture de Walter Scott à écrire un roman en prose. Walter Scott, dit-il, a révélé une carrière nouvelle aux romanciers; le parti qu'on peut tirer des moeurs, des habitudes domestiques, des idées, qui ont influé sur le bonheur et sur les malheurs de la vie à différentes époques de l'histoire de chaque pays. Alexandre donc a entrepris de représenter les Milanais de 1630 (les passions, l'anarchie, les désordres, les folies, les ridicules de ce temps-là). Une peste qui a ravagé la Lombardie précisément à cette époque; quelques anecdotes très intéressantes de la vie de Cardinal Borromeo, le fondateur de notre Ambrosienne; le fameux procès que nous appellons de la *Colonne Infâme*, chef d'oeuvre d'autorité, de superstition et de bêtise, va lui fournir assez de matière pour enter la fable du Roman sur des faits avérés. Mais dans ce mélange de la partie historique avec la poétique, Alexandre est bien décidé à éviter la faute où est tombé Walter Scott. Walter Scott, vous savez, ne se gêne pas quand il croit trouver son compte à s'éloigner de la vérité historique. Tout en conservant les résultats généraux, il se permet tant de changements aux circonstances et aux moyens qui les ont amenées, que le fond des événements n'est plus le même. Manzoni au contraire se propose de conserver dans son intégrité le positif des faits auxquels il doit faire allusion; sauf à ne les effleurer que très rapidement. Les développements et les détails seront réservés à l'exposition des fictions qui doivent figurer comme partie principale dans son ouvrage.

Manzoni's new novel has its starting point in the mythology of the historical picturesque, *à la* Scott, which so exalted Thierry and Pushkin, to name but two, in those very years. However, in Manzoni, there is a conscious internal reform, only apparently an integrating factor, which, behind the themes of folly, disorder, and society, conceals a disturbing objection, even if it was familiar to the author, which is forced upon him by painful research, without illusions, into the very meaning of history, just when, in fact, one wishes to trace in it "the various developments and adaptations of human nature in the history of society; of that state, so natural to man, so violent, so desired, and so full of suffering, which creates so many goals while making their attainment impossible, which tolerates all the evils and all the remedies, rather than cease for one moment; of that state which is a mystery of contradictions where the intelligence loses itself if it does not see it as a state of trial and as a preparation for another life." And, strangely enough, this conviction which Manzoni the historian expresses in his *Discorso su alcuni punti della storia longobardica in Italia* (Discourse on Some Points of the History of the Longobards in Italy) will also be the final discovery of two simple characters like Renzo and Lucia. Besides, on reflection, we realize that the principle of negation governs all the devices of a novel where the fictional space is subjected to the doubling of the narrative conscience, where literature in its aspect of a social institution, or induced prejudice, and the relationship between writer and public constitute a problem within a story which should already consider this resolved as an indispensable prerequisite of its literary code. It must also be added that the broadening of the novel's perspective and the breaking down of traditional networks provoke a kind of clogging of all Manzoni's themes and obsessions. The effect is almost to prove Friedrich Schlegel right in his view that the novel is a compendium, an encyclopedia of the whole spiritual life of an individual, such as, in fact, each man has within him.

Recently, Erich Heller, a critic with an Anglo-German cultural background, has reminded us that, in Hegel's prophetic diagnosis, the course of European literature from romanticism onward has only two possible destinations if it is to escape the fate of a prosaic age which will end by denying art its ancient significance. On the one hand, says Heller, it may attempt to come to terms with the rational demands of the modern world through realism, naturalism, psychology, anti-illusionism, and the passion for understanding, the urge for a delimitation of the mystery. On the other hand, Heller continues, it may attempt, instead, to divorce the creative imagination from the forms of a real universe which is the realm of the intellect, by exploring in an interior journey the sphere of pure subjectivity. One of Manzoni's paradoxes lies, perhaps, in the operation, which reveals itself as the basis of *Fermo e Lucia*, the first version of the novel, of transferring his own inner myths, the most secret adventures of his soul, into the objective reality of history while neutralizing the suggestions or echoes of heroic and pathetic introspection in a world of common characters from seventeenth-century provincial life, dragged into the "events" of a "social machine" which dissolves the illusion of the "romanesque" in a "mixture of greatness and meanness, reasonableness and madness." Once more it is a bold, intricate operation, insofar as it involves, through the relentless exercise of control and censorship, the transition from *Fermo e Lucia* to *I Promessi Sposi*, from the violent turmoil of a tumultuous encyclopedia to the order of a new narrative organism in which the writer has settled all his problems.

Nowadays, it seems correct to consider these two versions as two widely different types of novel, and to take even *Fermo e Lucia* as a work in its own right; but this should then enable us to measure the extent of Manzoni's experiment with narrative form, and the vigor of his choices, even when they bear the appearance of a renunciation. What is certain is that, from a Manzonian point of view, the real narrator seems to be that of *I Promessi Sposi*, who has now shed the indignation, the gaudy outbursts of the commentator in *Fermo e Lucia*. This is due not to a toning down of his ideology but to a consistent development of the function of the characters, to whom history, rather than providing a picturesque, "precious" background, must lend social consistency, a foundation of ideas and prejudices that are decisive for their roles and for the "modifications" of their psychology within the course of events. But in this way the level of consciousness of the character is lowered to that of the surrounding historical society. The character is limited and stripped of its heroic aura (as Visconti required when he annotated the manuscript of *Fermo e Lucia*, "it is Signor Don Alessandro who is reflecting on this, but Fermo would never have thought of it"), while the first-person narrator, in his dialogue with the manuscript, occupies a higher plane. It is from this higher plane that there emanate flashes of irony destined to involve the narrator later, for there is no such thing as a privileged time which can put aside the ambiguous truth of "men in general." The device of irony, of which the smile on the surface represents only the simplest aspect, takes over the novel and sets up a contrapuntal pattern on several levels and in various keys in a network of allusions or parodies that, the writer is well aware, risks passing unobserved. One would be tempted to compare it with the work of Thomas Mann, if it were not tempered by a thoughtful vein of modesty or, rather, of creatural piety. The transition from *Fermo e Lucia* to *I Promessi Sposi* has been wittily defined as a conversion from the profusion of the self to honest dissimulation; and the cognitive and poetical peak which the language of the 1827 novel attains, in its transposition from the level of the immediate meaning to a symbolic meaning in a key of metaphysical realism, has also been underlined. This intelligent formula of an Italian critic is apt, in the first place, for the harmonizing irony of the *Promessi Sposi*, but it also turns out to be appropriate for retracing the argument, by natural affinity, to the analogical system of Manzoni's technique and to its grip on the narrative layers of the prose, so much more rich in associations, as one might expect, than the closed measure of the verse. It must be added straightaway that here, too, Manzoni's creative genius is equal to his coherence as a writer who continues to probe deeply into his personal lyrical universe, but who at the same time keeps faith with his intention to "de-lyricize" himself and to approach things in the familiar atmosphere of humble everyday life. In our case, however, we do not find a substantial difference between *Fermo e Lucia* and *I Promessi Sposi*, except for a different degree of success with the style, which in the earlier text is at times loaded with rather unfortunate allegorical implications, as, for example, in one of the pages on the Nun, which reads, "The tree of knowledge had ripened a bitter, loathsome fruit, but Gertrude had passion in her heart and the snake at her side, and seized the fruit," or in the words, legitimate though they may be in the mouth of a friar, uttered by Fra Cristoforo, "Great God! This scourge does not correct the world: it is hail which beats upon an already cursed vineyard; it cuts down bunches of grapes in great numbers and those that remain are sadder, sourer, and more rotten than before." When Manzoni the narrator of *I Promessi Sposi* takes over the image, the vineyard of Renzo is born, and the result is entirely different, both in the ironical extravagance of the material and in the highly refined play of the plot.

There is, however, a page of *Fermo e Lucia* which it is impossible not to dwell upon, since it depicts the process of interpenetration of soul and nature as if at its origin, at the heart of the archetype, the spiritual etymon that supports and explains it. Lucia is at once the subject and the protagonist of this process:

> ... it had been a most turbulent and confused joy at first; and now, as she grew calm, her joy was gradually dampened by memories of recent events and thoughts of the future. The heart freed from a great misfortune is like the earth from which a great tree has been uprooted: for a while the soil appears cleared and empty, but little by little it begins to show signs of tiny shoots here and there, and then to cover itself with weeds, showing clearly that what is called

"the earth's rest or repose" is a metaphor or a mistake. Thus the troubles which had been buried and almost smothered in the heart when a great misfortune took possession of it and, so to speak, overshadowed it, begin to put forth shoots and reappear soon after the misfortune has ceased."

The profound matrix of Manzoni's inner landscapes stands revealed to us also in the polemical reasoning even against the quietism of the conscience. This will no longer occur in *I Promessi Sposi*, where the image, transferred from man to nature for the great scene in the lazaretto (the "weeds" become, instead, part of a moral portrait of Don Abbondio), grows sharper and dizzier, but also more secret, descending into the "days which forerun a storm, when Nature, outwardly calm but in the grip of an inward travail, seems to oppress everything and add an indefinable heaviness to every action, even to idleness, even to existence itself." But the basic attitude remains the same: whether Manzoni is describing a human being, or whether he is talking about the soil of a field, he sees life from the inside, in the processes of the mysterious forces that flow through an organism, in the discontinuous tension of the vital dialectic in which opacity and awakening, drowsiness and ardor, sterility and germination, darkness and light, alternate one with the other, and whose most typical figure of speech seems to be a restrained antithesis. It was not without reason that Manzoni, in a self-confession to Fauriel, with the analytical bent of a Maine de Biran, alluded to *"ce qu'il a d'incertain, de périlleux, je dirai même de terrible, dans le bonheur même le plus calme."*

It is also clear, in this way, how the conflicts, suspensions, and annoyances of the inner life acquire a new physical density of sensations that go below the surface, and of unexplored half-lights (penumbras) that reveal themselves in a kind of tremor, which is immediately dominated by the insinuating firmness of a "gaze" that observes without ever aiding or abetting. The great thematic opening in Chapter 10 comes spontaneously to mind: "There are times when the mind, particularly the mind of the young, is disposed to yield to the slightest pressure of anything that has an appearance of virtue and self-sacrifice; it is like a newly opened flower, sinking languidly back on its fragile stem and ready to yield its fragrance to the first breeze that plays around it. These moments, which should be regarded by others with delicate respect, are just the ones for which the cunning schemer watches, and catches on the wing, so as to ensnare the unguarded will." But even more, perhaps we ought to return to another study of disturbed emotions, in the same Gertrude episode: "To the majestic, but cold and limited prospects called forth by the idea of being the head of a convent, they would oppose the varied and glittering visions of weddings and banquets, of parties and balls, of summers in countryhouses, of clothes and carriages. Such visions made Gertrude's mind stir and flutter as if a great basket of fresh flowers had been set down before a hive of bees." And here, incidentally, it is necessary to pause and consider the dynamic value of the enumerative series in its process of approximation to a composite and unstable reality. We may also note the almost symbolic presence of the word "*brulichio*" (fluttering, swarming) at the summit, one might say, of a family of frequentatives for which Manzoni shows a predilection, and by no means accidentally.

Critics have already observed the dynamic nature of Manzoni's prose, the energy of which ferments inside the words and almost thrusts them one into the other, now slackening, now surging forward, while one has the impression that a serene order is harmonizing all their limpid interrelations. And it now seems clear that this depends, to a large extent, on that process of active internalization of which the *Promessi Sposi* shows so many signs, for example, in just such terms as "*brulichio*" (swarming), "*ronzio*" (buzzing), "*mugolio*" (whimpering), "*fischio*" (whistling), and "*mormorio*" (murmuring), in which one might detect the shadow of an exasperated sensibility, or almost a neurosis, if this did not involve the risk of superimposing a view as improper as it is evocative. On the other hand, the inner space of the novel is populated with voices, sounds, fears, ghosts, with "*guazzabugli*" (muddles), especially at the level of the uncultivated, common experience of the antiheroes and of the choices they are called upon to make. The Lucia episode in the nocturnal castle where the "light" theme of "Pentecost" also reappears, but as if distorted and reduced to the everyday world of prose and its fragmentary, chaotic sensations, speaks, we feel, for every such experience. "But all of a sudden she was aroused as if by some internal call, and felt she must arouse herself completely, retain all her scattered senses, and find out where she was and how and why she had got there. A sound made her prick up her ears; it was the slow, hoarse snoring of the old woman. She opened her eyes wide, and saw a faint light flickering and disappearing; it was the expiring wick of the lamp, whose tremulous gleams were rising, then quickly falling, like waves ebbing and flowing on a shore, and whose light withdrew from the surrounding objects before they could take clear shape or color from it, leaving only a succession of muddled glimpses."

In the great narrative counterpoint of *I Promessi Sposi* it has always to be remembered, as we have said, that the inner dimension of a character is conditioned by his social status. The more the story stresses this status, set, as it is, into the web of relationships which make up the story, the greater are the possibilities for irony on the part of the narrator, an irony which wrests a distressing play of dissonances and contingencies, on the verge of the absurd, from the actions of men, when they clash and mingle in the tumultuous dialectic of the whole. If the system remains that of the natural analogy or metaphysical realism, the proportions change in favor of the world and at the expense of the character, who shrinks into very fragile, minor images. This can be seen, for example, in the wonderful finale to Chapter 27, amid echoes of the Bible and Dante, transcribed into the score of a stately, joyous symphony, which is more ambiguous than ever:

> The autumn, when Agnese and Lucia had counted on meeting again, came round; but a great public event sent these hopes up in the air (which was certainly one of its most trifling effects). There followed other great events which, however, brought no important change in the destinies of our characters. At length new and more general, graver, extremer disasters involved even them, even the lowest of them, according to the world's scale—just as a vast, sweeping, wandering hurricane, which uproots and strips trees, unroofs houses, untops spires, tears down walls, and scatters rubbish everywhere, even stirs up the bits of straw hidden in the grass and searches out of corners the light dry leaves that a gentler wind had borne there, and whirls them off on its headlong course of destruction.

A step farther and we come, in the end, to the grotesque character of history in a reality where there exists no law valid for all levels of society other than that of power, where things forever go astray, lost in a web of heterogeneous gestures, or are rediscovered only in the artificial, suspended space of the narrator. The Governor of Milan and Renzo Tramaglino meet in this way:

> Don Gonzalo had far too many important matters on his hands to bother himself very much about the doings of Renzo; and, if he did appear to worry over them, this was due to a singular combination of events by which poor Renzo, without wanting to, and without being aware of it either then or later, was linked with those same important matters by the thinnest and most invisible of threads.
>
> . . . .
>
> After that he took no further interest in such a trivial matter, which was over and done with so far as he was concerned; and when, a long time afterwards, the reply reached him in his camp above Casale, whither he had returned and where he had quite different preoccupations, he got up and threw back his head like a silkworm looking for a leaf, stood there a moment to bring back into his mind a matter of which only a vague shadow now remained, recalled the episode, had a dim, fleeting idea of the person involved, passed on to something else, and thought no more about it.

In the last analysis, and not without a further paradox, the counterpart of inwardness at the average level of everyday life seems to be precisely the grotesque. It is assimilated in a realistic manner which anticipates in its own way, though without the bourgeois nihilism, the Flaubert of the *"ridicule intrinsèque à la vie humaine,"* and which, since it overturns the emotional conclusions, rejects in advance Constant's *Réflexions sur la Tragédie* with its hypothesis for the construction of a high modern drama around the *"action de la société sur les passions et les caractères"* when *"l'homme faible, aveugle, sans intelligence pour se guider, sans armes pour se défendre, est, à son insu et sans son aveu, jeté dans ce labyrinthe qu'on nomme le monde."* But the author of *Adolphe* would never have thought of the journey of Renzo, the *"homme faible,"* amid anarchy and a plague.

The truth is that *I Promessi Sposi* puts not only the past but also the future of literature and its myths on trial. Manzoni's declaration, later to strike a blow at the whole genre of the historical novel, fits closely into the logic of a poetic career (which the author took pleasure in referring to as a "trade"). In this career the alternative between poetry and history, imagination and science, present since the years of the passionate exchanges with Fauriel, is, after the burst of narrative synthesis, resolved in favor of truth to facts of a positive and complex reality. As this reality gradually affirms itself in the modern critical consciousness, it also destroys the illusion (from which, however, the *Promessi Sposi* was born) that it was possible to rediscover within the past the profound truth of the heart, the adventure of the human soul, through the mediation of poetry. Beneath the arguments of a ruthless analysis, heedful even of what today would be called the sociology of literature, one seems, at the same time, to detect a more radical suspicion, a certain mistrust, an irreducible antinomy. If the world of the poet-storyteller is the inside of history, it is necessary, to give an impression of truth, for him to divine the secret of another heart, whose fate is linked with his own by a law which transcends history. But, as Nicole said long before: *"Il y a toujours dans le coeur de l'homme, tant qu'il est en cette vie, des abîmes impénétrables à toutes ses recherches"; "on ne connait jamais avec certitude ce qu'on appelle le fond du coeur."* And so history becomes impenetrable and opaque to poetry. The myths of the heart disappear into the silence of time before the poet can seize them, unless he returns to the choral monologue of the *Inni Sacri*, renouncing the *"secret de l'âme humaine,"* and there remains only historical science, strictly confined to a study of human society and events and the choices of individuals or groups. Flaubert, too, would later conclude anyway that *"l'histoire absorbera bientôt toute la littérature."*

Manzoni's silence after the *Promessi Sposi* reveals one more aspect of the tension which was inherent in the novel as the danger of self-denial, the risk of an irony that one would like to define as Christian, which, however paradoxically modern it may be, is not contemplated in the subjective metaphysics of Schlegel. In regard to Manzoni also, one can repeat with René Girard that the writer "*reconnaît . . . qu'il n'est pas Dieu. . . . c'est là la première démarche de l'art vrai, la plus essentielle peut-être et la plus méconnue.*" Yet it would be an error to go on to see Manzoni, his great romantic season behind him, as a figure gradually losing his powers, losing sight of the "spirit of the age," or accepting, as an honest moderate, his role as an intellectual within the revolution of bourgeois nationalist liberalism, dividing his time between historical studies, Rosminian meditations, and linguistic investigations. Disguised in the mawkish forms of *Biedermeier* world, which may at times be unpleasant, there is in Manzoni a secret, unrhetorical loyalty to the great themes of his own inner history, sustained by an intelligence ever alert to contemporary events and problems, which, not to mention his long dispute with utilitarianism, carries him as far as Tocqueville's *De la démocratie en Amérique*. It is no mere chance, in fact, that, to an English traveler, an Anglican, who paid him a visit in 1840, Manzoni's spiritual position—distinguished, in the Anglican's opinion, by a "disordered state of mind," ever in search of an "infallible authority" on which to lean—appeared identical to Newman's, "whose history," the Englishman then explained to the writer, "was the same, and who reasoned in the same way."

Besides, even the accents of certain pages have not changed compared with the former passion of "proud" Alessandro. A footnote to Madame de Staël's *Considérations sur les principaux évènements de la révolution française* comments on the thought: "Le pouvoir abstrait des gouvernements représentatifs n'irrite en rien l'orgueil des hommes, et c'est par cette institution que doivent s'éteindre les flambeaux des furies. Ils se sont allumés dans un pays où tout était amour-propre, et l'amour-propre irrité, chez le peuple, ne ressemble point à nos nuances fugitives; c'est le besoin de donner la mort." Manzoni says, with the profound, almost violent irony of the *Fermo e Lucia* years, in the same crude light of cutting observation, "Savez-vous ce qui faisait qu'un paysan français trouvait la corvée insupportable? c'était l'amour-propre. Que lui faisait la lièvre du seigneur qui venait impunément manger ses choux? Il irritait son orgueil: en effet cela n'était pas abstrait. Car la perte des choux en elle-même, comment pouvait-elle être compté pour quelque chose dans un pays, où tout était amour-propre? Et lorsqu'il devait payer en impôt le sou dont il aurait voulu acheter du pain, que croyez-vous qu'il sentit? La faim peut-être? Non: c'était le besoin de donner la mort."

This page suffices, after all, to remind us how Manzoni is still the romantic writer, the "true" narrator so dear to Giuseppe Verdi, who introduced into an aristocratic literature in which hunger had been a theme of jest, the modest verbal reality of the *"stufato"* (stew), the *"polpette"* (meatballs), and the *"polenta bigia"* (gray maize pudding). The pastoral world is finished.

II

On more than one occasion, Raymond Queneau has observed that the tradition of the Western novel up to Joyce can be traced back to two poles, to two great story types, represented, respectively, by *The Iliad* and *The Odyssey*. What is important in the former, and what also comes to be its definition, is the involvement of the characters in history and the interrelation between them and historical reality. The latter, however, takes its shape from the story of an individual who, through various experiences, acquires a personality, or affirms or rediscovers his own, as does Ulysses. It must also be added that the autobiographical *"récit"* almost always constitutes an odyssey, in the profound sense of an existence which turns back upon itself. If we argue according to these categories, the character of Renzo in *I Promessi Sposi* makes the novel into a kind of odyssey, not only because he is the "leading man" of the action, with his adventures as "pilgrim," fugitive, and "traveler," but also because the information about him, as will be seen in Chapter 37, is derived from his conversations with, and confessions to, the anonymous storyteller. It is as if, at the origin of the purported seventeenth-century story, there lies, at least to a great extent, the pleasure a reminiscing countryman, a survivor, takes in evoking his past, in telling his story, even imagining it in advance, while it is still in course. And it is actually Renzo who, safe now across the river Adda, murmurs to himself in one of his imaginative monologues: "How pleasant it will be to go strolling, all of us together, along this very road! And go right up to the Adda in a cart, and picnic on the bank, right on the bank, and show the women the place I embarked, the brambles I came down through, the place where I stood looking for a road."

Certainly Renzo's odyssey falls within the pattern of the historical novel and fits perfectly, completed by that of Lucia, into Scott's novel archetype, as described recently, and not without biting irony, by Professor Leslie Fiedler:

> Initially confused about his own ambitions or the true identity and character of those who surround him, often himself maligned and misrepresented, the hero is forced to flee—usually into the midst of some famous historic conflict just then conveniently approaching its climax. The heroine meanwhile has been abducted or is off on some private evasion of her own, for reasons only revealed in the final pages. The two are kept apart as long as possible, but are finally joined by the intervention of either some noble figure out of history or some

> notorious outlaw fresh from the greenwood (if possible, both). By the same
> agency, their problems are resolved, their enemies discomfited, all confusions
> cleared up. The good is revealed as good—and triumphant; the evil as evil—
> and defeated [*Love and Death in the American Novel* (New York, 1962),
> p. 155].

But a composite novel like *I Promessi Sposi*, even while it takes plots and
machinery from the narrative tradition, always transfers them into a completely
different type of context, which deforms them and modifies them radically in
the mischievous light of a subtle polemic against sentimentality and romanticiz-
ing, which implies an acute awareness of evil, sin, and the sophistries of the passions and the prejudices in the "abyss of the human heart." (But the "abyss of
the human heart" is a formula from the *Osservazioni sulla Morale Cattolica*; in
the novel it will become the "hotchpotch of the human heart.")

Even the theme of the two young people persecuted by the evil man thus
takes on a very different coloring, with structural functions that cannot escape
the reader who considers the story in its total movement. In fact, if the first eight
chapters present the characters as still united in the face of the "misfortune" (or
misadventure), as Propp would say, which befalls them and forces them to
depart, Chapters 9 and 10 follow Lucia to Monza, into Gertrude's convent; then
in Chapter 11, through the link with his antagonist, we return to Renzo, who
remains at the center of the story, whether in or out of Milan, through Chapter 17,
after which, for the next two chapters, he turns into a kind of ghost who crops
up in the conversation of men of power and finally disappears, along with Fra
Cristoforo, leaving the field to Don Rodrigo and the Innominato, the Unnamed.
Chapter 20 returns to Lucia, to her misadventures and the encounters that ensue, ending, after the brief parenthesis of Chapter 28 with the domestic picture
of Don Abbondio in Chapter 30. At this point, if we interpret Chapters 31 and
32 as a necessary preliminary to what happens immediately afterward, the Renzo
theme resumes with him once more in Milan, in the midst of the plague, searching
for Lucia; and thus we reach Chapter 36, which marks the reunion of the sur-
viving characters, now nearing the conclusion, the so-called happy ending.

Bound to each other by a common fate and an internal counterpoint of
memories echoing sentiments, the two adventures of Renzo and Lucia, from the
moment they part company, proceed alternately and determine the double axis
along which the story unfolds, so as to become what Burckhardt was later to
call a chapter of universal history. However, their linking functions work in two
different directions, since on the axis of Lucia we meet Gertrude, the Unnamed,
Cardinal Federigo, and even Donna Prassede or Don Ferrante, whereas on that
of Renzo (with the exception of the Chancellor, Antonio Ferrer) are arrayed

the men of the roads and squares, innkeepers, lawyers, tramps, merchants, sheriffs, honest fellows, artisans, *monatti*, poverty-stricken peasants. Both, as we see, give a stratified, representative picture of Lombard society. But only Renzo actually fulfills an authentic public experience, comes into contact with the machinery of a social system, experiences its absurdities at the lowest level, and makes an attempt to understand something of it. He is the antihero of the picaresque tradition, a "poor man" cast into a world of unforeseen snares and forced, in his journey from the country to Milan, into a kind of *Bildungs-roman* in which, often without his knowing it, the mystery of existence seems almost to reveal itself. And, to use Propp's paradigms again, it is he who in the end fills the role of the protagonist, both victim and searcher in the face of that complex yet terribly simple reality, justice.

In fact, it is not by chance that he first appears in an indirect way, after the two "bravoes" have uttered the names Renzo Tramaglino and Lucia Mondella, in the portrait which Don Abbondio, head bowed, and muttering to himself, peevishly gives of him: "Oh . . . oh . . . oh . . . he's tough too; as quiet as a lamb while left to himself, but if anyone puts his back up . . . ugh . . .! And then, and then, his head's quite turned by that girl Lucia, in love like. . . . What silly young fools they are, going and falling in love because they've got nothing better to do, and then wanting to get married, and not thinking about anything else. Little they care what trouble they let a poor honest man in for." Before he has even appeared on the scene, in our eyes he is already involved in the system of violence and disorder which has produced the proclamations, the bravoes, and Don Abbondio, and which is now preparing to assail him with the complicity of another" peaceful and defenseless citizen," accustomed to sticking to "the stronger, but always in the rear guard." The judgment of an "honest man" like Don Abbondio, the "severe critic of those who did not behave as he did," immediately sets up a hierarchy in which the law of the strong is not only confirmed but even extended to another "weak man" according to the logic of time-serving and fear, in a relationship which, from the start, postulates a master-slave dialectic. On the other hand, in spite of all the embarrassments by which he is seized, it is Don Abbondio who has to act as mediator between Renzo and the spirit of the system and to convince a "callow youth," as he calls him while awaiting his arrival, of the need for caution and renunciation; Renzo's journey into the dark universe of absolute power actually begins with him, in a village priest's house.

Now Renzo is confronted with the reality of the plot against him, and learns what it means to be a "poor man" ("It's a bad thing to be born poor, Renzo, my boy") in a world where "it isn't a question of right or wrong" but only "of might," as Don Abbondio, from his long experience, at once explains to him. This remark is terrible, even if the context seems comic, the more so because it is made by a "priest" who, out of weakness, has chosen the path of never opposing power—a priest without love, sadly human and honest, to whom it matters little that "every unjust power, in order to harm men, needs collaborators who will give up obeying the divine law"; "and thus the failure to carry out this law is the most essential condition for such power to be able to act," as the *Osservazioni sulla Morale Cattolica* teaches us on a page of vital importance. Renzo, of course, is incapable of such moralist's subtleties, for which we must wait until Cardinal Federigo enters the story. As regards the narrator, what interests him as he follows the peasant toward Lucia's house, in the confused impulsiveness of his protest, is to observe that the state of mind of the "oppressed man" is still the responsibility of the "oppressor"; it is almost as if he is suggesting, from another point of view, that the idea of murder, which momentarily comes into Renzo's mind, originates in the very state of society and is the sign of a corruption which contaminates even the thoughts of a man who is "averse to bloodshed."

Although the situation continually postulates it, the word "justice" has not yet occurred, except obliquely in the flat quotation of a proclamation ("the great mischief this kind of person is to public weal, in contempt of justice") or in the officious, agitated words of Don Abbondio ("But you gentlemen are too fair, too reasonable. . . ."). The person who finally utters the word aloud is again Renzo, in the presence of Doctor Quibble-Weaver (Azzecca-garbugli); but it is a grotesque situation of hypocrisy and ambiguity, which serves only to emphasize the solitude of a naïve fellow and to deepen his disappointment. The "Doctor," for whom "no one's guilty, and no one's innocent," introduces Renzo into a cynical, grasping, servile province of law degraded, and of public life reduced to a spectacle of swindling, trickery, and bribery. The visitor's first reaction is exactly like that of a "yokel in the village square [who] is gazing at a conjurer, a sleight of hand performer." Then he begins to understand, and is obliged to talk of "justice," not in the false sense of the lawyer ("if it was a question of deciding between the law and you . . ."), but in the true and painful sense of his very recent experience of oppression. "I haven't threatened anyone; I don't do that kind of thing, I don't; you can ask all round my village, and they'll tell you I've never been up against the law [*"giustizia"* in Italian]. It's I who've been put upon; and I've come to you to find out how I'm to get redress [again *"giustizia"* in the Italian text].

As we have said, this is the first time that the term "justice" has appeared in the novel without qualification, in its naked essence as a denial of arbitrary power. But no sooner has it been brought up than the process of distortion begins again, both on the part of Quibble-Weaver, who, on hearing the name Don Rodrigo, immediately opposes the "nonsense, fiddlesticks" of the peasant with his "honest man's" common sense, and, on the part of Renzo, who returns to his women, disconsolate but determined to do something, and this in the name of the justice that he cannot obtain. And while he is conversing with Agnese and Lucia in an atmosphere of general sadness, we hear him declare, at the possibility that the remedy may come from Fra Cristoforo: ". . . in any case I'll get my rights, or have them got for me. There's justice in this world in the long run." The narrator then hastens to add that "a man overwhelmed by grief no longer knows what he is saying," which is by no means a witticism, as it might seem, if it is understood in connection with what has taken shape in Renzo's mind since leaving Don Abbondio and with the "perversion" that can affect the intentions of even an honest man such as he. What he is contemplating, in the last analysis, is murder, revenge; and yet he calls it justice, with the same logic that serves his opponents, thus unsuspectingly contaminating the suffering that he undergoes as an innocent man and his right as an immortal soul.

That this is how the matter stands can be seen at once from the next chapter, where, at a certain point in the flashback to the story of Lodovico–Fra Cristoforo, we read the phrase: "thus hand him over to justice, or rather to the vengeance of his enemies." This connection, however, is not a result of chance, since in the structure of the novel, so symmetrical and so rich in internal echoes, the figure of Fra Cristoforo has a profound link with the situation of Renzo, which often is not sufficiently observed or is interpreted in conventional terms. If there is anyone in whom the friar can almost recognize a part of himself, it is Renzo, who, for a moment, is planning to assault his enemy and is looking forward to a revenge which he considers just; and this explains exactly why his function, in relation to Renzo's spiritual voyage, becomes that of guiding him toward another idea of justice which involves not violence but respect for man. Only to Renzo can he say on meeting him that "the weak gain nothing by showing their claws," and add, from the depths of his own memories, a mysterious "and if . . . ," which is sufficient in itself to convince the listener. In fact, if we wish to clarify this completely, we must go back to the *Osservazioni sulla Morale Cattolica*, to the same place from which we quoted with reference to Don Abbondio, where it is concluded that "the divine law preaches justice to all men, and if in many cases it only proposes patience to those who wish to pursue it, it is proposing the sole means to happiness, since all other means, by rendering them guilty, as a result make them abject and miserable." Don Abbondio, as we have seen, has a very different view of it; and, in fact, his patience follows another route.

Fra Cristoforo's, however, drives him to the mansion of Don Rodrigo "the lair of the wild beast," with the illusion that he will be able to "tame" it, even if all this smacks of the fairy tale. In effect, the good Capuchin obtains nothing, although he invokes justice, charity, innocence, and honor; and, in the end, nothing remains—apart from the biblical appeal to God's justice—but to go back to his "poor creatures" and try to help them in some other manner, and explain to Renzo, who would like at least to know why Don Rodrigo has vetoed his marriage, that the man of power does not even need to give reasons for his whims: "he can insult you and make himself out to be the injured party, jeer at you and pretend he is in right, bully and yet complain." However, Renzo is still far from the "patience" that Fra Cristoforo counsels him and he has by no means abandoned his intention of taking the law into his own hands. He proclaims it once more while Agnese is repeating to him that "justice is always against the poor" and insists, with a mixture of stubbornness and histrionics, until Lucia lets herself be talked into attempting a surprise marriage at the house of Don Abbondio. We return to the level of comedy in a plot with a melodramatic flavor which once again reverses all the situations and all the roles in the game showing us the paradox of the dialectic of power concentrated again on Renzo before the flight from home when Fra Cristoforo takes leave of the fugitives. Even here, however, the experience of the characters passes through the "reflection" of the narrator, who interrupts the story of the night of confusion at the highest point of the force and observes: "We cannot forbear pausing a moment to make a reflection in the midst of all this uproar. Renzo, who had raised all this noise in someone else's house, who had got in by a trick, and was now keeping the master of the house himself besieged in a room, has all the appearance of being the aggressor; and yet, if one thinks it out, he was the injured party. Don Abbondio, surprised, terrified, and put to flight while peacefully attending to his own affairs, might seem the victim; and yet, it was he who was the wrongdoer."

Before Renzo begins, in his turn, to reflect on what has happened to him, we must wait until he enters Milan, until the new events which he witnesses or takes part in drive him time and again into a comparison, into a dialogue with his own memories which is perhaps, on the artistic level, one of Manzoni's greatest discoveries. Now begins his public adventure, his journey as a peasant *"déraciné"* among the monsters of a city in disorder, in the labyrinth of people and crowds which sweeps him as if into a "whirlpool." Together with the curiosity that arises from his certainty that this is a "day of conquest," what drives him on, without his knowing exactly what he is seeking, is a secret indignation, one might almost say a protest, against the morality of Don Abbondio; and little by little it changes into a hope for justice for himself and for others. In the midst of the turmoil the most generous words, in fact, are his, both when he expresses his "humble opinion" in the "press of people" ("And, as we've seen plainly enough today that we can get our rights by making ourselves heard, we ought to go on like this, until we've set all the other wrongs to rights, and made the world a decent place to live in . . . we would also be there to lend a hand"), and when he confides in the false cutler at the inn of the full moon: "Enough; they ought to put an end to these things! Today, luckily, everything was in plain language and without pen, ink, or paper; and tomorrow, if people know how to set about it, things will be done even better—without touching a hair of anyone's head, though all done legally ["*per via di giustizia*"]."

Yet Renzo's good sense and peasant's wisdom, while it helps the narrator to obtain extraordinary effects of alienation or estrangement behind his back, does not save him from the snares of the system, which immediately seizes him in its meshes and once more imposes its own rules and roles upon him, in accordance with the Machiavellian logic of public order. Thus Renzo himself undergoes the fate that awaits justice when everyone wants to appropriate it for himself: and so there grows up around his figure no less than around the term "justice" a kind of linguistic perspectivism and gloomy masquerade, in the same style as the Quibble-Weaver scene, but with stranger, more taunting complications. In the words of the crowd, he becomes, from episode to episode, a "rascally peasant," a "Commissioner's man, a spy" (and this only because he opposes brutality: "Shame! Do we want to do the executioner's job? Commit murder? How d'you expect God to give us bread if we go and do atrocities like that?"), and then he is also a "good friend from the country," an "honest fellow," a "stubborn mountaineer," a "good laddie," a "bad character," a "thief caught red-handed." And finally, when he manages to escape after the night of drunkenness and his arrest, reaching the inn at Gorgonzola, the fugitive even finds himself transformed into a mysterious, almost legendary agitator.

> One of them was arrested in some inn. . . . They're not quite sure yet exactly where this man came from, or who had sent him, or what kind of man he was; but he was certainly one of the ringleaders. He'd been raising the devil the day before in the middle of the rioting; and then, not content with that, he had

begun to make speeches, and put forward the gallant idea that the whole of the gentry should be murdered. The blackguard! Who'd keep the poor going if the gentry were all murdered? The police had marked him down, and got their clutches on him. They found a bundle of letters on him and were just taking him off to prison. But what d'you think happened then? His confederates, who were patrolling round the inn, came up in large numbers and freed him, the scoundrel.

While Ulysses heard his own story sung by a bard, the traveler of the *Promessi Sposi* finds only a merchant, in the midst of a group of curious persons (bystanders), telling the tale of his adventure in Milan, distorting it from the beginning with an exaggerated caution: the caution of Don Abbondio again, more triumphant than ever. Two other speakers immediately echo him, and one confesses: "Knowing how these things go, and that honest folk aren't safe in riots, I wouldn't let myself be carried away by curiosity, and stayed at home." The other makes it clear again, still in contrast with what Renzo had done: "Or I? . . . Why, if by any chance I'd been in Milan, I'd have left my business unfinished and come back home at once. I've a wife and children; and, to tell the truth, I don't like uproars." From the narrative point of view, this game of mirrors under the intent gaze of Renzo is a fine invention, the more so because it prompts him to cross-examine himself, to question his conscience, not straight away of course, because of his fear of being discovered, but soon afterward, when he has left the inn and, alone in the darkness, thinks over the words he has heard, in honest indignation, drawing the moral that it is never worth putting oneself out to "help the gentry," even if they are "fellow creatures."

Meanwhile, in the solitude of the countryside, something more profound ripens in the pilgrim, in a mingling of affections, anxieties, and remorse which gives movement to one of the most memorable chapters of the whole novel, pervaded as it is by an aura of sensations rising in a lucid "crescendo" until the discovery of the river Adda and the sky of Lombardy. As he moves forward once again in a world of simple men and things, gradually, in the inner chronicle of his soul, a feeling of serenity and a ready faith spring up; and the word "Providence" resounds, innocent and joyful, in this poor man's speech. But around him, the landscape again takes on and deepens the gloom that had already accompanied Fra Cristoforo at the beginning of the story: ". . . his eye was saddened every moment by gloomy sights, which made him realize that he would find the same scarcity in the country he was entering as he had left at home. The whole way along, and particularly in the fields and villages, he met beggars at every step —not professional beggars, for they showed their distress more by their faces than by their clothes—peasants, mountaineers, artisans, complete families, from whom came a confused mutter of entreaties, lamentations, and sobs."

At this point, the first phase of his urban odyssey completed, Renzo passes for the time being out of the narrative, even if his image does not in fact altogether disappear, being brought up several times in the conversation of the other characters and distorted, along with that of Fra Cristoforo (a "villager" and an "impudent friar," "a plebeian") among others, in the diplomatic interview between the Father Provincial and the "right-honorable Uncle," as seems to be his fate as long as he is in exile. However, the link always remains indirect, as if following an underground course from which Renzo re-emerges, gathering the principal plot of the story around him only when the plague finally gives him the opportunity to set off again, immunized as he is against the infection, in search of Agnese or his own house. Renzo's role coincides with that of the questing hero (or hero-searcher) in a world where death holds sway, a world made perilous by corruption and by the great fear of cosmic disorder; at the same time his journey takes on the character of a trial and of an initiation on the level of bare, almost elementary humanity. This begins to come clear as soon as Renzo sets foot in his troubled village and meets Tonio, now no better than the "poor half-wit Gervasio," then Don Abbondio, with his "list of individuals and families" buried, and lastly his friend, whose name we never learn, alone: "sitting on a wooden stool at the door, with his arms crossed and his eyes raised to the sky, like a man overwhelmed by misfortune and grown animal-like through solitude." While it is increasingly affected by horror, his peasant's heart at the same time opens up to the anguished tenderness of his memories, to the solidarity of the affections that survive, to the joy of consoling another man with his own presence, over a little *polenta* and a pail of milk: it is as if he divines that only benevolence can save a man from desperation.

Yet it is clear that his visit to the village is only a preamble, a preparation. The decisive experience is yet to be undergone in Milan, at the heart of the suffering and absurdity. Here the "stranger" with the "knotty stick" to drive him away, who later tells how he ran into an *untore*, an "anointer" with a "meek and humble air," immediately gives Renzo the impression that he has plunged once more into the city of madness, error, and excess. And his "journey," or "itinerary" as it is called several times in the story, with remote symbolic implications, is not slow to reveal other contrasts to him in the livid, grim color of death which is now ubiquitous: from the woman on the "balcony" with a "cluster of children," to the "instrument of torture"; from the death carts heaped with "naked corpses," to the "priest" who answers politely; from the "silence" interrupted only by the "lamentations of the poor" or "the shrieks of the delirious," to Cecilia's mother, who commands respect even from a "filthy *monatto*," or to the "lying witch," who shouts accusations that he is an anointer while Renzo is asking her desperately for news of Lucia. In the reversal of roles that now begins, the "traveler" is forced to protect himself by pretending to be an anointer and to play along with the atrocious *monatti*, who carry him to safety on their cart, joining together in an "infernal chant," almost as if for Renzo too, in keeping with the requirements of the mythical archetype of the journey, a descent into hell is necessary before the right to rediscover the truest part of the self is earned.

Moreover, even the search for Lucia, and this has already been pointed out, is a renewal of the old myth of the *quête*. It is not without reason that in Chapter 33 the sole *filo*, the only thread (Colquhoun translates as "clue") available "for going in search of Lucia," is mentioned, and the whole lazaretto episode is interwoven with ritual gestures and liturgical cadences. But the conversation between Renzo and Fra Cristoforo (for it was necessary to come to him in the end) is something more than a rite or an indispensable purification once it is interpreted in the light of the correspondences that echo throughout the novel. It is here, in fact, that the concept of justice returns to the scene. It has followed us throughout the story, hidden among the rags of the plague like a shadow, a desperate absence. Nor is it surprising, after what we have seen in the early chapters, that it is again Renzo who raises the question, the Renzo who is tormented by the thought that Lucia may be dead, and who is once more set on revenge, as if nothing had happened, as if the plague meant merely a compensation for the oppressed, an equal right to kill for all. Let us observe his words carefully: "if the plague hasn't already done justice. . . . The time's past when a coward with his bravoes around him could drive folk to desperation and get off all free; the time's come when men meet one another face to face; and. . . . I'll do my own justice, I will!"

These words fill Fra Cristoforo with indignation mingled with sadness and dismay. For an instant they represent his defeat by a false, proud justice built upon contempt for man, whereas in Fra Cristoforo's view Renzo must find the road to foregiveness so that the violent destiny which torments the old friar's soul may not repeat itself, not even if it is what Renzo desires in his heart. We mentioned, at the beginning of this essay, the very special relationship which unites Renzo and Fra Cristoforo, as regards the framework of the novel. Now the conversation in the lazaretto throws light on the profound motives for this, since the time has come for the Capuchin to reveal the secret of his existence to Renzo: "I also have hated; I, who have rebuked you for a thought, for a word, I killed the man I hated deeply, whom I had hated for a long time." It is time also to confess to him that the image of that dead man, even if he was a "bully," as Renzo retorts in confusion, continues to haunt his memory in the darkness of a logic which has lost its sense: "D'you think that if there had been a good reason I would not have found it out in thirty years?" It is as if, in the end, Fra Cristoforo wishes to see his own story freed from the obsession with blood which is reflected in the story of Renzo, the story of a man forced to commit an evil deed to learn the justice of God, which is the justice of the free and patient heart. Certainly he is the dramatic "double" of Renzo's Christian conscience and, as such, accompanies him on his mysterious journey as far as the deathbed of Don Rodrigo for a "face to face" meeting, where there is no more room for violence or hatred. And now it will be possible to find Lucia too.

Some readers of *I Promessi Sposi* have remarked that the story could even end at Chapter 36 and that, in any case, the "idyl" of the epilogue sinks to the level of a minor chronicle, of a domestic comedy which has lost the pace of the novel and the cadence of the great adventure. But perhaps insufficient attention has been paid to the circular construction of the story and to the irony which governs the return of the survivors to everyday life, the irony which is so clear, to say the least, in the disappointment of the curious villagers on seeing the real Lucia, who seems too mediocre in their eyes to be a romantic heroine (who, of course, should be splendid and perfect); the reader of *Ivanhoe* knows perfectly well that Rebecca's admiration of Lady Rowena was unqualified ("long, long will I remember your features, and bless God that I leave my noble deliverer united with"). In other words, the detachment which one notices in the narration after the downpour at the lazaretto and the "sudden turn in Nature" around Renzo, now on his last journey, seems intended to juxtapose a cycle of exceptional occurrences with a world that has become ordinary once more and that has retained little more than a memory, a more or less opaque reflection of them. The great season of dramatic choices is over; the reality of prose, of everyday meetings and conversations in the recaptured warmth of the home and the family, takes over again. And yet the problems that set the story in motion continue to project themselves onto the mirror of their consciences, if only one is capable of detecting the presence of the past in the inner texture of the final conversations. Nor can it be excluded that the irony of the conclusion consists, among other things, in this challenge to the reader.

As to Renzo, it is convenient to turn to Don Abbondio and put him to the test when, his mind at peace, he permits himself to joke with Agnese and the "lady" of the lazaretto in his sly, coarse way. He says: "We've been through some bad times, haven't we, my children, some bad times? Let's hope these few days we've still got in the world will be better. Ah, well! You're lucky in having a bit of time to talk over your past troubles, if no new ones come up; but I, on the other hand, am three-quarters past the eleventh hour, and ... rascals may die, and one may recover from the plague, but there's no remedy for the years; and, as they say, *senectus ipsa est morbus.*" As ever, Don Abbondio is human, colorful, prodigiously alive; but it is also true that he has learned nothing or, rather, that he has wasted what had moved him at the time of the great adventure, since the phrase "three-quarters past the eleventh hour" is nothing less than a quotation from Cardinal Federigo translated into a comic figure of speech and vulgarized. It was Borromeo who said to him, in his warmer tones: "Let us redeem the time; midnight is near; the bridegroom cannot be far off; let us keep our lamps lighted."

But Renzo, for his part, has learned something of lasting value and declares as much to Don Abbondio himself when the latter, now that he is sure that Don Rodrigo is dead, exalts the plague as the scourge of tyrants and the instrument of Providence. The contrast between the two speeches is striking and by no means accidental. Don Abbondio's overflow in all directions, joyful and unfettered as a *danse macabre.* "Ah! So he's dead, then. He's really gone," exclaimed Don Abbondio.

> Just see, my children, if Providence doesn't get people like that in the end. D'you know, it's a wonderful thing. A great relief for this poor neighborhood. For the man was impossible to live with. This plague's been a great scourge, but it's also been a great broom: it's swept away certain folk, my children, whom we never thought we'd be rid of any more; in their prime and vigor and prosperity, too; and we'd thought the man who'd conduct their funeral was still doing his Latin exercises at the seminary; and then in the twinkle of an eye they've disappeared hundreds at a time. We shan't see him going round any more with that pack of cut-throats behind him, with his show and his haughty airs and his stuck-up way of looking at people as if we were all in the world just by his gracious permission. Anyway, he's not here any more, and we are. He won't send honest folk any more of those messages. He's given us all a great deal of trouble, you see; we can say that now.

Renzo's answer, however, is extremely terse: "I have forgiven him from the bottom of my heart"; but the reader remembers that they are the very words he had pronounced in the presence of Fra Cristoforo in his trial at the lazaretto. Something has remained in his heart ("I realize I had never really forgiven him; I realize that I spoke like a dog and not like a Christian; and now, by God's grace, yes, I forgive him from the bottom of the heart").

If this system of cross-references and allusions has a meaning, and with a writer like Manzoni it seems unlikely not to have one, it is natural to conclude that in the conversation between Renzo and Don Abbondio we see in play once more the great theme of justice in the alternative between fear and love, time-serving and liberty, pride and patience: it is as if for a moment the morality of Fra Cristoforo and the code of Don Abbondio confront each other. But Fra Cristoforo is dead while Don Abbondio continues to live, ready to sit at the table of Don Rodrigo's heir and to share his class prejudices, even on a day of folk festivity, against a newly married peasant couple. In the end the plague has changed nothing: men soon forget and adapt themselves to the rules of the world. Even someone who, like Renzo, remembers and recounts his adventures risks falling back into time-serving and drawing from what has happened the easiest moral lesson of cautious, passive honesty. "I've learnt ... not to get into riots; I've learnt not to make speeches in the street; I've learnt not to raise my elbow too much; I've learnt not to hold door knockers when there are excited people about; I've learnt not to fasten a bell to my feet before thinking of the consequences. And a hundred other things of the kind." It now seems as if Renzo is admitting that Don Abbondio is right, as if he is accepting his principle, his "favorite phrase," according to which "unpleasant accidents do not happen to the honest man who keeps to himself and minds his own business."

As regards the "hundred other things" which Renzo thinks he has learned, the reader has to guess at what they are, although it is permissible to suspect that the number, with its fairy-tale ring, added to the string of "I've learnt's," conceals a hint of irony against Renzo and his would-be "doctrine." Besides, it is enough for Lucia to intervene with her "smiling" remark that the "troubles" were the ones which came looking for her, for her "moralist's" certainty to be baffled and undermined. In truth, Renzo, as a poor peasant, has to admit that the suffering of the world cannot be explained with reference only to itself, and that "trust in God" remains the sole comfort in man's mysterious journey on the earth. But it is precisely in this that justice consists, the justice for which man may suffer and feel himself brother to all the oppressed, even if he is more familiar with fear than with courage. While there is an impression of having reached a peaceful epilogue, in obedience to renunciation or resignation, the secret discourse of the whole novel starts off again, drawing behind it the anguish of history, the inquietude of contradiction, the feeling of the absurd, as it may reach even the "lowest" on the "world" scale (if we remember the closing of Chapter 27). And the anguish of history is the afflicted stupefaction of their memories as "men lost on the earth" ("as good as lost to the world"), men who have not "even got a land-lord." Where Renzo's quest ends, the reader's, perhaps, begins.

5

STEPHEN GILMAN

The Novelist and His Readers:
Meditations on a Stendhalian Metaphor

THE present essay is not intended as a manifesto. It does not propose to prescribe or describe critical methods but rather to invite meditation on the novel as a phenomenon, as one of the strangest phenomena—despite its familiarity to all of us—of the cultural history of the West. As a result, what I shall have to say is at once wider in scope (involving social, existential, and even technical factors) and anterior to our traditional critical concerns. What is the novel? What is the nature of its value? Only after answering or at least defining consciously our often unexpressed answers to these awesomely simple questions may we approach with full responsibility those other queries beginning with the word "how," with which most of us are more comfortable. For, if we think of the novel as an "epic in prose" or as an expression of our age not substantially different from, say, one of Ibsen's plays, or simply as an area of imaginative literature, each of these views (the first is rhetorical, the second, historical, and the third, aesthetic) will condition subsequent judgment and methodology. It so happens that, as a Hispanist concerned with Cervantes and the history of the genre in Spain prior to the *Quijote*, I believe these answers are too simple. Discussions of novelistic structure, style, characterization, theme, intention, point of view, and the rest—all of which I would be the last to deny are worthwhile—based on them are often misleading. Therefore, as preparation for criticism of how given novels and novelists operate, I have here tried to explain as explicitly as possible the kind of definition many of us in Spanish as well as French studies find more meaningful.

I had originally hoped to publish an expanded version of the present essay in an effort to incorporate the many suggestions and objections of those who listened to its oral presentation (at the English Institute and at Johns Hopkins). But unfortunately, because of my travel plans and because of Charles Singleton's generous desire to include it in the annual volume of the Humanities Center, this has been impossible. All I have had time to do is to add a few bibliographical and expository notes to the text as first written.

*   *   *

The definition of the novel which most of us identify with Stendhal is that of a mirror *"qu'on promène au long d'un chemin."*[1] And, in spite of the fact that over the years it has been quoted so frequently as to become commonplace, it is not a definition to be dismissed. In so affirming, however, we must recognize that the later realists and naturalists who repeated it failed to notice that the operative word therein was not *"miroir"* but *"chemin."* Seeing in Stendhal a precursor, they overlooked his far greater concern with open structure than with collection—or reflection—of contents. By that I mean his concern to revive the loose, semiplotless form of the centuries-old picaresque novel as a way of communicating for the first time a personal experience of the nineteenth-century discovery called history. Here were wayside encounters in which the wayside was Restoration France instead of the eternal and literal (which is to say, the moral and brutal) wayside of Gil Blas de Santillana. Balzac saw contemporary history as a layer cake of fascinating milieux; Stendhal viewed it as a string of people and ironical adventures. Hence his stress on the erratic *"chemin"* of the novel. It is no accident that Cervantes and Fielding (who called his readers "fellow travelers") were among Stendhal's own favorite precursors.

But, in spite of its fame and in spite of its relevance to the American novel I propose to employ as an example (*Huck Finn* being as much a *"chemin"* through contemporary history as *Le Rouge et le Noir*), this is not the definition upon which I invite meditation. Years after *Le Rouge et le Noir* had been published and ignored, while composing the autobiographical *Henri Brûlard* (1835) and thinking over his long experience of reading (as well as writing) novels, Stendhal proposed a second definition far more suggestive than that of the mirror and the road. The trouble with the earlier formulation, Stendhal now realized, was that it presented each novel as a game of solitaire. The author and his character join together in order to sustain and aim their mirror toward the passing historical show. In a sense we can think of them as one paradoxically double man. However, the fact of printing and publishing invalidates the comparison. There is another new, unknown traveler along the road (eventually an endless band of travelers) who will inevitably take over the author's prerogative of intimacy: the reader. It was he and his fellows who would go on traveling with Fabrice and Julien—not Stendhal. Hence the renewed effort at definition.

Stendhal, as he tells us himself, was particularly preoccupied with readers

---

[1] Stendhal first proposed this definition in the Preface to *Armance* (1827) and went on to repeat it on a number of occasions. See my complementary essay, *The Tower as Emblem* (Frankfurt am Main, 1967), p. 9.

because of their extreme scarcity. Other novelists might take them for granted or even make fun of them. But Stendhal was justifiably concerned about the unknown consciousnesses who might adopt his spiritual children. Would there be anyone at all? Would there be anyone worthy (the select Happy Few)? Would there exist by 1880 or 1935 a public trained by more historical experience than was available to Stendhal's contemporaries for the happy and demanding enterprise? Continuing worry about such questions resulted in Stendhal's being the first to comprehend the hybrid and long underestimated form of the novel as a means of distributing a marvelous product: fresh and unprocessed experience for its reading clientele. In Stendhal's time Goethe had pondered on the novel as peculiarly suited to certain areas of existence (sentiments and chance events) hitherto distorted, unadmired, or ignored. Schelling and others had proclaimed it as the epic of the new century. But, of these and other pioneering meditations, the following is to my mind the most illuminating: "Un roman est comme un archet; la caisse du violon qui rend les sons, c'est l'âme du lecteur." (The novel is like a fiddle bow; the violin that gives forth the sounds is the soul of the reader.)[2]

The significance of Stendhal's comparison is clearly this: in the act of reading, the reader provides from the accumulated experience of his particular life a new flow of novelistic experience suggested to him and drawn from him by the printed signs he so rapidly absorbs. As a result each reader—and indeed each reading—is qualitatively distinct, to a greater or lesser extent depending on epoch and culture as well as on the individual age, sensitivity, and momentary state of what Stendhal called his "soul." It is all very well to speak of an essential Huck Finn, of a determining matrix of being, but Huck's existence takes the form of numberless incarnations over generations of readers. In order to come alive (which is what really matters) he must be born again in our lives. As we shall see, however, incarnation is not necessarily the same thing as identification. The reader is not Huck Finn (perhaps it would be better to say "need not be") in the sense that Don Quijote is Amadís of Gaul or that readers of my generation have been Tom Swift. But there is an identity of our experience with his—in that, according to Stendhal, we have provided him with it.

It goes without saying that the imaginative collaboration of reader, observer, or listener (the "apprehender" in the jargon of aesthetics) is indispensable to all literary or artistic experience. But what Stendhal proposes more radically is that the novel, because of its silent performance in the reader's mind, is charac-

---

[2] *Henri Brûlard* (Paris: Le Divan, 1949), p. 227.

terized by extreme dependence on this ultimate "factor" in the aesthetic equation. Of all forms of literature, it is the one which demands the most from us and can do—as Cervantes and Flaubert knew—the most to us. We have all had the marvelous experience of being taken over—spiritually infiltrated—by a novel. Who is there among us who does not confer special qualities on rafts and islands, not because they are symbols of anything but themselves, but because for a few intense hours we have experienced Huck's experience as if it were our own, indeed, because we have made it out of our own and rediscovered it as his? The novel is not a story we hear mentally but a shared present experience.

The usual way of explaining this parasitical intimacy of the novel is in terms of absorption. "So and so is deep in a book," we frequently say, and Ortega y Gasset goes on to amplify the commonplace into a definition comparable to Stendhal's:

> Let us observe ourselves at the moment we finish reading a great novel.
> It seems to us as if we are emerging from another existence, that we have escaped
> from a world out of communication with our authentic world. This lack of com-
> munication is shown by the fact that transition from one to another is imper-
> ceptible. An instant ago we found ourselves in Parma with Count Mosca, Clélia,
> and Fabrice; we were living with them, immersed in their air, their space,
> their time. Now suddenly, without any intermission, we find ourselves in our
> chamber, in our city, in our date; already our habitual preoccupations begin to
> awaken at the nerve ends. There is, of course, an interval of indecision, of
> uncertainty. Perhaps a brusque wing stroke of memory will suddenly submerge
> us again in the universe of the novel, and then with an effort, as if struggling
> in a liquid element, we try to swim to the shore of our own existence. If someone
> should observe us then, he would see the dilation of eyelids which characterizes
> those who have been shipwrecked.
> *I define the novel as the kind of literature which produces this effect.* Such
> is the enormous, unique, glorious, and magic power of this sovereign of modern
> literary forms. And the novel that lacks it is a failure whatever its other merits.
> Oh sublime, benign power which multiplies our existence, which frees us
> and pluralizes us, which enriches us with generous transmigration![3]

But, in spite of this optimistic exclamation, there are also, as novelists have always known, latent dangers in such a genre. Using Ortega's comparison, we might well interpret the *Quijote* or *Madame Bovary* as novels about novel-

---

[3] *Obras completas* (Madrid, 1946), vol. 3, "Ideas sobre la novela"; translation and italics mine.

readers, about a sad squire and an errant wife, who cannot swim to the shore of their provincial existences.

Ortega, while agreeing with Stendhal that a valid definition of the novel can be derived only from the reading experience, gets carried away by the terms of his comparison. As a result, he fails to see that it is not we who are inside the world of the novel but rather the novel which is inside us—providing us with what Cervantes long before had explained as *"nueva vida"* (new life).[4] As a metaphor Stendhal's fiddle bow is more exact and revealing than Ortega's immersion.

Such a notion of the novel, although self-evident to most students of Cervantes, may be of difficult acceptance to others. In that, subordinating form to performance, they put into reverse our habitual order of critical thinking, Stendhal and Ortega may well be accused of putting the cart before the horse. And if we proceed from the definition to its inevitable corollaries, the objections will be multiplied. Taken negatively, Stendhal's comparison denies a proposition which most critics (Albert Thibaudet being a notable exception[5]) are committed to affirm. The novel—we are forced to conclude—should not be thought of as a stable literary object to be characterized critically by such features as structure, style, theme, plot, intention, point of view, or whatever. The novel *is* not anything; it *happens*—or, perhaps it is better to say, it is made to happen. And the strategies the novelist uses to make it happen—style, structure, and the rest—while of great critical interest, are both anterior to and absorbed by the happening. We cannot, in other words, fabricate a definition of *the* novel from, or justify an evaluation of *a* novel on the basis of, the kind of critical dissection to which most of us are accustomed. A definition based on structure, length, subject matter, or point of view quite simply takes the life out of the novel while an evaluation which attempts to cross the perilous span from form to merit, however interesting intellectually, is necessarily precarious. Let me try to be as clear as I can. I do not intend to say that structural and stylistic analyses are worthless or misleading, but rather that they should not be used as a preliminary catechism. At most, the novice or "common" reader may need preparation for the experience, help in getting "inside," of the sort Virginia Woolf knew so well how to

[4] Cervantes proposes this fundamental notion of the novel first in the persona of the illiterate innkeeper (pt. I, chap. 32), who remarks that romances of chivalry *"verdaderamente me han dado la vida y no solo a mí sino a otros muchos."* As a matter of fact they are so rejuvenating that they take away gray hair (*nos quitan mil canas*)! These naïve observations are confirmed and meditated upon by the learned canon in Chapter 49 when he refers to novelists as "inventors" of a *"nuevo modo de vida."*

[5] See his fundamental collection of essays, *Réflexions sur le roman* (Paris, 1938).

supply. But after that, he should be left alone. A novel properly read by an adequate soul is its own guidebook. Only when the journey is ended is map-tracing—critical exegesis—a profitable occupation.

Two extreme examples may be useful. The first is Nabokov's notorious underestimation and, indeed, active dislike of Dostoevski. On one occasion he actually referred to him as the Blasco Ibáñez of Russia, an odious comparison that in its way is also unfair to Blasco Ibáñez! What Nabokov is really saying, I think, is that he is not attuned to Dostoevski, and readers attuned to Nabokov's novels should not find it hard to intuit why, in spite of their undeniable greatness, *The Idiot* and the others cannot happen in the "Nabokovian" soul. For such a reader, as for Henry James, who held much the same opinion, destructive criticism is easy. Because they as readers are immovable and the novels immobile, the surgery proceeds rapidly. For both novelist-readers, Dostoevski's style is crude; structure, irregular and indecisive; plots, melodramatic; and thought, murky. At the opposite extreme is the Spanish philosopher, Unamuno, so deeply attuned to the *Quijote* that his discussion of it amounted only to a re-creation of his own reading experience, of his private incarnation. Ignoring Cervantes, disdainful of a literary form he refused to comprehend except insofar as it worked in him, he actually (or at least he so proclaimed) preferred to read the novel in translation. The result was a book—*La vida de Don Quijote y Sancho*—which can best be understood as a novel about a novelistic experience and which is more interesting for students of Unamuno than for those of Cervantes.

Only full comprehension of what we as readers and critics are up against when dealing with novels will allow us to avoid these extremes. We may sum up our efforts thus far in the tried and true manner: by taking note of our discrepancy with Aristotle. The author of the *Poetics* was able to subdivide tragedy into its five famous components because he began by defining it as an imitation of an action. But if we accept Stendhal's implicit doctrine that the novel is an action, not an imitation of one—that it acts in us with our passive and entranced, violin-like collaboration—we must revise our intellectual behavior.

A proper first step toward this necessary revision would be to ask ourselves why it is that novels operate in this fashion. How do they differ from other literary genres and, in particular, from other kinds of narration? We Hispanists, because of our preoccupation with the phenomenon of the *Quijote*, should have welcomed with joy Marshall McLuhan's assertion that the novel is the characteristic literary expression of print culture.[6] From our point of view McLuhan has

[6] *The Gutenberg Galaxy* (Toronto, 1962), pp. 207–8.

158

given effective new statement and new relevance to a truth insistently suggested by the history of the novel in Spain prior to Cervantes. In 1506—so the lesson goes—a now-lost medieval romance (a prose narrative of the adventures of a knight called Amadís of Gaul) was revised, rewritten, and sent to be printed for sale to the general public. Its success was immediate. As the world's first best-seller, it provided welcome substitute life for readers (barbers, curates, idle girls, lawyers, and, above all, village squires proudly and boredly committed to poverty-stricken idleness), readers who a generation before had witnessed the last flourish of chivalric prowess in their peninsula. I refer to the taking of Moorish Granada, which at the time was thought to be the major event of the year 1492. It was something like the upsurge of the Western novel after the loss of our own frontier. The printing press was no longer a mere means of producing in larger quantity hard-to-get medieval books; it was suddenly the organ of a public, with the result that the *Amadís* was, as Cervantes put it, the "origin and beginning" of numberless imitations. The best-seller, as best-sellers still today have a habit of doing, gave birth to a genre.

Reading rapidly and silently (a kind of reading extremely rare before printed standardization of the page), the new human market was able to absorb reams of grotesque adventures. And the more it read, the better it learned to read—driven on by its sudden addiction to what Thibaudet called one of the two varieties of "voluptuousness" denied to the ancients;[7] the other was tobacco. Not only the form of print on the page (stressed by McLuhan), but also the capacity of straining and ever-multiplying presses to supply (as well as stimulate) the demand for more and more resulted in a brand new kind of reading. In addition to its silence, it was avid, insatiable, self-accelerating—reading which moved into the soul like heroin into the mainline.

We today may not react to novels with the intoxication of such sixteenth-century Spaniards as Bernal Díaz del Castillo, Teresa of Avila, Ignatius of Loyola, Miguel de Cervantes, or his creature Alonso Quijano the Good. Perhaps the last human beings alive who have read in a way even remotely comparable to theirs are we diminishing few fortunate enough to have grown up in a world free of television. But I think, as I said before, we can recognize in our own reading—however tepid and desultory it may appear when compared with the reading of our childhood or of our ancestors—the way the novel depends on the rapid scanning of the eye, on the compulsive push forward from page to page, on a greediness for artificial time antithetical to the slow motion of literature which depends

[7] *Op. cit.*, p. 239.

on pronunciation.[8] This is not quite the same contrast that McLuhan makes when he distinguishes voiced literature from silent. In *The Gutenberg Galaxy*, McLuhan stresses the linear, abstract, rationally ordered, commodity-minded qualities of "typographic man." Put in the novel we see a very different set of possibilities, the possibility to resuscitate lost time, to evoke half-forgotten experience as a gift for another life, to refresh ourselves and our stale memories with the raw immediacy of present adventure. What we might call "novelistic man," although a creature of print, is as irrational, concrete, three-dimensional, and spiritual as they come. He is a member of the adventure.

To be as precise as possible, training in submission, not to more or less solemnly intoned phrases (whether lyric, epic, or dramatic), but to unpronounced, immediately assimilated clusters of words is essential to the novel. Why? Because the novel may be defined as the kind of literature which presents a fictional world not necessarily resembling our own but in a fashion resembling the way we experience our own—thus its natural realism less of mirrored content than of unfolding process. And it does this because its printed language reaches directly into our inner store of experience, draws upon it, and rearranges it imaginatively into a new spatiotemporal sequence—which is to say into Cervantes' "new life." As Ortega reminded us, the here and now of lamp, page, and chair, the very awareness that we are engaged in reading, is temporarily suppressed. We are now incarnating—vivifying—Huck Finn on the raft with the river around us floating past, down, along, with distant perspectives (some described, others implicit and added by us) opening and closing like fans. The river is neither a geographical reality (like the Bay of Naples described in a guidebook) nor a myth; it is a process, a symphony of experiential music in action.

Let us pause for just one example, an example that is for me one of the most intense forms of "new life" in this novel: the storm over Jackson's Island seen from the cave. Read aloud, the passage becomes a prose poem about a past storm

---

[8] This was remarked on in negative terms by A. W. von Schlegel at the beginning of the ninteenth century (*Vorlesungen uber schöne Litteratur und Kunst* [Heilbronn, 1884], pt. II, pp. 19–20): "Man lobt den jetzt allgemeiner verbreiteten Geschmack am Lesen, aber hilf Himmel! Welch eine Leserei ist das! Sie verdammt sich selbst schon dadurch, das sie *so rastlos nach dem neuen greift* was doch kein wirklich neues ist. Nur die leidigste Passivität kann zu dieser Liebhaberen führen, die weder denken noch handeln mag; ja nicht einmal zu träumen mussen solche Menscen verstehen, denn sonst wurden sie sich weit etwas besseres imaginieren konnen als in ihren *Romanen* steht. Ihr eignes Leben ist unbedeutend und leer...." Schlegel clearly refers here to the kind of reader later to be termed in this essay the "adventure addict," not realizing, as Cervantes realized, that it is through such addiction that one learns to read in the way all novels—including the greatest—should be read.

160

congealed into lasting beauty, a storm susceptible to aural appreciation or stylistic analysis. But that is not the way most of us read it or, I dare say, the way it should be read. Properly and silently performed, the storm is a synthesis of the best storms of our childhood reanimated and transformed into a new, present storm that is uniquely Huck's, immeasurably more laden with danger and tense with adventure than the memories we contribute. It is Huck's storm now and forever, but at the same time (and here again we encounter the underlying paradox of the novel) it is for each reader in each reading a storm made out of different materials and, depending on the state of the soul, possessing different qualities and levels of intensity. Américo Castro wrote not long ago: "The novel does not consist in telling what happens to a person, but instead, of how that person feels himself existing in a happening."[9] To this we would answer, "Yes," provided we understand that it is the reader who is induced to provide the experience of existing within the happening.[10]

At this point—having meditated historically and autobiographically on Stendhal's metaphorical definition—we still sense its inherent incompletion. After all, an individual novel is *there* in front of us on the table, where it can be picked up and read again and again. What kind of characters, what kind of language, and even what kind of authors—we want to know—are most typically and efficiently novelistic? What can we say, not about the music, but about the musician and his score? Obviously a reasonably satisfactory answer to any one of these questions would require an essay of its own, but we may at least offer a

[9] *De la edad conflictiva* (Madrid, 1961), p. 202.

[10] The obvious objection that such novelists as a Dickens or a Mark Twain enjoyed reading passages from their novels to the public or that in past centuries many novels were read aloud within families seems to me to be beside the point. There are clearly, in any good novel, moments of dramatic interchange as well as a line of story (Castro's "happening"), both of which permit and benefit from oral reading. But the kind of reading that is most appropriately novelesque—as we know from our own experience— is both silent and solitary. Only by reading in this way can we savor the special voluptuousness of immediate participation in the feeling of "existing in a happening." Achilles, Hamlet, and Snow White, all of them oral characters, live either in their own speech or in the intonations ("And *then* . . .") of a skilled narrator. Huck Finn, Julien Sorel, and Don Quijote, on the other hand, live as we do, in a process of accumulation of experiential data—visual, auditory, tactile, olfactory, tasted. This raw material—told in words but perceived in terms of experience supplied from our warehouse of *"durée vécue"*—is modified by character and mood. What results is a sequence of human situations (each one a synthesis of sensation and consciousness) which is the character's life—hence the possibility of continuing change, of unpredictable spiritual dynamism, which distinguishes these lives from their oral counterparts. I think it is significant that Mark Twain preferred to read from those parts of *Huck Finn* in which Tom Sawyer —a creature of story and a maker of stories—was present.

few provisional conclusions. As far as the "characters" are concerned, comparison of Huck with Robinson Crusoe, Marcel, Werther, or Yossarian (lives chosen more or less at random) indicates, not surprisingly, that they have in common a special openness, receptivity, even vulnerability, to experience. The frequently advanced notion of antiheroism is negative in its connotations; such lives as these are antiheroic not because they are less than heroes but because they are more. That is, they are incredibly more sensitive than any recognized and self-conscious hero would permit himself to be. Goethe was sniffing around this truth when he spoke of the passivity of these new protagonists, but he would have come closer to the mark had he recognized that extreme vulnerability and spiritual impetus are, as in the case of Don Quijote, not mutually exclusive. Indeed, as Castro insists, many of the greatest combine extraordinary ability to register experience with indomitable self-propulsion. As against the superficial excitement of adventure, they are possessed with inner "incitation,"[11] at times a mere obsession, at times the noblest of vocations, but always a source of forward movement. All of which is a way of saying people in novels are more intensely alive in both active and passive modes than most of us; hence their special attraction for our lives.[12]

The language of the novel, as against the styles of individual novelists, has been explored from various points of view by such critics as Thibaudet, Stephen Ullmann, and Kathe Hamburger.[13] But a central question has, as far as I know, never been adequately answered: how does this special language express the fact that novelistic experience is not a thing to be described on its own terms (as in some of the "*nouveaux romans*") but as *somebody's* experience? How does lan-

[11] This fundamental comprehension of the special nature of "novelistic" life was formulated in 1947 by Américo Castro in his "La estructura del *Quijote*." An English translation (which should be read by all serious students of the novel) appeared in *Cervantes across the Centuries*, ed. J. Benardete and A. Flores (New York, 1947), while the original has been reprinted in Castro's *Hacia Cervantes* (Madrid, 1960).

[12] One result of this condition is the intense mutual sensitivity and interaction among the inhabitants of given novels. As Robert Petsch points out (and as Dostoevski exemplifies perhaps more than any other novelist), they intuit and know each other so profoundly and so beyond the limits of our daily experience as to seem uncanny (*Wesen und Formen der Erzahlkunst* [Halle, 1942], p. 119). Interpersonal relations of this highly concentrated variety are what the greatest novels can be said to be about —beneath the levels of thesis and theme.

[13] In addition to the collection cited, Thibaudet has a splendid study of Flaubert's use of spoken language in his *Gustave Flaubert* (Paris, 1922). K. Hamburger's work on the novelistic conversion of past tenses into equivalents of the present is gathered in *Die Logik der Dichtung* (Stuttgart, 1957). Ullmann gives an informative "*état présent*" of work on indirect novelistic dialogue (see note 14 below) in his *Style in the French Novel* (Cambridge: At the University Press, 1957).

162

guage confer the indispensable otherness—Stendhal's human musical score—on sounds drawn from our souls? How can what we have lived be transformed, by the act of reading words, into the provoking, immensely stimulating newness (not mere novelty) of an alien life? In the cases of *Huck Finn, Don Quijote, Tom Jones, Pickwick Papers*, and many others, we might answer these questions by pointing to their authors' mastery of expressive speech in both dialogue and narration.

Here is a language that is ours—English, French, or Spanish, as the case may be—but spoken differently, a language possessing the uniquely personal otherness that only speech rhythms and intonations can convey. But it should not be thought of as a dramatic performance. In *Huck Finn*, I would maintain, however controversial such a position may appear, the rural speech of mid-America in its several human variants is not used to slow down our reading by creating a pseudo-oral experience. Rather, it is used because Huck's "Huckness" is his speech. We forget the use of dialect (a general notion) precisely because Huck's unique way of saying things is the vehicle of his (and our) new experience. It is in fact the very shape of that experience. There is nothing more awkward than reading a so-called dialect novel consciously. As in the novels of Thames Williamson or of some of Mark Twain's predecessors, the oral and printed experiences get in each other's way. But in *Huck Finn* the contrary is the case. Its language is completely personal but at the same time restrained, never a hindrance to rapid assimilation. By attuning the process of our silent reading to Huck's particular accents, vocabulary, intonations, rhythms, and, above all, grammar (even though we might be incapable of reading properly a single sentence aloud), we allow the course of his existence to be transported into ours. The language of the novel is, then, a strange kind of transformed speech, speech accelerated and silenced, personalized and intensified—transformed into print but retaining its ancient creative magic when played in our souls.[14]

The special suitability of the novel to translation is clearly a result of its special language. Foreign languages, as we know, are far more capable, in the process of translation, of doing justice to novels than to literature that depends on the precise oral connotations of words and phrases. The fact that novelistic

---

[14] These observations should be modified by taking into account the later evolution of the novelistic idiom toward increasing speech interiorization: indirect dialogue accompanied by the use of the imperfect tense (in languages fortunate enough to possess that superbly novelistic tool), the stream of consciousness, and ultimately the new mental languages which made Proust and Virginia Woolf seem difficult two generations ago and which since then have become ever more arcane. As far as the printed speech of novels is concerned, the medium has been capable of many messages!

speech is not only dynamic but accelerated (assimilated in clusters, often whole sentences at a time) permits translation by cluster, the discovery of equivalents for the process rather than for the exact meaning. I have never read the Spanish translation of *Huck Finn* (it is probably bad, though it is much loved by Spanish readers), but I can state with moderate authority that certain translations of the *Don Quijote* (notably Jarvis and Ormsby, Cohen being flat and unvoiced) use a range of English speech which works almost as well as Cervantes' Spanish, which is more than can be said for even the best translations of Lope de Vega or García Lorca. In the novel the gravest sort of differences abound on every page and in every phase; yet the over-all effect—the living process—is not necessarily lost.

These rapid, sketchy, and hypothetical extensions of Stendhal's definition demand scrupulous amplification and at the same time suggest the further branching out of tempting paths of speculation. Chief among these is the much-discussed problem of novelistic irony. The simultaneous presence and absence of the ironical author takes many forms. It is explicit and comic in *Tom Jones*, for example, while implicit and simultaneously tender and bitter in *Huck Finn*. Each novel has its own pattern, but the authors of the greatest novels, I would propose, dedicate their capacity for irony to an end common to all. They dedicate it to keeping the reader from identifying with the character. A public of Madame Bovarys is a poor incentive to creation, and, if an escapist or habitual identifier (most of us are from time to time, though we know it is wrong) should begin to read an authentically great novel, he must be quickly retrained. He must learn new habits. The guise of cowboy or private eye wandering through the purple sage or the corpse-infested motel to which he is used will not serve for reading *Huck Finn* or *The American Dream*—even though one is western and the other urban. In other words, only by ironical interference (interruptions, tonal implications, etc.) with our inborn urge to be the character (in the way we all were Tom Sawyer) can the author arrange for us to fulfill our far more important function. That is, to allow the character, as another person, to identify with us, to come alive by feeding on our life and its accumulated experience. Novelistic irony—and Stendhal, as Victor Brombert shows, was a consummate master of this use—is a way of teaching us, within our individual limitations, to become a Stradivarius.

The contrast just made between active identification with a character and passive incarnation, provision of life for a character, may seem at this point obscure and oversubtle. A good part of the difficulty, however, may well lie in the unexamined assumptions about the value of novels on which it is based. A concluding excursion into this perilous terrain would therefore seem advisable. On the face of it, Stendhal's metaphor (and Ortega's, too, for that matter) suggests that all novels are created equal. If a novel works, it is good; if it fails to work, it is an abortion; and there is nothing more to say. The absurd *Amadís of Gaul* (an immediately efficient novel if there ever was one) and the syrupy fiction lapped up by Madame Bovary would then be as estimable as the *Don Quijote* or Flaubert's masterpiece. We know, of course, that this is false, but it is a knowledge which definitions of the sort considered here seem to be unable to account for.

The obvious solution is to measure quantitatively and historically the range of efficient performance—the notion of range being taken to mean not merely the number of readers but also the duration (the number of generations and centuries) and the extension (the number of different countries, cultures, and languages) of each novel's acceptance. A major novel, such as *Huck Finn*, can provoke the imaginations and invoke the disparate stores of experience of American boys, elderly British gentlemen, and, going farther afield, an enormous public of Russians—including one young writer, whose name I have forgotten, who went down the Volga on a raft after reading it. Here is eloquent testimony to the value of a novel. The adjective "immortal" is both excessive and misleading; it is revivability, the power to come alive again across reaches of time and space and disparities of culture, that *is* in a sense a novel's greatness.

The *Amadís of Gaul* worked for, at most, four generations of Spaniards and perhaps two of Englishmen, Frenchmen, and Italians—its ability to sell having quickly reached the ears of translators and printers on the other side of the Pyrenees. Now it is at best a curiosity and at worst a disagreeable chore—often shirked—for graduate students in Spanish. But the *Quijote*, perhaps with somewhat more teaching than our typographic grandparents needed, still can be played in us and in our novelists too (in a Moravia or a Bellow)[15] as movingly as it was played in seventeenth-century readers or in Mark Twain and his generation.

Range, however, is an *ex post facto* measurement of value as well as often being misleading and unfair. I happen to know (as well as I know that the *Don Quijote* is better than *Amadís*) that Mark Twain's Spanish contemporary Benito Pérez Galdós is a novelist as great as any produced by the nineteenth century.

[15] The *Quijote* was deftly exploited in *Henderson the Rain King* as a creative point of departure, while Moravia (whose novels bear no apparent resemblance to those of Cervantes) has recently re-evaluated the "*miracolo*" of the *Quijote* with superb critical insight, explaining Cervantes not as an ironist but fully "*dentro e fuori del suo mondo*" (*Corriere della Sera*, September 29, 1963).

165

Nevertheless, he is still unrecognized abroad, and only in the last few years has he begun to be revived in the Spanish-speaking world. And, without the evidence of range, how can this claim to a knowledge that is not mere opinion be justified? If we refrain, as we agreed to do earlier, from demonstrations based on more or less objective analyses of structure, style, point of view, and the rest, the question of value would seem to be unanswerable.

However, it is precisely in novels, in the course of endowing one novel after another with our lives, that we discover at first hand the heterogeneous nature of reading experiences Not only do they differ in our perception of them —each novelistic world possessing its individual spectrum, dimensionality, and gravity (a matter of much concern to recent French criticism)—but also they vary widely in quality. This is perhaps best demonstrated by a whole region of less valuable novelistic experience, a region which self-evidently detaches itself from the rest as distinct and inferior. I refer to the variety of experience ascribed by Mark Twain to the life of Huck Finn: adventure.

The unadulterated adventure novel is, as we know, both primordial and perennial. Doomed to go out of fashion in a generation or two, it is always reborn, disguising its identity with new milieux and revised predicaments. A low-grade form of "new life," its history from Amadís to James Bond constitutes a lurid chronicle of reaction against the successive limitations, the prosaic forms of "old life," imposed on us by society. But it would be wrong, on the basis of such reading, to dismiss adventure as cheap escapism or as a constantly mutating sociological virus. Not only does adventure, along with its sibling, sentimentality, provide the pseudo novelty of an infinite number of novels; it also (as we shall see, and as readers of Mark Twain already know) is indispensable leavening for novels that plunge far deeper into human life. Adventure is at once a clearly inferior brand of experience and a stimulus for heightened perception—and for both reasons demands our attention as a phenomenon.

At this point an acute essay—"The Adventure"—by Georg Simmel will be of great help. Adventure, Simmel observes, is essentially a closed and hermetic form of experience:

> The most general form of adventure is its dropping out of the continuity of life.... An adventure is certainly a part of our existence, directly contiguous with other parts which proceed or follow it; at the same time, however, in its deeper meaning, it occurs outside the usual continuity of this life.... We ascribe to an adventure a beginning and end much sharper than those to be discovered in other forms of experience.... The adventure lacks that reciprocal

interpenetration with adjacent parts of life which constitutes "life-as-a-whole." It is like an island in life which determines its beginning and end according to its own formative powers.[16]

Simmel speaks here of an actual adventure, an adventure of the sort we may have had or may be fortunate enough to live through. But, applied to the novel, conceived of as the fictitious life of a professional adventurer who proceeds furiously from one adventure to the next, we can understand its inherent inferiority. In these novels the parts become a whole only through the artifice of plot. There is for such an adventurous protagonist no deeper continuity of "life-as-a-whole" which integrates happenings and experiences of happenings into the singularity of a complete human existence, of a Huck Finn. The adventure novel is a freight-train sequence of stimulating but hermetic situations—transitory apartments which we furnish hastily with the necessary minimum of *décor* because we know we shall not be staying very long. Simmel goes on to say that, because of the enclosed nature of adventures, even the non-fictional variety (those we actually have had) often tend "to take on the quality of a dream" or seem to have been "experienced by another person," which would imply that, as far as adventures in books are concerned, the author lures us into putting most of our own life between parentheses, into flattening our attention out through a series of absolute present moments of love and danger. As a musical score, adventure, by inviting us to lose ourselves, fails to utilize all that we as living instruments have to offer. Instead of finding more of ourselves, more experience in ourselves than we may have known to exist (as Mark Twain, Stendhal, and Cervantes demand), we surrender ourselves. And, like our fictional surrogates, we make a profession of forgetting as we move from page to page.[17]

[16] *Georg Simmel*, ed. Kurt H. Wolff (Columbus, Ohio, 1959), pp. 243–44.

[17] Ortega provides an admirable sequel to Simmel's essay in his discussion of certain seventeenth-century memoirs, the *Aventuras del Capitán Alonso de Contreras* (*Obras completas*, 6: 505–6):

La impulsividad es, pues, quien crea mecánicamente los destinos del aventurero. Su vida es la serie espasmódica de disparos automáticos que sus impulsos ejecutan. . . . La acción en Contreras y afines no está al servicio de nada. Rebota sobre sí misma. Llevan una existencia puntiforme, hilván de puros y aislados momentos. El futuro, con sus preocupaciones, no les lastra y apesadumbra el presente. Tampoco rememoran el pasado: por eso hay tan pocas memorias de auténticos hombres de acción. He aquí porque todas las energías del aventurero, exentas del ayer y el mañana, se condensan en la punta del tiempo que es cada instante como la electricidad en la punta de la antena. Contemplada en cada momento una vida así, es algo incomparable, sublime, soberano; pero no hay modo de ensamblar dos momentos, y mientras ofrece al espectador el más divertido espectáculo, es, para sí misma, una existencia vacía.

André Wurmser, like all Marxist critics fascinated by the phenomenon of the novel, has remarked that it is the peculiar feature of detective novels that they can be reread with equal pleasure after an appropriate lapse of time.[18] In my own case five years would seem about right, which means I am about ready for my third or fourth rehearsal of Dashiell Hammett (who had the same virtue of innovation that Cervantes granted to the author of *Amadís*). But this is for a reason antithetical to that which leads us back again and again to such novels as *Huck Finn* and *Don Quijote*. We have given so much of ourselves to them that time cannot erase them from the tape of our mental recorder. They are still vividly present, but we return to them because we know that the time that elapsed in us, with its accumulation of experience, will enrich and deepen reading after reading. As we grow older, these novels have more to draw on; they can ask more from us since we have more to give them.

Examination of novels of adventure as a distinct category of lesser value (which is not to deny the existence of adventure "classics") demonstrates the unreality of the dilemma posed earlier. It is not *whether* a novel works (for a trained and insatiable lover of novels almost any reasonably coherent fictional sequence may be operative) that is decisive to value judgment. Rather, it is *how* and *where*. Adventure addicts are limited to a shallow and hermetic pleasure; in skimming their novels, they skim their souls. On the other hand, great novels, we conclude (since polarity is the essential condition of value), are profound and engage our lives "as-a-whole." But we must take care to interpret the apparently facile antithesis in Stendhalian terms. "Shallow" and "profound" do not necessarily refer to the absence or presence of deep ideas, complex symbolism, or coherent philosophy. Rather, it is a question of depth of penetration into us, depths of potential reanimation of our lives. Intellectual profundity, although easier to teach, is neither good nor bad novelistically speaking. What matters is a novel's capacity to enrich and intensify its reader's existence by transporting it into a new life more alive—more sentient and charged, exalted by hazardous coping with non-being in its manifold forms and on its manifold frontiers.

It is this notion of novelistic value which is implied by Mark Twain (whose foxiness has at times been underestimated) in the curious initial warning:

> *Notice.* Persons attempting to find a motive in this narrative will be prosecuted; persons attempting to find a moral in it will be banished; persons attempting to find a plot in it will be shot. By Order of the Author, per G. G. Chief of Ordinance.

[18] In the Prologue to *L'Assassin est mort le 1'er* (Paris, 1960).

168

For Mark Twain, motives, morals, and plots (and, had he heard about them, structures, themes, and myths) are all abstractions, which is to say lies. Therefore, those who discuss them must be punished. The truth was to be found in the sheer, immediate, concrete experience of Huck, a running, cumulative experience which was his narrative's only claim to importance. Adventure novels have plots and, if their authors are pretentious, morals and motives too. But *Huck Finn* opposes the superficial tempo and prevarication of adventure (represented at beginning and end by Tom Sawyer) with the slow time of "life-as-a-whole" drawn from us with that kind of irrefutable, unarguable freshness which only Huck's genius for truth can tap. The first paragraph, immediately following the above "Notice," sets up a novel-long dialectic of truth and lie: "That book was made by Mr. Mark Twain, and he told the truth mainly. There was things which he stretched but mainly he told the truth." Huck's ability to judge and tell the truth (as well as to build lies from truth) may be moral in its implications, but, as "the Author" states, it is not a moral. Novelistically it serves to authenticate experience.

This contrast of novels of adventure against novels of experience (the first being inferior insofar as they foreshorten life, the second superior insofar as they enhance it) is as much an abstraction as the three Mark Twain warns us against. It may be useful as a way of comprehending what we called at the beginning the nature of novelistic value, but, as a way of categorization of individual novels, it is a falsehood. Therefore, in order to avoid being drawn and quartered, or whatever other punishment the author might have decided it fitting to legislate, I must admit the truth that adventure is a kind of experience and that every experience, by the very fact that it is individualized, has an element of adventure. As a result it is impossible (as Cervantes discovered and as major novelists have known ever since) to trace a boundary between the two. The one blends into the other imperceptibly, thereby providing a Twain, a Balzac, a Conrad, or a Dickens with an enchanting frontier zone. Here is the region we as readers all adore, a region which submits the daily time of our lives, our sense of living an unfolding process, to more marvelous possibilities, coincidences, emotions, and fatalities than we may reasonably expect to encounter tomorrow or a year from now. The world of the novel instead of sifting all the adventure out of experience always is to greater or lesser degree an amalgamation of the two.

It is precisely for this reason that novelists have always, as we pointed out, attempted ironically to train their readers to avoid identification with the protagonist. The elements of adventure present in *Huck Finn* perhaps more openly than in other novels (although it is never in one form or another entirely absent from any, as the so-called human documents of the Naturalists demonstrate) are a temptation hard for a youthful or unprepared reader to resist. One wants to read the book as a sequel to *Tom Sawyer*, which is why Mark Twain's intuition led him to frame the experience of Huck, and Jim, adventure-prone but never professionals, with the contrived piracies and escapes of Tom. Tom is no longer a boy but a self-styled professional whose absurd behavior is meant to reveal the fallacy and impoverishment of identification. And it does. In the difference of narrative power between the great central chapters in which Huck narrates "how it felt to exist in the happening" of the river and those in which he narrates Tom's adventures, we learn (often as early as the second reading) to avoid identification. We learn, instead, how to accept and vivify Huck's profound otherness from ourselves, to respect it, and, in every new reading, to realize it more. We know we are not he. But we also learn that not being Huck allows him, as it were, to identify with us, to flesh out his words from our experience. He comes alive suddenly with poignant intensity because he receives and forms anew both the ongoing nowness of our lives as readers *and* all that we have lived through as fellow human beings.

When Thackeray shocks us by referring ironically to his characters at their moments of most intense living as "puppets," it is not because he believes them so to be, but because he wants us to be fully aware of the strange, vital duplication (observance of ourselves in somebody else) that only great novels can provide. Before rejecting this paradox—the paradox of at once being ourselves and recognizing consciously a purified, intensified, sanctified incarnation of our experience in another—let my reader think back again, let him remember the storm over Jackson's Island. He will, I trust, recognize the doubleness of the memory. He will recognize how much the novel has done for him and to him—and how important it is that it should have been done.

In our admiration at the otherness and actual aliveness of the inhabitants of novels, we should not be misled into studying them psychologically or measuring the stages of their "growth." If we stop to think about it, how unreasonable it is that the Huck of *Tom Sawyer* or the Huck of the beginning of *Huck Finn* should so have expanded his awareness and so superbly have narrated the Mississippi experience. How outside the bounds of calculated characterization or verisimilitude! How little the resemblance to biographical growth in a change which occurs explosively, at the exact moment when Huck is caught by Pap and taken away from Tom, or when he submits again meekly to Tom's adventurous flair at the Phelpses'! Although psychological construction may be important to other fictional lives, in this case (as in the *Quijote*) we can see how nonessential it is to the creation of living experience. What has happened is something else. Huck has entranced us with the naïve hypersensitivity of his wondering gaze; we have revived him once again with the breath of our life. We are not one, but each of us in his own way knows the other with a symbiotic intimacy that is strange both to psychology and to other forms of literature.

Although very much alive, Huck and Jim should not be explained as if they were real people or like real people—which they are not. Instead, we must understand them as caricatures (Mark Twain's pair, like Cervantes', constitute extreme cases within the genre) suddenly temporalized, which is to say suddenly conscious. As against the impoverishment of adventure fiction, a loss of time in the profoundest sense, the novelistic transaction just outlined is a Comstock Lode of temporal enrichment. When recent critics speak of the novel as the genre of passing time, a portrait of life in time, they tend to think mostly about the years, days, and minutes of chronicled rise and fall—a time of diapers, crutches, and autumn days. But beneath this epidermis there is something more important: the temporal consciousness of novelistic life, the duration it was designed to excavate from the mines of readers' souls. If adventure fiction is voluptuous, the novel in full flower offers a far more intense and lasting joy: that of encountering the best we have lived, cleansed of daily compromise and impurity, incarnated in a new life, once more free to search for meaning along the uncertain path.

There are, of course, novelists who, instead of freeing, put their characters in chains, who bind them to evil or render them the helpless prey of naturalistic circumstances. We all know, admire, and teach such novels—although to furnish them with life we must magnify our miseries. But we should not ignore the other side of the coin. We should not ignore the power of the novel to give birth to Don Quijote, Prince Myshkin, Huck Finn, Fabrice del Dongo, Parson Adams, the eccentric latter-day saints of an age the values of which are—as Lukács explains and Cervantes first discovered—in a state of abject devaluation.

6

PAUL DE MAN

The Rhetoric of Temporality

I. ALLEGORY AND SYMBOL

SINCE the advent, in the course of the ninteenth century, of a subjectivistic critical vocabulary, the traditional forms of rhetoric have fallen into disrepute. It is becoming increasingly clear, however, that this was only a temporary eclipse: recent developments in criticism[1] reveal the possibility of a rhetoric that would no longer be normative or descriptive but that would more or less openly raise the question of the intentionality of rhetorical figures. Such concerns are implicitly present in many works in which the terms "mimesis," "metaphor," "allegory," or "irony" play a prominent part. One of the main difficulties that still hamper these investigations stems from the association of rhetorical terms with value judgments that blur distinctions and hide the real structures. In most cases, their use is governed by assumptions that go back at least as far as the romantic period; hence the need for historical clarification as a preliminary to a more systematic treatment of an intentional rhetoric. One has to return, in the history of European literature, to the moment when the rhetorical key-terms undergo significant changes and are at the center of important tensions. A first and obvious example would be the change that takes place in the latter half of the eighteenth century, when the word "symbol" tends to supplant other denominations for figural language, including that of "allegory."

Although the problem is perhaps most in evidence in the history of German literature, we do not intend to retrace the itinerary that led the German writers of the age of Goethe to consider symbol and allegory as antithetical, when they

[1] The trend is apparent in various critical movements that develop independently of one another in several countries. Thus, for example, in the attempt of some French critics to fuse the conceptual terminology of structural linguistics with traditional terms of rhetoric (see, among others, Roland Barthes, "Eléments de sémiologie," in *Communications*, 1964; Gérard Genette, *Figures* (Paris, 1966); Michel Foucault, *Les Mots et les choses* (Paris, 1966). In Germany a similar trend often takes the form of a rediscovery and reinterpretation of the allegorical and emblematic style of the baroque (see, among others, Walter Benjamin, *Ursprung des deutschen Trauerspiels* [1928; reissued in Frankfurt, 1963]; Albrecht Schöne, *Emblematik und Drama im Zeitalter des Barock* [Munich, 1964]). The evolution from the New Criticism to the criticism of Northrop Frye in North America tends in the same direction.

were still synonymous for Winckelmann. The itinerary is too complex for cursory treatment. In *Wahrheit und Methode*, Hans-Georg Gadamer makes the valorization of symbol at the expense of allegory coincide with the growth of an aesthetics that refuses to distinguish between experience and the representation of this experience. The poetic language of genius is capable of transcending this distinction and can thus transform all individual experience directly into general truth. The subjectivity of experience is preserved when it is translated into language; the world is then no longer seen as a configuration of entities that designate a plurality of distinct and isolated meanings, but as a configuration of symbols ultimately leading to a total, single, and universal meaning. This appeal to the infinity of a totality constitutes the main attraction of the symbol as opposed to allegory, a sign that refers to one specific meaning and thus exhausts its suggestive potentialities once it has been deciphered. "Symbol and allegory," writes Gadamer, "are opposed as art is opposed to non-art, in that the former seems endlessly suggestive in the indefiniteness of its meaning, whereas the latter, as soon as its meaning is reached, has run its full course."[2] Allegory appears as dryly rational and dogmatic in its reference to a meaning that it does not itself constitute, whereas the symbol is founded on an intimate unity between the image that rises up before the senses and the supersensory totality that the image suggests. In this historical perspective, the names of Goethe, Schiller, and Schelling stand out from the background of the classical idea of a unity between incarnate and ideal beauty.

Even within the area of German thought other currents complicate this historical scheme. In the perspective of traditional German classicism, allegory appears as the product of the age of Enlightenment and is vulnerable to the reproach of excessive rationality. Other trends, however, consider allegory as the very place where the contact with a superhuman origin of language has been preserved. Thus the polemical utterances of Hamann against Herder on the problem of the origin of language are closely related to Hamann's considerations on the allegorical nature of all language,[3] as well as with his literary praxis that mingles allegory with irony. It is certainly not in the name of an enlightened rationalism that the idea of a transcendental distance between the incarnate world of man and the divine origin of the word is here being defended. Herder's

---

[2] Hans-Georg Gadamer, *Wahrheit und Methode* (Tübingen, 1960; 2d ed., 1965), p. 70.

[3] Johann Georg Hamann, "Die Rezension der Herderschen Preisschrift," in *J. G. Hamann's Hauptschriften erklärt*, vol. 4 (*Über den Ursprung der Sprache*), ed. Elfriede Büchsel (Gütersloh, 1963).

humanism encounters in Hamann a resistance that reveals the complexity of the intellectual climate in which the debate between symbol and allegory will take place.

These questions have been treated at length in the historiography of the period. We do not have to return to them here, except to indicate how contradictory the origins of the debate appear to be. It is therefore not at all surprising that, even in the case of Goethe, the choice in favor of the symbol is accompanied by all kinds of reservations and qualifications. But, as one progresses into the nineteenth century, these qualifications tend to disappear. The supremacy of the symbol, conceived as an expression of unity between the representative and the semantic function of language, becomes a commonplace that underlies literary taste, literary criticism, and literary history. The supremacy of the symbol still functions as the basis of recent French and English studies of the romantic and post-romantic eras, to such an extent that allegory is frequently considered an anachronism and dismissed as non-poetic.

Yet certain questions remain unsolved. At the very moment when properly symbolic modes, in the full strength of their development, are supplanting allegory, we can witness the growth of metaphorical styles in no way related to the decorative allegorism of the rococo, but that cannot be called "symbolic" in the Goethian sense. Thus it would be difficult to assert that in the poems of Hölderlin, the island Patmos, the river Rhine, or, more generally, the landscapes and places that are often described at the beginning of the poems would be symbolic landscapes or entities that represent, as by analogy, the spiritual truths that appear in the more abstract parts of the text. To state this would be to misjudge the literality of these passages, to ignore that they derive their considerable poetic authority from the fact that they are not synecdoches designating a totality of which they are a part, but are themselves already this totality. They are not the sensorial equivalence of a more general, ideal meaning; they are themselves this idea, just as much as the abstract expression that will appear in philosophical or historical form in the later parts of the poem. A metaphorical style such as Hölderlin's can at any rate not be described in terms of the antinomy between allegory and symbol—and the same could be said, albeit in a very different way, of Goethe's late style. Also, when the term "allegory" continues to appear in the writers of the period, such as Friedrich Schlegel, or later in Solger or E. T. H. Hoffmann, one should not assume that its use is merely a matter of habit, devoid of deeper meaning. Between 1800 and 1832, under the influence of Creuzer and Schelling, Friedrich Schlegel substitutes the word "symbolic" for "allegorical" in the oft-quoted passage of the "Gespräch über die Poesie": ". . . alle Schönheit ist

Allegorie. Das Höchste kann man eben weil es unaussprechlich ist, nur allegorisch sagen."[4] But can we deduce from this, with Schlegel's editor Hans Eichner, that Schlegel "simply uses allegory where we would nowadays say symbol"?[5] It could be shown that, precisely because it suggests a disjunction between the way in which the world appears in reality and the way it appears in language, the word "allegory" fits the general prolematic of the "Gespräch," whereas the word "symbol" becomes an alien presence in the later version.

We must go even further than this. Ever since the study of *topoi* has made us more aware of the importance of tradition in the choice of images, the symbol, in the post-romantic sense of the terms, appears more and more as a special case of figural language in general, a special case that can lay no claim to historical or philosophical priority over other figures. After such otherwise divergent studies as those of E. R. Curtius, of Erich Auerbach, of Walter Benjamin,[6] and of H.-G. Gadamer, we can no longer consider the supremacy of the symbol as a "solution" to the problem of metaphorical diction. "The basis of aesthetics during the nineteenth century," writes Gadamer, "was the freedom of the symbolizing power of the mind. But is this still a firm basis? Is the symbolizing activity not actually still bound today by the survival of a mythological and allegorical tradition?"[7]

To make some headway in this difficult question, it may be useful to leave the field of German literature and see how the same problem appears in English and French writers of the same period. Some help may be gained from a broader perspective.

The English contemporary of Goethe who has expressed himself most explicitly on the relationship between allegory and symbol is, of course, Coleridge. We find in Coleridge what appears to be, at first sight, an unqualified assertion of the superiority of the symbol over allegory. The symbol is the product of the organic growth of form; in the world of the symbol, life and form are identical: "such as the life is, such is the form."[8] Its structure is that of the synecdoche, for the symbol is always a part of the totality that it represents. Consequently, in the symbolical imagination, no disjunction of the constitutive faculties takes place,

---

[4] Friedrich Schlegel, *Kritische Ausgabe*, vol. 2 (*Karakteristiken und Kritiken I, 1796–1801*), ed. Hans Eichner (Paderborn, 1967), "Gespräch über die Poesie," pp. 324ff.

[5] *Ibid.*, p. xci, n. 2.

[6] *Loc. cit.*

[7] Gadamer, *op. cit.*, p. 76.

[8] S. T. Coleridge, *Essays and Lectures on Shakespeare and Some Other Old Poets and Dramatists*, Everyman ed. (London, 1907), p. 46.

since the material perception and the symbolical imagination are continuous, as the part is continuous with the whole. In contrast, the allegorical form appears purely mechanical, an abstraction whose original meaning is even more devoid of substance than its "phantom proxy," the allegorical representative; it is an immaterial shape that represents a sheer phantom devoid of shape and substance.[9]

But even in the passage from *The Statesman's Manual,* from which this quotation is taken, a certain degree of ambiguity is manifest. After associating the essential thinness of allegory with a lack of substantiality, Coleridge wants to stress, by contrast, the worth of the symbol. One would expect the latter to be valued for its organic or material richness, but instead the notion of "translucence" is suddenly put in evidence: "The symbol is characterized by the translucence of the special in the individual, or of the general in the special, or of the universal in the general; above all by the translucence of the eternal through and in the temporal."[10]

The material substantiality dissolves and becomes a mere reflection of a more original unity that does not exist in the material world. It is all the more surprising to see Coleridge, in the final part of the passage, characterize allegory negatively as being *merely* a reflection. In truth, the spiritualization of the symbol has been carried so far that the moment of material existence by which it was originally defined has now become altogether unimportant; symbol and allegory alike now have a common origin beyond the world of matter. The reference, in both cases, to a transcendental source, is now more important than the kind of relationship that exists between the reflection and its source. It becomes of secondary importance whether this relationship is based, as in the case of the symbol, on the organic coherence of the synecdoche, or whether, as in the case of allegory, it is a pure decision of the mind. Both figures designate, in fact, the transcendental source, albeit in an oblique and ambiguous way. Coleridge stresses the ambiguity in a definition of allegory in which it is said that allegory "... convey[s], while in disguise, either moral qualities or conceptions of the mind that are not in themselves objects of the senses ...," but then goes on to state that, on the level of language, allegory can "combine the parts to form a consistent whole."[11] Starting out from the assumed superiority of the symbol in terms of organic substantiality, we end up with a description of figural language

[9] S. T. Coleridge, *The Statesman's Manual,* ed. W. G. T. Shedd (New York, 1875), pp. 437–38, quoted in Angus Fletcher, *Allegory: The Theory of a Symbolic Mode* (Ithaca, N.Y., 1964), p. 16, n. 29.
[10] *Ibid.*
[11] S. T. Coleridge, *Miscellaneous Criticism,* ed. T. M. Raysor (London, 1936), p. 30; also quoted by Fletcher, *op. cit.,* p. 19.

177

as translucence, a description in which the distinction between allegory and symbol has become of secondary importance.

It is not, however, in this direction that Coleridge's considerable influence on later English and American criticism has been most manifest. The very prominent place given in this criticism to the study of metaphor and imagery, often considered as more important than problems of metrics or thematic considerations, is well enough known. But the conception of metaphor that is being assumed, often with explicit reference to Coleridge, is that of a dialectic between object and subject, in which the experience of the object takes on the form of a perception or a sensation. The ultimate intent of the image is not, however, as in Coleridge, translucence, but synthesis, and the mode of this synthesis is defined as "symbolic" by the priority conferred on the initial moment of sensory perception.

The main interpretative effort of English and American historians of romanticism has focused on the transition that leads from eighteenth-century to romantic nature poetry. Among American interpreters of romanticism, there is general agreement about the importance of eighteenth-century antecedents for Wordsworth and Coleridge, but when it comes to describing just in what way romantic nature poetry differs from the earlier forms, certain difficulties arise. They center on the tendency shared by all commentators to define the romantic image as a relationship between mind and nature, between subject and object. The fluent transition in romantic diction, from descriptive to inward, meditative passages, bears out the notion that this relationship is indeed of fundamental importance. The same applies to a large extent to eighteenth-century landscape poets who constantly mix descriptions of nature with abstract moralizings; commentators tend to agree, however, that the relationship between mind and nature becomes much more intimate toward the end of the century. Wimsatt was the first to show convincingly, by the juxtaposition of a sonnet of Coleridge and a sonnet of Bowles that, for all external similitudes, a fundamental change in substance and in tone separated the two texts.[12] He points to a greater specificity in Coleridge's details, thus revealing a closer, more faithful observation of the outside object. But this finer attention given to the natural surfaces is accompanied, paradoxically enough, by a greater inwardness, by experiences of memory and of reverie that stem from deeper regions of subjectivity than in the earlier writer. How this closer attention to surfaces engenders greater depth remains problematic. Wimsatt writes: "The common feat of the romantic nature poets was to

[12] W. K. Wimsatt, Jr., "The Structure of Romantic Nature Imagery," *The Verbal Icon* (Lexington, 1954), pp. 106–10.

178

read meanings into the landscape. The meaning might be such as we have seen in Coleridge's sonnet, but it might more characteristically be more profound, concerning the spirit or soul of things—'the one life within us and abroad.' And that meaning especially was summoned out of the very surface of nature itself."[13] The synthesis of surface and depth would then be the manifestation, in language, of a fundamental unity that encompasses both mind and object, "the one life within us and abroad." It appears, however, that this unity can be hidden from a subject, who then has to look outside, in nature, for the confirmation of its existence. For Wimsatt, the unifying principle seems to reside primarily within nature, hence the necessity for the poets to start out from natural landscapes, the sources of the unifying, "symbolic" power.

The point receives more development and ampler documentation in recent articles by Meyer Abrams and Earl Wasserman that make use of very similar, at times even identical material.[14] The two interpreters agree on many issues, to the point of overlapping. Both name, for instance, the principle of analogy between mind and nature as the basis for the eighteenth-century habit of treating a moral issue in terms of a descriptive landscape. Abrams refers to Renaissance concepts of theology and philosophy as a main source for the later *paysage moralisé*: "... the divine Architect has designed the universe analogically, relating the physical, moral, and spiritual realms by an elaborate system of correspondences.... The metaphysics of a symbolic and analogical universe underlay the figurative tactics of the seventeenth-century metaphysical poets."[15] A "tamed and ordered" version of this cosmology, "smoothed to a neo-classic decency" and decorum, then becomes the origin of the eighteenth-century loco-descriptive poem, in which "sensuous phenomena are coupled with moral statements." And Wasserman points to eighteenth-century theoreticians of the imagination, such as Akenside, who "can find [the most intimate relation] between subject and object is that of associative analogy, so that man beholds "in lifeless things / The Inexpressive semblance of himself, / Of thought and passion.' "[16]

The key concept here is, in Wasserman's correct phrasing, that of an *associative* analogy, as contrasted with a more vital form of analogy in the romantics. Abrams makes it seem, at times, as if the romantic theory of imagination did

[13] *Ibid.*, p. 110.
[14] Meyer Abrams, "Structure and Style in the Greater Romantic Lyric," in *From Sensibility to Romanticism: Essays Presented to F. A. Pottle*, ed. F. W. Hillis and H. Bloom (New York, 1965). Earl Wasserman, "The English Romantics, The Grounds of Knowledge," *Essays in Romanticism*, 4 (Autumn, 1964).
[15] Abrams, *op. cit.*, p. 536.
[16] Wasserman, *op. cit.*, p. 19.

away with analogy altogether and that Coleridge in particular replaced it by a genuine and working monism. "Nature is made thought and thought nature," he writes, "both by their sustained interaction and by their seamless metaphoric continuity."[17] But he does not really claim that this degree of fusion is achieved and sustained—at most that it corresponds to Coleridge's desire for a unity toward which his thought and poetic strategy strive. Analogy as such is certainly never abandoned as an epistemological pattern for natural images; even within the esoteric vocabulary of as late a version of a monistic universe as Baudelaire's correspondences, the expression *"analogie universelle"* is still being used.[18] Nevertheless, the relationship between mind and nature becomes indeed a lot less formal, less purely associative and external than it is in the eighteenth century. As a result, the critical—and even, at times, the poetic—vocabulary attempts to find terms better suited to express this relationship than is the somewhat formal concept of analogy. Words such as "affinity," or "sympathy," appear instead of the more abstract "analogy." This does not change the fundamental pattern of the structure, which remains that of a formal resemblance between entities that, in other respects, can be antithetical. But the new terminology indicates a gliding away from the formal problem of a congruence between the two poles to that of the ontological priority of the one over the other. For terms such as "affinity" or "sympathy" apply to the relationships between subjects rather than to relationships between a subject and an object. The relationship with nature has been superseded by an intersubjective, interpersonal relationship that, in the last analysis, is a relationship of the subject toward itself. Thus the priority has passed from the outside world entirely within the subject, and we end up with something that resembles a radical idealism. Both Abrams and Wasserman offer quotations from Wordsworth and Coleridge, as well as summarizing comments of their own, that seem to suggest that romanticism is, in fact, such an idealism. Both quote Wordsworth: "I was often unable to think of external things as having external existence, and I communed with all that I saw as something not apart from, but inherent in, my own immaterial nature"—and Wasserman comments that "Wordsworth's poetic experience seeks to recapture that condition."[19]

Since the assertion of a radical priority of the subject over objective nature is not easily compatible with the poetic praxis of the romantic poets, who all gave a great deal of importance to the presence of nature, a certain degree of con-

---

[17] Abrams, *op. cit.*, p. 551.

[18] Charles Baudelaire, "Réflexions sur quelques-uns de mes contemporains, Victor Hugo," in *Curiosités esthétiques: L'Art romantique et autres Oeuvres critiques*, ed. H. Lemaître (Paris: Garnier, 1962), p. 735.

[19] Wasserman, *op. cit.*, p. 26.

fusion ensues. One can find numerous quotations and examples that plead for the predominance, in romantic poetry, of an analogical imagination that is founded on the priority of natural substances over the consciousness of the self. Coleridge can speak, in nearly Fichtean terms, of the infinite self in opposition to the "necessarily finite" character of natural objects, and insist on the need for the self to give life to the dead forms of nature.[20] But the finite nature of the objective world is seen, at that moment, in spatial terms, and the substitution of vital (i.e., in Coleridge, intersubjective) relationships that are dynamic, for the physical relationships that exist between entities in the natural world is not necessarily convincing. It could very well be argued that Coleridge's own concept of organic unity as a dynamic principle is derived from the movements of nature, not from those of the self. Wordsworth is more clearly conscious of what is involved here when he sees the same dialectic between the self and nature in temporal terms. The movements of nature are for him instances of what Goethe calls *Dauer im Wechsel*, endurance within a pattern of change, the assertion of a metatemporal, stationary state beyond the apparent decay of a mutability that attacks certain outward aspects of nature but leaves the core intact. Hence we have famous passages such as the description of the mountain scenes in *The Prelude* in which a striking temporal paradox is evoked:

> . . . these majestic floods—these shining cliffs
> The untransmuted shapes of many worlds,
> Cerulian ether's pure inhabitants,
> These forests unapproachable by death,
> That shall endure as long as man endures . . . ;

or

> The immeasurable height
> Of woods decaying, never to be decayed
> The stationary blast of waterfalls. . . .

Such paradoxical assertions of eternity in motion can be applied to nature but not to a self caught up entirely within mutability. The temptation exists, then, for the self to borrow, so to speak, the temporal stability that it lacks from nature, and to devise strategies by means of which nature is brought down to a human level while still escaping from "the unimaginable touch of time." This strategy is certainly present in Coleridge. And it is present, though perhaps not consciously, in critics such as Abrams and Wasserman, who see Coleridge as the

[20] *Ibid.*, p. 29.

great synthetizer and who take his dialectic of subject and object to be the authentic pattern of romantic imagery. But this forces them, in fact, into a persistent contradiction. They are obliged, on the one hand, to assert the priority of object over subject that is implicit in an organic conception of language. So Abrams states: "The best Romantic meditations on a landscape, following Coleridge's example, all manifest a transaction between subject and object in which the thought incorporates and makes explicit what was already implicit in the outer scene."[21] This puts the priority unquestionably in the natural world, limiting the task of the mind to interpreting what is given in nature. Yet this statement is taken from the same paragraph in which Abrams quotes the passages from Wordsworth and Coleridge that confer an equally absolute priority to the self over nature. The contradiction reaches a genuine impasse. For what are we to believe? Is romanticism a subjective idealism, open to all the attacks of solipsism that, from Hazlitt to the French structuralists, a succession of de-mystifiers of the self have directed against it? Or is it instead a return to a certain form of naturalism after the forced abstraction of the Enlightenment, but a return which our urban and alienated world can conceive of only as a nostalgic and unreachable past? Wasserman is caught in the same impasse: for him, Wordsworth represents the extreme form of subjectivism whereas Keats, as a quasi-Shakespearean poet of negative capability, exemplifies a sympathetic and objective form of material imagination. Coleridge acts as the synthesis of this antithetical polarity. But Wasserman's claim for Coleridge as the reconciler of what he calls "the phenomenal world of understanding with the noumenal world of reason"[22] is based on a quotation in which Coleridge simply substitutes another self for the category of the object and thus removes the problem from nature altogether, reducing it to a purely intersubjective pattern. "To make the object one with us, we must become one with the object—ergo, an object. Ergo, the object must be itself a subject—partially a favorite dog, principally a friend, wholly God, *the* Friend."[23] Wordsworth was never guilty of thus reducing a theocentric to an interpersonal relationship.

Does the confusion originate with the critics, or does it reside in the romantic poets themselves? Were they really unable to move beyond the analogism that they inherited from the eighteenth century and were they trapped in the

---

[21] Abrams, *op. cit.*, p. 551.
[22] Wasserman, *loc. cit.*, p. 30.
[23] *Ibid.*, pp. 29–30.

contradiction of a pseudo dialectic between subject and object? Certain commentators believe this to be the case;[24] before following them, we should make certain that we have indeed been dealing with the main romantic problem when we interpret the romantic image in terms of a subject-object tension. For this dialectic originates, it must be remembered, in the assumed predominance of the symbol as the outstanding characteristic of romantic diction, and this predominance must, in its turn, be put into question.

It might be helpful, at this point, to shift attention from English to French literary history. Because French pre-romanticism occurs, with Rousseau, so early in the eighteenth century, and because the Lockian heritage in France never reached, not even with Condillac, the degree of automaticism against which Coleridge and Wordsworth had to rebel in Hartley, the entire problem of analogy, as connected with the use of nature imagery, is somewhat clearer there than in England. Some of the writers of the period were at least as aware as their later commentators of what was involved in a development of the general taste that felt attracted toward a new kind of landscape. To take one example: in his *De la composition des paysages sur le terrain*, which dates from 1777, the Marquis de Girardin describes a landscape explicitly designated as "romantic," made up of dark woods, snow-capped mountains, and a crystalline lake with an island on which an idyllic "*ménage rustique*" enjoys a happy combination of sociability and solitude among cascades and rushing brooks. And he comments on the scene as follows: "It is in situations like this that one feels all the strength of this analogy between natural beauty and moral sentiment."[25] One could establish a long list of similar quotations dating from the same general period, all expressing the intimate proximity between nature and its beholder in a language that evokes the material shape of the landscape as well as the mood of its inhabitants.

Later historians and critics have stressed this close unity between mind and nature as a fundamental characteristic of romantic diction. "Often the outer and the inner world are so deeply intermingled," writes Daniel Mornet, "that nothing distinguishes the images perceived by the senses from the chimera of the imagination."[26] The same emphasis, still present in more recent writings on the

---

[24] As one instance among others, see E. E. Bostetter, *The Romantic Ventriloquists* (Seattle, 1963).

[25] Quoted by Daniel Mornet, *Le Sentiment de la Nature en France au XVIIIe siècle de Jean-Jacques Rousseau à Bernardin de Saint-Pierre* (Paris, 1932), p. 248.

[26] *Ibid.*, p. 187.

period,[27] closely resembles the opinion expressed in Anglo-American criticism. There is the same stress on the analogical unity of nature and consciousness, the same priority given to the symbol as the unit of language in which the subject-object synthesis can take place, the same tendency to transfer into nature attributes of consciousness and to unify it organically with respect to a center that acts, for natural objects, as the identity of the self functions for a consciousness. In French literary history dealing with the period of Rousseau to the present, ambivalences closely akin to those found in the American historians of romanticism could be pointed out, ambivalences derived from an illusionary priority of a subject that had, in fact, to borrow from the outside world a temporal stability which it lacked within itself.

In the case of French romanticism, it is perhaps easier than it is in English literature to designate the historical origin of this tendency. One can point to a certain number of specific texts in which a symbolic language, based on the close interpenetration between observation and passion, begins to acquire a priority that it will never relinquish during the nineteenth and twentieth centuries. Among these texts none is more often singled out than Rousseau's novel *La Nouvelle Héloise*. It forms the basis of Daniel Mornet's study on the sentiment of nature in the eighteenth century.[28] In more recent works, such as Robert Mauzi's *Idée du bonheur dans la littérature française du 18ème siècle*,[29] the same predominant importance is given to Rousseau's novel. "When one knows *Cleveland* and *La Nouvelle Héloise*, there is little left to discover about the 18th century," Mauzi asserts in his preface.[30] There is certainly no better reference to be found than *La Nouvelle Héloise* for putting to the test the nearly unanimous conviction that the origins of romanticism coincide with the beginnings of a predominantly symbolical diction.

Interpreters of Rousseau's epistolary novel have had no difficulty in pointing out the close correspondence between inner states of soul and the outward aspect of nature, especially in passages such as the Meillerie episode in the fourth part of the novel.[31] In this letter, St. Preux revisits, in the company of the now-

[27] See, for example, Herbert Dieckmann, "Zur Theorie der Lyrik im 18. Jahrhundert in Frankreich, mit gelegentlicher Berücksichtigung der Englischen Kritik," in *Poetik und Hermeneutik*, vol. 2, ed. W. Iser (Munich, 1966), p. 108.

[28] Mornet, *op. cit.*

[29] Robert Mauzi, *L'Idée du bonheur dans la littérature et la pensée française du XVIIIe siècle* (Paris, 1960).

[30] *Ibid.*, p. 10.

[31] J. J. Rousseau, *Julie ou la Nouvelle Héloise*, pt. 4, letter 17, in *Oeuvres complètes*, ed B. Gagnebin and Marcel Raymond (Paris, 1961), 2: 514ff.

184

married Julie, the deserted region on the northern bank of the lake from which he had, in earlier days, written the letter that sealed their destiny. Rousseau stresses that the *lieu solitaire* he describes is like a wild desert *"sauvage et désert; mais plein de ces sortes de beautés qui ne plaisent qu'aux âmes sensibles et paraissent horribles aux autres."*[32] A polemical reference to current taste is certainly present here, and such passages can be cited to illustrate the transition from the eighteenth-century, idyllic landscape that we still find in Girardin to the somber, tormented scenes that are soon to predominate in Macpherson. But this polemic of taste is superficial, for Rousseau's concerns are clearly entirely different. It is true that the intimate analogy between scenery and emotion serves as a basis for some of the dramatic and poetic effects of the passage: the sensuous passion, reawakened by memory and threatening to disturb a precarious tranquillity, is conveyed by the contrasting effects of light and setting which give the passage its dramatic power. The analogism of the style and the sensuous intensity of the passion are closely related. But this should not blind us to the explicit thematic function of the letter, which is one of temptation and near-fatal relapse into former error, openly and explicitly condemned, without any trace of ambiguity, in the larger context of Rousseau's novel.

In this respect, the reference to the Meillerie landscape as a wilderness is particularly revealing, especially when contrasted with other landscapes in the novel that are not emblematic of error, but of the virtue associated with the figure of Julie. This is the case for the central emblem of the novel, the garden that Julie has created on the Wolmar estate as a place of refuge. On the allegorical level the garden functions as the landscape representative of the "beautiful soul." Our question is whether this garden, the Elysium described at length in the eleventh letter of the fourth part of the novel, is based on the same kind of subject/object relationship that was thematically and stylistically present in the Meillerie episode.

A brief consideration of Rousseau's sources for the passage is enlightening. The main non-literary source has been all too strongly emphasized by Mornet in his critical edition of the novel:[33] Rousseau derives several of the exterior aspects of his garden from the so-called *jardins anglais*, which, well before him, were being preferred to the geometrical abstraction of the classical French gardens. The excessive symmetry of Le Nôtre, writes Rousseau, echoing a commonplace of

[32] *Ibid.*, p. 518.
[33] *La Nouvelle Héloïse*, ed. by Daniel Mornet (Paris, 1925), Introduction, 1: 67–74, and notes, 3: 223–47.

sophisticated taste at the time, is *"ennemie de la nature et de la variété."*[34] But this "natural" look of the garden is by no means the main theme of the passage. From the beginning we are told that the natural aspect of the site is in fact the result of extreme artifice, that in this bower of bliss, contrary to the tradition of the *topos*, we are entirely in the realm of art and not that of nature. "Il est vrai," Rousseau has Julie say, "que la nature a tout fait [dans ce jardin] mais sous ma direction, et il n'y a rien là que je n'aie ordonné."[35] The statement should at least alert us to the literary sources of the passage which Mornet, preoccupied as he was with the outward history of taste, was led to neglect.

Confining ourselves to the explicit literary allusions that can be found in the text, the reference to *"une Ile déserte . . . (où) je n'aperçois aucuns pas d'hommes"*[36] points directly toward Rousseau's favorite contemporary novel, the only one considered suitable for Emile's education, Defoe's *Robinson Crusoe*, whereas the allusion to the *Roman de la rose* in the pages immediately preceding the letter on Julie's Elysium[37] is equally revealing. The combination of *Robinson Crusoe* with the *Roman de la rose* may not look very promising at first sight, but it has, in fact, considerable hidden possibilities. The fact that the medieval romance, re-issued in 1735 and widely read in Rousseau's time,[38] had given the novel its subtitle of *"la nouvelle Héloise"* is well known, but its influence is manifest in many other ways as well. The close similarity between Julie's garden and the love garden of Deduit which appears in the first part of Guillaume de Lorris' poem is obvious. There is hardly a detail of Rousseau's description that does not find its counterpart in the medieval text: the self-enclosed, isolated space of the *"asile"*; the special privilege reserved to the happy few who possess a key that unlocks the gate; the traditional enumeration of natural attributes—a catalogue of the various flowers, trees, fruits, perfumes, and, above all, of the birds, culminating in the description of their song.[39] Most revealing of all is the emphasis on water, on fountains and pools that, in *Julie* as in the *Roman de la rose*, are controlled not by nature but by the ingenuity of the inhabitants.[40] Far from

[34] Rousseau, *op. cit.*, p. 483.

[35] *Ibid.*, p. 472.

[36] *Ibid.*, p. 479.

[37] "Richesse ne fait pas riche, dit le Roman de la Rose," quoted in letter 10 of pt. 4, *ibid.*, p. 466 and n.

[38] *Ibid.*, p. 1606, n. 2. I have consulted a copy of the Lenglet du Fresnoy edition which, at first sight, offers no variants that are immediately relevant to our question.

[39] Guillaume de Lorris and Jean de Meun, *Le Roman de la Rose* ed. Félix Lecoy (Paris: Champion, 1965), vol. 1, esp. ll. 499ff., 629ff., 1345ff.

[40] *Ibid.*, ll. 1385ff.

186

being an observed scene or the expression of a personal *état d'âme*, it is clear that Rousseau has deliberately taken all the details of his setting from the medieval literary source, one of the best-known versions of the traditional *topos* of the erotic garden.

In linguistic terms, we have something very different, then, from the descriptive and metaphorical language that, from Chateaubriand on, will predominate in French romantic diction. Rousseau does not even pretend to be observing. The language is purely figural, not based on perception, less still on an experienced dialectic between nature and consciousness. Julie's claim of domination and control over nature (*"il n'y a rien là que je n'aie ordonné"*) may well be considered as the fitting emblem for a language that submits the outside world entirely to its own purposes, contrary to what happens in the Meillerie episode, where the language fuses together the parallel movements of nature and of passion.

In the first part of the *Roman de la rose*, however, the use of figural language in no way conflicts with the exalted treatment of erotic themes; quite to the contrary, the erotic aspects of the allegory hardly need to be stressed. But in *La Nouvelle Héloise* the emphasis on an ethic of renunciation conveys a moral climate that differs entirely from the moralizing sections of the medieval romance. Rousseau's theme of renunciation is far from being one-sided and is certainly not to be equated with a puritanical denial of the world of the senses. Nevertheless, it is in the use of allegorical diction rather than of the language of correspondences that the medieval and eighteenth-century sources converge. Recent studies of Defoe, such as G. A. Starr's *Defoe and Spiritual Autobiography*[41] and Paul Hunter's *The Reluctant Pilgrim*,[42] have reversed the trend to see in Defoe one of the inventors of a modern "realistic" idiom and have rediscovered the importance of the puritanical, religious element to which Rousseau responded. Paul Hunter has strongly emphasized the stylistic importance of this element, which led Defoe to make an allegorical rather than a metaphorical and descriptive use of nature. Thus Defoe's gardens, far from being realistic natural settings, are stylized emblems, quite similar in structure and detail to the gardens of the *Roman de la rose*. But they serve primarily a redemptive, ethical function. Defoe's garden, writes Paul Hunter, "is not ... a prelapsarian paradise but rather an earthly paradise *in posse,* for Crusoe is postlapsarian man who has to

[41] G. A. Starr, *Defoe and Spiritual Autobiography* (Princeton, 1965).
[42] J. Paul Hunter, *The Reluctant Pilgrim: Defoe's Emblematic Method and Quest in Robinson Crusoe* (Baltimore, 1966).

toil to cultivate his land into full abundance."[43] The same stress on hardship, toil, and virtue is present in Julie's garden, relating the scene closely to the Protestant allegorical tradition of which the English version, culminating in Bunyan, reached Rousseau through a variety of sources, including Defoe. The stylistic likeness of the sources supersedes all further differences between them; the tension arises not between the two distant literary sources, the one erotic, the other puritanical, but between the allegorical language of a scene such as Julie's Elysium and the symbolic language of passages such as the Meillerie episode. The moral contrast between these two worlds epitomizes the dramatic conflict of the novel. This conflict is ultimately resolved in the triumph of a controlled and lucid renunciation of the values associated with a cult of the moment, and this renunciation establishes the priority of an allegorical over a symbolic diction. The novel could not exist without the simultaneous presence of both meta-phorical modes, nor could it reach its conclusion without the implied choice in favor of allegory over symbol.

Subsequent interpreters of *La Nouvelle Héloise* have, in general, ignored the presence of allegorical elements in shaping the diction of the novel, and it is only recently that one begins to realize how false the image of Rousseau as a primitivist or as a naturalist actually is. These false interpretations, very revealing in their own right, resist correction with a remarkable tenacity, thereby indicating how deeply this correction conflicts with the widespread *"idées reçues"* on the nature and the origins of European romanticism.

For, if the dialectic between subject and object does not designate the main romantic experience, but only one passing moment in a dialectic, and a negative moment at that, since it represents a temptation that has to be overcome, then the entire historical and philosophical pattern changes a great deal. Similar allegorizing tendencies, though often in a very different form, are present not only in Rousseau but in all European literature between 1760 and 1800. Far from being a mannerism inherited from the exterior aspects of the baroque and the rococo, they appear at the most original and profound moments in the works, when an authentic voice becomes audible. The historians of English romanticism have been forced, by the nature of things, to mention allegory, although it is often a problem of secondary importance. Wimsatt has to encounter it in deal-ing with Blake; he quotes two brief poems by Blake, entitled "To Spring" and "To Summer," and comments: "Blake's starting point . . . is the opposite of Wordsworth's and Byron's, not the landscape but a spirit personified or alle-gorized. Nevertheless, this spirit as it approaches the 'western isle' takes on cer-

[43] *Ibid.*, p. 172.

188

tain distinctly terrestrial hues. . . . These early romantic poets are examples of the Biblical, classical, and Renaissance tradition of allegory as it approaches the romantic condition of landscape naturalism—as Spring and Summer descend into the landscape and are fused with it."[44] Rather than such a continuous development from allegory to romantic naturalism, the example of Rousseau shows that we are dealing instead with the rediscovery of an allegorical tradition beyond the sensualistic analogism of the eighteenth century. This rediscovery, far from being spontaneous and easy, implies instead the discontinuity of a renunciation, even of a sacrifice. Taking for his starting point the descriptive poem of the eighteenth century, Abrams can speak with more historical precision. After having stressed the thematic resemblance between the romantic lyric and the metaphysical poem of the seventeenth century, he writes: "There is a very conspicuous and significant difference between the Romantic lyric and the seventeenth-century meditation on created nature. . . . [In the seventeenth century] the 'composition of place' was not a specific locality, nor did it need to be present to the eyes of the speaker, but was a typical scene or object, usually called up . . . before 'the eyes of the imagination' in order to set off and guide the thought by means of correspondences whose interpretation was firmly controlled by an inherited typology."[45] The distinction between seventeenth- and late eighteenth-century poetry is made in terms of the determining role played by the geographical *place* as establishing the link between the language of the poem and the empirical experience of the reader. However, in observing the development of even as geographically concrete a poet as Wordsworth, the significance of the locale can extend so far as to include a meaning that is no longer circumscribed by the literal horizon of a given place. The meaning of the site is often made problematic by a sequence of spatial ambiguities, to such an extent that one ends up no longer at a specific place but with a mere name whose geographical significance has become almost meaningless. Raising the question of the geographical locale of a given metaphorical object (in this case, a river), Wordsworth writes: "The spirit of the answer [as to the whereabouts of the river] through the word might be a certain stream, accompanied perhaps with an image gathered from a Map, or from a real object in nature—these might have been the letter, but the spirit of the answer must have been, as inevitably—a receptacle without bounds or dimensions;—nothing less than infinity."[46] Passages in Wordsworth such as

---

[44] Wimsatt, *op. cit.*, p. 113.
[45] Abrams, *op. cit.*, p. 556.
[46] W. Wordsworth, "Essay upon Epitaphs," in *The Poetical Works* (Oxford, 1949), 4: 446.

the crossing of the Alps or the ascent of Mount Snowden, or texts less sublime in character, such as the sequence of poems on the river Duddon, can no longer be classified with the locodescriptive poem of the eighteenth century. In the terminology proposed by Abrams, passages of this kind no longer depend on the choice of a specific locale, but are controlled by "a traditional and inherited typology," exactly as in the case of the poems from the sixteenth and seventeenth centuries—with this distinction, however, that the typology is no longer the same and that the poet, sometimes after long and difficult inner struggle, had to renounce the seductiveness and the poetic resources of a symbolical diction.

Whether it occurs in the form of an ethical conflict, as in *La Nouvelle Héloise*, or as an allegorization of the geographical site, as in Wordsworth, the prevalence of allegory always corresponds to the unveiling of an authentically temporal destiny. This unveiling takes place in a subject that has sought refuge against the impact of time in a natural world to which, in truth, it bears no resemblance. The secularized thought of the pre-romantic period no longer allows a transcendence of the antinomies between the created world and the act of creation by means of a positive recourse to the notion of a divine will; the failure of the attempt to conceive of a language that would be symbolical as well as allegorical, the suppression, in the allegory, of the analogical and anagogical levels, is one of the ways in which this impossibility becomes manifest. In the world of the symbol it would be possible for the image to coincide with the substance, since the substance and its representation do not differ in their being but only in their extension: they are part and whole of the same set of categories. Their relationship is one of simultaneity, which, in truth, is spatial in kind, and in which the intervention of time is merely a matter of contingency, whereas, in the world of allegory, time is the originary constitutive category. The relationship between the allegorical sign and its meaning (*signifié*) is not decreed by dogma; in the instances we have seen in Rousseau and in Wordsworth, this is not at all the case. We have, instead, a relationship between signs in which the reference to their respective meanings has become of secondary importance. But this relationship between signs necessarily contains a constitutive temporal element; it remains necessary, if there is to be allegory, that the allegorical sign refer to another sign that precedes it. The meaning constituted by the allegorical sign can then consist only in the *repetition* (in the Kierkegaardian sense of the term) of a previous sign with which it can never coincide, since it is of the essence of this previous sign to be pure anteriority. The secularized allegory of the early romantics thus necessarily contains the negative moment which in Rousseau is that of renunciation, in Wordsworth that of the loss of self in death or in error.

190

Whereas the symbol postulates the possibility of an identity or identification, allegory designates primarily a distance in relation to its own origin, and, renouncing the nostalgia and the desire to coincide, it establishes its language in the void of this temporal difference. In so doing, it prevents the self from an illusory identification with the non-self, which is now fully, though painfully, recognized as a non-self. It is this painful knowledge that we perceive at the moments when early romantic literature finds its true voice. It is ironically revealing that this voice is so rarely recognized for what it really is and that the literary movement in which it appears has repeatedly been called a primitive naturalism or a mystified solipsism. The authors with whom we are dealing had often gone out of their way to designate their theological and philosophical sources; too little attention has been paid to the complex and controlled set of literary allusions which, in *La Nouvelle Héloise*, establishes the link between Rousseau and his Augustinian sources, mostly by way of Petrarch.

We are led, in conclusion, to a historical scheme that differs entirely from the customary picture. The dialectical relationship between subject and object is no longer the central statement of romantic thought, but this dialectic is now located entirely in the temporal relationships that exist within a system of allegorical signs. It becomes a conflict between a conception of the self seen in its authentically temporal predicament and a defensive strategy that tries to hide from this negative self-knowledge. On the level of language the asserted superiority of the symbol over allegory, so frequent during the nineteenth century, is one of the forms taken by this tenacious self-mystification. Wide areas of European literature of the nineteenth and twentieth centuries appear as regressive with regard to the truths that come to light in the last quarter of the eighteenth century. For the lucidity of the pre-romantic writers does not persist. It does not take long for a symbolic conception of metaphorical language to establish itself everywhere, despite the ambiguities that persist in aesthetic theory and poetic practice. But this symbolical style will never be allowed to exist in serenity; since it is a veil thrown over a light one no longer wishes to perceive, it will never be able to gain an entirely good poetic conscience.

II. IRONY

Around the same time that the tension between symbol and allegory finds expression in the works and the theoretical speculations of the early romantics, the problem of irony also receives more and more self-conscious attention. At times, a concern with the figural aspects of language and, more specifically, an awareness of the persistence of allegorical modes go hand in hand with a theoretical concern for the trope "irony" as such. This is by no means always the case. We cited Rousseau and Wordsworth, and alluded to Hölderlin, as possible instances of romantic allegorism; the use of irony is conspicuously absent from all these poets. In others, however, the implicit and rather enigmatic link between allegory and irony which runs through the history of rhetoric seems to prevail. We mentioned Hamann;[47] in Germany alone, the names of Friedrich Schlegel, Friedrich Solger, E. T. H. Hoffmann, and Kierkegaard would be obvious additions to the list. In all these instances a more-or-less systematic theory of figural language, with explicit stress on allegory, runs parallel with an equally prevalent stress on irony. Friedrich Schlegel, of course, is well known as the main theoretician of romantic irony. That he was also affected, as well as somewhat puzzled, by the problem of metaphorical diction is clear from many of the *Fragmenten*, as well as from the revisions he made between the 1800 and 1823 editions of his works.[48] A similar parallelism between the problem of allegory and that of irony is certainly present in Solger, who elevates irony to the constitutive mode of all literature and suggestively distinguishes between symbol and allegory in terms of a dialectic of identity and difference.[49]

Nevertheless, the connection and the distinction between allegory and irony never become, at that time, independent subjects for reflection. The terms are rarely used as a means to reach a sharper definition, which, especially in the case of irony, is greatly needed. It obviously does not suffice to refer back to the descriptive rhetorical tradition which, from Aristotle to the eighteenth century, defines irony as "saying one thing and meaning another" or, in an even more restrictive context, as "blame-by-praise and praise-by-blame."[50] This definition points to a structure shared by irony and allegory in that, in both cases, the relationship between sign and meaning is discontinuous, involving an extraneous principle that determines the point and the manner at and in which the relationship is articulated. In both cases, the sign points to something that differs from its literal meaning and has for its function the thematization of this difference. But this important structural aspect may well be a description of figural language in general; it clearly lacks discriminatory precision. The relationship between

[47] See note 3 above.

[48] Schlegel, *op. cit.*, p. xci.

[49] Friedrich Solger, *Erwin: Vier Gespräche über das Schöne und die Kunst* (Leipzig, 1829).

[50] Norman Knox, *The Word Irony and its Context, 1500–1755* (Durham, N.C.: Duke University Press, 1961).

allegory and irony appears in history as a casual and apparently contingent fact, in the form of a common concern of some writers with both modes. It is this empirical event that has to receive a more general and theoretical interpretation.

The question is made more complex, but also somewhat more concrete, by an additional connection between a concern with irony and the development of the modern novel. The link is made in many critical texts: in Goethe, in Friedrich Schlegel, more recently in Lukács and in structuralist studies of narrative form. The tie between irony and the novel seems to be so strong that one feels tempted to follow Lukács in making the novel into the equivalent, in the history of literary genres, of irony itself. From the very beginning, the possibility of extending the trope to make it encompass lengthy narratives existed; in the *Institutio*, Quintilian described irony as capable of coloring an entire discourse pronounced in a tone of voice that did not correspond to the true situation, or even, with reference to Socrates, as pervading an entire life.[51] The passage from the localized trope to the extended novel is tempting, although the correlation between irony and the novel is far from simple. Even the superficial and empirical observation of literary history reveals this complexity. The growth of theoretical insight into irony around 1800 bears a by no means obvious relationship to the growth of the nineteenth-century novel. In Germany, for instance, the advent of a full-fledged ironic consciousness, which will persist from Friedrich Schlegel to Kierkegaard and to Nietzsche, certainly does not coincide with a parallel blossoming of the novel. Friedrich Schlegel, writing on the novel, has to take his recent examples from Sterne and Diderot and has to strain to find a comparable level of ironic insight in *Wilhelm Meisters Lehrjahre* and in Jean Paul Richter.[52] The opposite is true in France and England, where the spectacular development of the novel is not necessarily accompanied by a parallel interest in the theory of irony; one has to wait until Baudelaire to find a French equivalent of Schlegel's penetration. It could be argued that the greatest ironists of the nineteenth century generally are not novelists: they often tend toward novelistic forms and devices—one thinks of Kierkegaard, Hoffmann, Baudelaire, Mallarmé, or Nietzsche—but they show a prevalent tendency toward aphoristic, rapid, and brief texts (which are incompatible with the duration that is the basis of the novel), as if there were something in the nature of irony that did not allow for sustained movements. The great and all-important exception is, of course, Stendhal. But it should be clear by now that, aside from having to give insight into the relation-

[51] Quintilian *Institutio* 9. 2. 44–53, quoted in Knox, *loc. cit.*
[52] Schlegel, "Brief über den Roman," in "Gespräch über die Poesie," *op. cit.*, pp. 331ff.

ship between irony and allegory, an intentional theory of irony should also deal with the relationship between irony and the novel.

In the case of irony one cannot so easily take refuge in the need for a historical de-mystification of the term, as when we tried to show that the term "symbol" had in fact been substituted for that of "allegory" in an act of ontological bad faith. The tension between allegory and symbol justified this procedure: the mystification is a fact of history and must therefore be dealt with in a historical manner before actual theorization can start. But in the case of irony one has to start out from the structure of the trope itself, taking one's cue from texts that are de-mystified and, to a large extent, themselves ironical. For that matter, the target of their irony is very often the claim to speak about human matters as if they were facts of history. It is a historical fact that irony becomes increasingly conscious of itself in the course of demonstrating the impossibility of our being historical. In speaking of irony we are dealing not with the history of an error but with a problem that exists within the self. We cannot escape, therefore, the need for a definition toward which this essay is oriented. On the other hand, a great deal of assistance can be gained from existing texts on irony. Curiously enough, it seems to be only in describing a mode of language which does not mean what it says that one can actually say what one means.

Thus freed from the necessity of respecting historical chronology, we can take Baudelaire's text *De l'essence du rire* as a starting point. Among the various examples of ridicule cited and analyzed, it is the simplest situation of all that best reveals the predominant traits of an ironic consciousness: the spectacle of a man tripping and falling in the street. "Le comique," writes Baudelaire, "la puissance du rire est dans le rieur et nullement dans l'objet du rire. Ce n'est point l'homme qui tombe qui rit de sa propre chute, à moins qu'il ne soit un philosophe, un homme qui ait acquis, par habitude, la force de se dédoubler rapidement et d'assister comme spectateur désintéressé aux phénomènes de son *moi*."[53] In this simple observation several key concepts are already present. In the first place, the accent falls on the notion of *dédoublement* as the characteristic that sets apart a reflective activity, such as that of the philosopher, from the activity of the ordinary self caught in everyday concerns. Hidden away at first in side-remarks such as this one, or masked behind a vocabulary of superiority and inferiority, of master and slave, the notion of self-duplication or self-multiplication emerges at the end of the essay as the key concept of the article, the concept for the sake of which the essay has in fact been written.

[53] Charles Baudelaire, "De l'essence du rire," in *Curiosités esthétiques: L'Art romantique et autres Oeuvres critiques*, ed. H. Lemaître (Paris: Garnier, 1962), pp. 215ff.

... pour qu'il y ait comique, c'est-à-dire émananation, explosion, dégagement de comique, il faut qu'il y ait deux êtres en présence; — que c'est spécialement dans le rieur, dans le spectateur, que gît le comique; — que cependant, relative- ment à cette loi d'ignorance, il faut faire une exception pour les hommes qui ont fait métier de développer en eux le sentiment du comique et de le tirer d'eux-mêmes pour le divertissement de leurs semblables, lequel phénomène rentre dans la classe de tous les phénomènes artistiques qui dénotent dans l'être humain l'existence d'une dualité permanente, la puissance d'être à la fois soi et un autre.[54]

The nature of this duplication is essential for an understanding of irony. It is a relationship, within consciousness, between two selves, yet it is not an inter- subjective relationship. Baudelaire spends several pages of his essay distinguishing between a simple sense of comedy that is oriented toward others, and thus exists on the necessarily empirical level of interpersonal relationships, and what he calls "*le comique absolu*" (by which he designates that which, at other moments in his work, he calls irony), where the relationship is not between man and man, two entities that are in essence similar, but between man and what he calls nature, that is, two entities that are in essence different. Within the realm of intersubjectivity one would indeed speak of difference in terms of the superiority of one subject over another, with all the implications of will to power, of vio- lence, and possession which come into play when a person is laughing at some- one else—including the will to educate and to improve. But, when the concept of "superiority" is still being used when the self is engaged in a relationship not to other subjects, but to what is precisely not a self, then the so-called superiority merely designates the *distance* constitutive of all acts of reflection. Superiority and inferiority then become merely spatial metaphors to indicate a discontinuity and a plurality of levels within a subject that comes to know itself by an increas- ing differentiation from what it is not. Baudelaire insists that irony, as "*comique absolu*," is an infinitely higher form of comedy than is the intersubjective kind of humor he finds so frequently among the French; hence his preference for Italian *commedia dell' arte*, English pantomime, or the tales of E. T. H. Hoffmann over Molière, the typical example of a certain French comic spirit that is unable to rise above the level of intersubjectivity. Daumier is dismissed in the same terms in favor of Hogarth and Goya in the essays on caricature.[55]

The *dédoublement* thus designates the activity of a consciousness by which a man differentiates himself from the non-human world. The capacity for such

---

[54] *Ibid.*, p. 262.
[55] Baudelaire, "Quelques caricaturistes français," *ibid.*, p. 281.

duplication is rare, says Baudelaire, but belongs specifically to those who, like artists or philosophers, deal in language. His emphasis on a professional vocabulary, on "*se faire un métier*," stresses the technicality of their action, the fact that language is their material, just as leather is the material of the cobbler or wood is that of the carpenter. In everyday, common existence, this is not how language usually operates; there it functions much more as does the cobbler's or the carpenter's hammer, not as the material itself, but as a tool by means of which the heterogeneous material of experience is more-or-less adequately made to fit. The reflective disjunction not only occurs *by means of* language as a privileged category, but it transfers the self out of the empirical world into a world constituted out of, and in, language—a language that it finds in the world like one entity among others, but that remains unique in being the only entity by means of which it can differentiate itself from the world. Language thus conceived divides the subject into an empirical self, immersed in the world, and a self that becomes like a sign in its attempt at differentiation and self-definition.

More important still, in Baudelaire's description the division of the subject into a multiple consciousness takes place in immediate connection with a fall. The element of falling introduces the specifically comical and ultimately ironical ingredient. At the moment that the artistic or philosophical, that is, the language-determined, man laughs at himself falling, he is laughing at a mistaken, mystified assumption he was making about himself. In a false feeling of pride the self has substituted, in its relationship to nature, an intersubjective feeling (of superiority) for the knowledge of a difference. As a being that stands upright (as in the passage at the beginning of Ovid's *Metamorphoses* to which Baudelaire alludes elsewhere[56]), man comes to believe that he dominates nature, just as he can, at times, dominate others or watch others dominate him. This is, of course, a major mystification. The Fall, in the literal as well as the theological sense, reminds him of the purely instrumental, reified character of his relationship to nature. Nature can at all times treat him as if he were a thing and remind him of his factitiousness, whereas he is quite powerless to convert even the smallest particle of nature into something human. In the idea of fall thus conceived, a progression in self-knowledge is certainly implicit: the man who has fallen is somewhat wiser than the fool who walks around oblivious of the crack in the pavement about to trip him up. And the fallen philosopher reflecting on the

---

[56] For example, in the poem "Le Cygne":
> Je vois ce malheureux, mythe étrange et fatal,
> Vers le ciel quelquefois, comme l'homme d'Ovide. . . .

The allusion is to *Metamorphoses* 1. 84–86.

discrepancy between the two successive stages is wiser still, but this does not in the least prevent him from stumbling in his turn. It seems instead that his wisdom can be gained only at the cost of such a fall. The mere falling of others does not suffice; he has to go down himself. The ironic, twofold self that the writer or philosopher constitutes by his language seems able to come into being only at the expense of his empirical self, falling (or rising) from a stage of mystified adjustment into the knowledge of his mystification. The ironic language splits the subject into an empirical self that exists in a state of inauthenticity and a self that exists only in the form of a language that asserts the knowledge of this inauthenticity. This does not, however, make it into an authentic language, for to know inauthenticity is not the same as to be authentic.

It becomes evident that the disjunction is by no means a reassuring and serene process, despite the fact that it involves laughter. When the contemporary French philosopher V. Jankélévitch entitled a book on irony *L'Ironie ou la bonne conscience,* he certainly was far removed from Baudelaire's conception of irony —unless, of course, the choice of the title itself was ironic. For Baudelaire, at any rate, the movement of the ironic consciousness is anything but reassuring. The moment the innocence or authenticity of our sense of being in the world is put into question, a far from harmless process gets underway. It may start as a casual bit of play with a stray loose end of the fabric, but before long the entire texture of the self is unraveled and comes apart. The whole process happens at an unsettling speed. Irony possesses an inherent tendency to gain momentum and not to stop until it has run its full course; from the small and apparently innocuous exposure of a small self-deception it soon reaches the dimensions of the absolute. Often starting as litotes or understatement, it contains within itself the power to become hyperbole. Baudelaire refers to this unsettling power as *"vertige de l'hyperbole"* and conveys the feeling of its effect in his description of the English pantomime he saw at the Théâtre des Variétés:

> Une des choses les plus remarquables comme comique absolu, et, pour ainsi dire, comme métaphysique du comique absolu, était certainement le début de cette belle pièce, un prologue plein d'une haute esthétique. Les principaux personnages de la pièce, Pierrot, Cassandre, Harlequin, Colombine ... sont [d'abord] à peu près raisonnables et ne diffèrent pas beaucoup des braves gens qui sont dans la salle. Le souffle merveilleux qui va les faire se mouvoir extraordinairement n'a pas encore soufflé sur leurs cervelles.... Une fée s'intéresse à Harlequin ... elle lui promet sa protection et, pour lui en donner une preuve immédiate, elle promène avec un geste mystérieux et plein d'autorité sa baguette dans les airs. Aussitôt le vertige est entré, le vertige circule dans l'air, on respire

le vertige; c'est le vertige qui remplit les poumons et renouvelle le sang dans le ventricule. Qu'est-ce que ce vertige? C'est le comique absolu; il s'est emparé de chaque être. Ils font des gestes extraordinaires, qui démontrent clairement qu'ils se sentent introduits de force dans une existence nouvelle.... Et ils s'élancent à travers l'oeuvre fantastique qui, à proprement parler, ne commence que là, c'est-à-dire sur la frontière du merveilleux.[57]

Irony is unrelieved *vertige*, dizziness to the point of madness. Sanity can exist only because we are willing to function within the conventions of duplicity and dissimulation, just as social language dissimulates the inherent violence of the actual relationships between human beings. Once this mask is shown to be a mask, the authentic being underneath appears necessarily as on the verge of madness. "Le rire est généralement l'apanage des fous," writes Baudelaire, and the term *"folie"* remains associated throughout with that of *"comique absolu."* "Il est notoire que tous les fous des hôpitaux ont l'idée de leur superiorité développée outre mesure. Je ne connais guère de fous d'humilité. Remarquez que le rire est une des expressions les plus fréquentes et les plus nombreuses de la folie.... [Le rire] sorti des conditions fondamentales de la vie ... est un rire qui ne dort jamais, comme une maladie qui va toujours son chemin et exécute un ordre providentiel."[58] And, most clearly of all, in the essay on caricature he states, in reference to Brueghel: "Je défie qu'on explique le capharnaüm diabolique et drôlatique de Breughel le Drôle autrement que par une espèce de grâce spéciale et satanique. Au mot grâce spéciale substituez, si vous voulez, le mot folie, ou hallucination; mais le mystère restera presque aussi noir."[59]

When we speak, then, of irony originating at the cost of the empirical self, the statement has to be taken seriously enough to be carried to the extreme: absolute irony is a consciousness of madness, itself the end of all consciousness; it is a consciousness of a non-consciousness, a reflection on madness from the inside of madness itself. But this reflection is made possible only by the double structure of ironic language: the ironist invents a form of himself that is "mad" but that does not know its own madness; he then proceeds to reflect on his madness thus objectified.

This might be construed to mean that irony, as a *"folie lucide"* which allows language to prevail even in extreme stages of self-alienation, could be a kind of therapy, a cure of madness by means of the spoken or written word. Baudelaire himself speaks of Hoffmann, whom he rightly considers to be an instance of ab-

---

[57] Baudelaire, "De l'essence du rire," pp. 259–60.
[58] *Ibid.*, pp. 248–50.
[59] Baudelaire, "Quelques caricturistes étrangers," *ibid.*, p. 303.

solute irony, as *"un physiologiste ou un médecin de fous des plus profonds, et qui s'amuserait à revêtir cette profonde science de formes poétiques.* Jean Starobinski, who has written very well on the subject, allows that irony can be considered a cure for a self lost in the alienation of its melancholy. He writes:

> Nothing prevents the ironist from conferring an expansive value to the freedom he has conquered for himself: he is then led to dream of a reconciliation of the spirit and the world, all things being reunited in the realm of the spirit. Then the great, eternal Return can take place, the universal reparation of what evil had temporarily disrupted. This general recovery is accomplished through the mediation of art. More than any other romantic, Hoffmann longed for such a return to the world. The symbol of this return could be the "bourgeois" happiness that the young comedian couple finds at the end of the *Prinzessin Brambilla*—the Hoffmann text to which Baudelaire had alluded in the essay on laughter as a *"haut bréviaire d'esthétique"* and which is also cited by Kierkegaard in his journals.[60]

Yet the effect of irony seems to be the opposite of what Starobinski here proposes. Almost simultaneously with the first duplication of the self, by means of which a purely "linguistic" subject replaces the original self, a new disjunction has to take place. The temptation at once arises for the ironic subject to construe its function as one of assistance to the original self and to act as if it existed for the sake of this world-bound person. This results in an immediate degradation to an intersubjective level, away from the *"comique absolu"* into what Baudelaire calls *"comique significatif,"* into a betrayal of the ironic mode. Instead, the ironic subject at once has to ironize its own predicament and observe in turn, with the detachment and disinterestedness that Baudelaire demands of this kind of spectator, the temptation to which it is about to succumb. It does so precisely by avoiding the return to the world mentioned by Starobinski, by reasserting the purely fictional nature of its own universe and by carefully maintaining the radical difference that separates fiction from the world of empirical reality.

Hoffmann's *Prinzessin Brambilla* is a good case in point. It tells the story of a young comedian couple thoroughly mystified into believing that the fine and moving parts they are made to play on the stage give them an equally exalted station in life. They are finally "cured" of this delusion by the discovery of irony, manifest in their shift from a tragic to a comical repertory, from the tearful tragedies of the Abbato Chiari to a Gozzi-like type of *commedia dell' arte*. Near the end of the story, they exist indeed in a state of domestic bliss that might give

---

[60] Jean Starobinski, "Ironie et mélancolie: Gozzi, Hoffmann, Kierkegaard," in *Estratto da Sensibilitá e Razionalitá nel Settecento* (Florence, 1967), p. 459.

credence to Starobinski's belief that art and the world have been reconciled by the right kind of art. But it takes no particular viciousness of character to notice that the bourgeois idyl of the end is treated by Hoffmann as pure parody, that the hero and the heroine, far from having returned to their natural selves, are more than ever playing the artificial parts of the happy couple. Their diction is more stilted, their minds more mystified, than ever before. Never have art and life been farther apart than at the moment they seem to be reconciled. Hoffmann has made the point clear enough throughout: at the very moment that irony is thought of as a knowledge able to order and to cure the world, the source of its invention immediately runs dry. The instant it construes the fall of the self as an event that could somehow benefit the self, it discovers that it has in fact substituted death for madness. "Der Moment, in dem der Mensch umfällt, ist der erste, in dem sein wahrhaftes Ich sich aufrichtet,"[61] Hoffmann has his mythical king, initiated into the mysteries of irony, proclaim—and, lest we imagine that this is the assertion of a positive, hopeful future for prince and country, he immediately drops dead on the spot. Similarly, in the last paragraph of the text, when the prince pompously proclaims that the magical source of irony has given humanity eternal happiness in its ascent to self-knowledge, Hoffmann pursues: "Hier, versiegt plötzlich die Quelle, aus der . . . der Herausgeber dieser Blätter geschöpft hat"—and the story breaks off with the evocation of the painter Callot, whose drawings have indeed been the "source" of the story. These drawings represent figures from the *commedia dell' arte* floating against a background that is precisely *not* the world, adrift in an empty sky.

Far from being a return to the world, the irony to the second power or "irony of irony" that all true irony at once has to engender asserts and maintains its fictional character by stating the continued impossibility of reconciling the world of fiction with the actual world. Well before Baudelaire and Hoffmann, Friedrich Schlegel knew this very well when he defined *irony*, in a note from 1797, as "*eine permanente Parekbase.*"[62] Parabasis is understood here as what is called in English criticism the "self-conscious narrator," the author's intrusion that disrupts the fictional illusion. Schlegel makes clear, however, that the effect of this intrusion is not a heightened realism, an affirmation of the priority of a historical over a fictional act, but that it has the very opposite aim and effect: it serves to prevent the all too readily mystified reader from confusing fact and fiction and from forgetting the essential negativity of the fiction. The problem is familiar to students of point of view in a fictional narrative, in the distinction they have learned to make between the persona of the author and the persona of the fic-

[61] E. T. H. Hoffmann, *Prinzessin Brambilla*, chap. 5.
[62] Schlegel, *Kritische Ausgabe*, 18: 85 (668).

tional narrator. The moment when this difference is asserted is precisely the moment when the author does not return to the world. He asserts instead the ironic necessity of not becoming the dupe of his own irony and discovers that there is no way back from his fictional self to his actual self.

It is also at this point that the link between irony and the novel becomes apparent. For it is at this same point that the temporal structure of irony begins to emerge. Starobinski's error in seeing irony as a preliminary movement toward a recovered unity, as a reconciliation of the self with the world by means of art, is a common (and morally admirable) mistake. In temporal terms it makes irony into the prefiguration of a future recovery, fiction into the promise of a future happiness that, for the time being, exists only ideally. Commentators of Friedrich Schlegel have read him in the same way. To quote one of the best among them, this is how Peter Szondi describes the function of the ironic consciousness in Schlegel:

> The subject of romantic irony is the isolated, alienated man who has become the object of his own reflection and whose consciousness has deprived him of his ability to act. He nostalgically aspires toward unity and infinity; the world appears to him divided and finite. What he calls irony is his attempt to bear up under his critical predicament, to change his situation by achieving distance toward it. In an ever-expanding act of reflection[63] he tries to establish a point of view beyond himself and to resolve the tension between himself and the world on the level of fiction [*des Scheins*]. He cannot overcome the negativity of his situation by means of an act in which the reconciliation of finite achievement with infinite longing could take place; through prefiguration of a future unity, *in which he believes*, the negative is described as temporary [*vorlaüfig*] and, by the same token, it is kept in check and reversed. This reversal makes it appear tolerable and allows the subject to dwell in the subjective region of fiction. Because irony designates and checks the power of negativity, it becomes itself, although originally conceived as the overcoming of negativity, the power of the negative. Irony allows for fulfillment only in the past and in the future; it measures whatever it encounters in the present by the yardstick of infinity and thus destroys it. The knowledge of his own impotence prevents the ironist from respecting his achievements: therein resides his danger. Making this assumption about himself, he closes off the way to his fulfillment. Each achievement becomes in turn inadequate and finally leads into a void: therein resides his tragedy.[64]

---

[63] "*In immer wieder potenzierter Reflexion ...*" is a quotation from Schlegel, "Athenäum Fragment 116," *ibid.*, p. 182.

[64] Peter Szondi, "Friedrich Schlegel und die Romantische Ironie," in *Satz und Gegensatz* (Frankfurt am Main, 1964), pp. 17–18; the italics are ours.

Every word in this admirable quotation is right from the point of view of the mystified self, but wrong from the point of view of the ironist. Szondi has to posit the belief in a reconciliation between the ideal and the real as the result of an action or the activity of the mind. But it is precisely this assumption that the ironist denies. Friedrich Schlegel is altogether clear on this. The dialectic of self-destruction and self-invention which for him, as for Baudelaire, characterizes the ironic mind is an endless process that leads to no synthesis. The positive name he gives to the infinity of this process is freedom, the unwillingness of the mind to accept any stage in its progression as definitive, since this would stop what he calls its "infinite agility." In temporal terms it designates the fact that irony engenders a temporal sequence of acts of consciousness which is endless. Contrary to Szondi's assertion, irony is not temporary (*vorlaüfig*) but repetitive, the recurrence of a self-escalating act of consciousness. Schlegel at times speaks of this endless process in exhilarating terms, understandably enough, since he is describing the freedom of a self-engendering invention. "(Die romantische Poesie)," he writes—and by this term he specifically designates a poetry of irony—

> kann . . . am meisten zwischen dem Dargestellten und dem Darstellenden, frei von allem realen und idealen Interesse, auf den Flügeln der poetischen Reflexion in der Mitte schweben, diese Reflexion immer wieder potenzieren und wie in einer endlosen Reihe von Spiegeln vervielfachen. . . . Die romantische Dichtart ist noch in Werden; ja das ist ihr eigentliches Wesen, daß sie ewig nur werden, nie vollendet sein kann. . . . Nur eine divinatorische Kritik dürfte es wagen, ihr Ideal charakterisieren zu wollen. Sie allein ist unendlich, wie sie allein frei ist, und das als ihr erstes Gesetz anerkennt, daß die Willkür des Dichters kein Gesetz über sich leide.[65]

But this same endless process, here stated from the positive viewpoint of the poetic self engaged in its own development, appears as something very close to Baudelaire's lucid madness when a slightly older Friedrich Schlegel describes it from a more personal point of view. The passage is from the curious essay in which he took leave from the readers of the *Athenäum*; written in 1798 and revised for the 1800 publication, it is entitled, ironically enough, "Über die Ünverständlichkeit." It evokes, in the language of criticism, the same experience of *"vertige de l'hyperbole"* that the spectacle of the pantomime awakened in Baudelaire. Schlegel has described various kinds of irony and finally comes to what he calls "the irony of irony."

[65] Schlegel, *op. cit.*, pp. 182–83.

202

... Im allgemeinen ist das wohl die gründlichste Ironie der Ironie, daß man sie doch eben auch überdrüssig wird, wenn sie uns überall und immer wieder geboten wird. Was wir aber hier zunächst unter Ironie der Ironie verstanden wissen wollen, das entsteht auf mehr als einem Wege. Wenn man ohne Ironie von der Ironie redet, wie es soeben der Fall war; wenn man mit Ironie von einer Ironie redet, ohne zu merken, daß man sich zu eben der Zeit in einer andren viel auffalenderen Ironie befindet; wenn man nicht wieder aus der Ironie herauskommen kann, wie es in diesem Versuch über die Unverständlichkeit zu sein scheint; wenn die Ironie Manier wird, und so den Dichter gleichsam wieder ironiert; wenn man Ironie zu einem überflüssigen Taschenbuche versprochen hat, ohne seinen Vorrat vorher zu überschlagen und nun wider Willen Ironie machen muß, wie ein Schauspielkunstler der Leibschmerzen hat; wenn die Ironie wild wird, und sich gar nicht mehr regieren läßt.

Welche Götter werden uns von allen diesen Ironien erretten können? das einzige wäre, wenn sich eine Ironie fände, welche die Eigenschaft hätte, alle jene großen und kleinen Ironien zu verschlucken und zu verschlingen, daß nichts mehr davon zu sehen wäre, und ich muß gestehen, daß ich eben dazu in der meinigen eine merkliche Disposition fühle. Aber auch das würde nur auf kurze Zeit helfen können. Ich fürchte ... es würde bald eine neue Generation von kleinen Ironien entstehn: denn wahrlich die Gestirne deuten auf phantastisch. Und gesetzt es blieb auch während eines langen Zeitraums alles ruhig, so wäre doch nicht zu trauen. Mit der Ironie ist durchaus nicht zu scherzen. Sie kann unglaublich lange nachwirken. ....[66]

Our description seems to have reached a provisional conclusion. The act of irony, as we now understand it, reveals the existence of a temporality that is definitely not organic, in that it relates to its source only in terms of distance and difference and allows for no end, for no totality. Irony divides the flow of temporal experience into a past that is pure mystification and a future that remains harassed forever by a relapse within the inauthentic. It can know this inauthenticity but can never overcome it. It can only restate and repeat it on an increasingly conscious level, but it remains endlessly caught in the impossibility of making this knowledge applicable to the empirical world. It dissolves in the narrowing spiral of a linguistic sign that becomes more and more remote from its meaning, and it can find no escape from this spiral. The temporal void that it reveals is the same void we encountered when we found allegory always implying an unreachable anteriority. Allegory and irony are thus linked in their common discovery of a truly temporal predicament. They are also linked in their common de-mystification of an organic world postulated in a symbolic mode of analogical

[66] Schlegel, "Über die Ünverständlichkeit," *op. cit.*, p. 369.

correspondences or in a mimetic mode of representation in which fiction and reality could coincide. It is especially against the latter mystification that irony is directed: the regression in critical insight found in the transition from an allegorical to a symbolic theory of poetry would find its historical equivalent in the regression from the eighteenth-century ironic novel, based on what Friedrich Schlegel called *"Parekbase,"* to nineteenth-century realism.

This conclusion is dangerously satisfying and highly vulnerable to irony in that it rescues a coherent historical picture at the expense of stated human incoherence. Things cannot be left to rest at the point we have reached. More clearly even than allegory, the rhetorical mode of irony takes us back to the predicament of the conscious subject; this consciousness is clearly an unhappy one that strives to move beyond and outside itself. Schlegel's rhetorical question "What gods will be able to rescue us from all these ironies?" can also be taken quite literally. For the later Friedrich Schlegel, as for Kierkegaard, the solution could only be a leap out of language into faith. Yet a question remains: certain poets, who were Schlegel's actual, and Baudelaire's spiritual, contemporaries, remained housed within language, refused to escape out of time into apocalyptic conceptions of human temporality, but nevertheless were not ironic. In his essay on laughter Baudelaire speaks, without apparent irony, of a semimythical poetic figure that would exist beyond the realm of irony: "si dans ces mêmes nations ultra-civilisées, une intelligence, poussée par une ambition supérieure, veut franchir les limites de l'orgueil mondain et s'élancer hardiment vers la poésie pure, dans cette poésie, limpide et profonde comme la nature, le rire fera défaut comme dans l'âme du Sage."[67] Could we think of certain texts of that period— and it is better to speak here of texts than of individual names—as being truly meta-ironical, as having transcended irony without falling into the myth of an organic totality or bypassing the temporality of all language? And, if we call these texts "allegorical," would the language of allegory then be the overcoming of irony? Would some of the definitely non-ironic, but, in our sense of the term, allegorical, texts of the late Hölderlin, of Wordsworth, or of Baudelaire himself be this "pure poetry from which laughter is absent as from the soul of the Sage"? It would be very tempting to think so, but, since the implications are far-reaching, it might be better to approach the question in a less exalted mood, by making a brief comparison of the temporal structure of allegory and of irony.

The text we can use for our demonstration has the advantage of being exceedingly brief and very well known. It would take some time to show that it

---

[67] Baudelaire, "De l'essence du rire," p. 251.

falls under the definition of what is here being referred to as "allegorical" poetry; suffice it to say that it has the fundamentally prefigurative pattern that is one of the characteristics of allegory. The text clearly is not ironic, either in its tonality or in its meaning. We are using one of Wordsworth's Lucy Gray poems:

> A slumber did my spirit seal;
> I had no human fears:
> She seemed a thing that could not feel
> The touch of earthly years.
>
> No motion has she now, no force;
> She neither hears nor sees;
> Rolled round in earth's diurnal course,
> With rocks, and stones, and trees.

Examining the temporal structure of this text, we can point to the successive description of two stages of consciousness, one belonging to the past and mystified, the other to the *now* of the poem, the stage that has recovered from the mystification of a past now presented as being in error; the "slumber" is a condition of non-awareness. The event that separates the two states is the radical discontinuity of a death that remains quite impersonal; the identity of the unnamed "she" is not divulged. Lines 3 and 4 are particularly important for our purpose:

> She seemed a thing that could not feel
> The touch of earthly years.

These lines are curiously ambiguous, with the full weight of the ambiguity concentrated in the word "thing." Within the mystified world of the past, when the temporal reality of death was repressed or forgotten, the word "thing" could be used quite innocently, perhaps even in a playfully amorous way (since the deceased entity is a "she"). The line could almost be a gallant compliment to the well-preserved youth of the lady, in spite of the somewhat ominous "seemed." The curious shock of the poem, the very Wordsworthian "shock of mild surprise," is that this innocuous statement becomes literally true in the retrospective perspective of the eternal "now" of the second part. She now has become a *thing* in the full sense of the word, not unlike Baudelaire's falling man who became a thing in the grip of gravity, and, indeed, she exists beyond the touch of earthly years. But the light-hearted compliment has turned into a grim awareness of the de-mystifying power of death, which makes all the past appear as a flight into the inauthenticity of a forgetting. It could be said that, read within the perspective of the entire poem, these two lines are ironic, though they are not ironic in themselves or within the context of the first stanza. Nor is the poem, as a whole, ironic. The stance of the speaker, who exists in the "now," is that of a subject whose insight is no longer in doubt and who is no longer vulnerable to irony. It could be.called, if one so wished, a stance of wisdom. There is no real disjunction of the subject; the poem is written from the point of view of a unified self that fully recognizes a past condition as one of error and stands in a present that, however painful, sees things as they actually are. This stance has been made possible by two things: first, the death alluded to is not the death of the speaker but apparently that of someone else; second, the poem is in the third person and uses the feminine gender throughout. If this were truly relevant, the question would remain whether Wordsworth could have written in the same manner about his own death. For the informed reader of Wordsworth the answer to this question is affirmative; Wordsworth is one of the few poets who can write proleptically about their own death and speak, as it were, from beyond their own graves. The "she" in the poem is in fact large enough to encompass Wordsworth as well. More important than the otherness of the dead person is the seemingly obvious fact that the poem describes the de-mystification as a temporal sequence: first there was error, then the death occurred, and now an eternal insight into the rocky barrenness of the human predicament prevails. The *difference* does not exist within the subject, which remains unique throughout and therefore can resolve the tragic irony of lines 3 and 4 in the wisdom of the concluding lines. The difference has been spread out over a temporality which is exclusively that of the poem and in which the conditions of error and of wisdom have become successive. This is possible within the ideal, self-created temporality engendered by the language of the poem, but it is not possible within the actual temporality of experience. The "now" of the poem is not an actual now, but the ideal "now," the duration of an acquired wisdom. The actual now, which is that of the moment of death, lies hidden in the blank space between the two stanzas. The fundamental structure of allegory reappears here in the tendency of the language toward narrative, the spreading out along the axis of an imaginary time in order to give duration to what is, in fact, simultaneous within the subject.

The structure of irony, however, is the reversed mirror-image of this form. In practically all the quotations from Baudelaire and Schlegel, irony appears as an instantaneous process that takes place rapidly, suddenly, in one single moment: Baudelaire speaks of *"la force de se dédoubler* rapidement," *"la puissance d'être* à la fois *soi-même et un autre"*; irony is instantaneous like an "explosion" and the fall is sudden. In describing the pantomime, he complains that his pen cannot possibly convey the simultaneity of the visual spectacle: *"avec une plume tout cela est pâle et glacé.*"[68] His later, most ironic works, the prose poems of the *Tableaux parisiens*, grow shorter and shorter and always climax in the single brief moment of a final *pointe*. This is the instant at which the two selves, the empirical as well as the ironic, are simultaneously present, juxtaposed within the same moment but as two irreconcilable and disjointed beings. The structure is precisely the opposite from that of the Wordsworth poem: the difference now resides in the subject, whereas time is reduced to one single moment. In this respect, irony comes closer to the pattern of factual experience and recaptures some of the factitiousness of human existence as a succession of isolated moments lived by a divided self. Essentially the mode of the present, it knows neither memory nor prefigurative duration, whereas allegory exists entirely within an ideal time that is never here and now but always a past or an endless future. Irony is a synchronic structure, while allegory appears as a successive mode capable of engendering duration as the illusion of a continuity that it knows to be illusionary. Yet the two modes, for all their profound distinctions in mood and structure, are the two faces of the same fundamental experience of time. One is tempted to play them off against each other and to attach value judgments to each, as if one were intrinsically superior to the other. We mentioned the temptation to confer on allegorical writers a wisdom superior to that of ironic writers; an equivalent temptation exists to consider ironists as more enlightened than their assumedly naïve counterparts, the allegorists. Both attitudes are in error. The knowledge derived from both modes is essentially the same; Hölderlin's or Wordsworth's wisdom could be stated ironically, and the rapidity of Schlegel or Baudelaire could be preserved in terms of general wisdom. Both modes are fully de-mystified when they remain within the realm of their respective languages but are totally vulnerable to renewed blindness as soon as they leave it for the empirical world. Both are determined by an authentic experience of temporality which, seen from the point of view of the self engaged in the world, is a negative one. The dialectical play between the two modes, as well their common interplay with mystified forms of language (such as symbolic or mimetic representation), which it is not in their power to eradicate, make up what is called literary history.

We can conclude with a brief remark on the novel, which is caught with the truly perverse assignment of using both the narrative duration of the diachronic allegory and the instantaneity of the narrative present; to try for less than a combination of the two is to betray the inherent *gageure* of the genre. Things seem very simple for the novel when author and narrator are considered

---

[68] *Ibid.*, p. 259.

to be one and the same subject and when the time of the narrative is also assumed to be the natural time of days and years. They get somewhat more complex when, as in the scheme proposed by René Girard, the novel begins in error but works itself almost unwittingly into the knowledge of this error; this allows for a mystified structure that falls apart at the end and makes the novel into a pre-ironic mode. The real difficulty starts when we allow for the existence of a novelist who has all these preliminary stages behind him, who is a full-fledged ironist as well as an allegorist and has to seal, so to speak, the ironic moments within the allegorical duration.

Stendhal, in the *Chartreuse de Parme*, is a good example. We readily grant him irony, as in the famous Stendhalian speed that allows him to dispose of a seduction or a murder in the span of two brief sentences. All perceptive critics have noticed the emphasis on the moment with the resulting discontinuity. Georges Poulet, among others, describes it very well:

> In none of [Stendhal's truly happy moments] is the moment connected with other moments to form a continuous totality of fulfilled existence, as we almost always find it, for instance, in the characters of Flaubert, of Tolstoi, of Thomas Hardy, of Roger Martin du Gard. They all seem, at all times, to carry the full weight of their past (and even in their future destiny) on their shoulders. But the opposite is true of Stendhal's characters. Always living exclusively in their moments, they are entirely free of what does not belong to these moments. Would this mean that they lack an essential dimension, a certain consistency which is the consistency of duration? It could be....[69]

This is true of Stendhal the ironist, whose reflective patterns are very thoroughly described in the rest of the article, although Poulet never uses the term "irony." But, especially in the *Chartreuse de Parme*, there clearly occur slow, meditative movements full of reverie, anticipation, and recollection: one thinks of Fabrice's return to his native town and the night he spends there in the church tower,[70] as well as of the famous courtship episodes in the high tower of the prison. Stephen Gilman[71] has very convincingly shown how these episodes, with their numerous antecedents in previous works of literature, are allegorical and emblematic, just as Julie's garden in *La Nouvelle Héloïse* was found to be. And he has also shown very well how these allegorical episodes act prefiguratively and give the novel a duration that the *staccato* of irony would never be able, by definition,

[69] Georges Poulet, *Mesure de l'instant* (Paris, 1968), p. 250.
[70] Stendhal, *La Chartreuse de Parme* (1839), chap. 8.
[71] Stephen Gilman, *The Tower as Emblem*, Analecta Romanica, vol. 22 (Frankfurt am Main, 1967).

to achieve. It remains to be said that this successful combination of allegory and irony also determines the thematic substance of the novel as a whole, the underlying *mythos* of the allegory. The novel tells the story of two lovers who, like Eros and Psyche, are never allowed to come into full contact with each other. When they can see each other they are separated by an unbreachable distance; when they can touch, it has to be in a darkness imposed by a totally arbitrary and irrational decision, an act of the gods. The myth is that of the unovercomable distance which must always prevail between the selves, and it thematizes the ironic distance that Stendhal the writer always believed prevailed between his pseudonymous and nominal identities. As such, it reaffirms Schlegel's definition of irony as a "permanent parabasis" and singles out this novel as one of the few novels of novels, as the allegory of irony.

7

MURRAY KRIEGER

Mediation, Language, and Vision
in the Reading of Literature

I

IT IS A special opportunity, and a special challenge—on an occasion sponsored by
The Johns Hopkins University—for me to discuss the problem of language as
mediation in literature, a problem increasingly at the forefront of recent theoretical discussion. I hope it is not also a presumption for me to do so. For it is largely
through the intellectual activities that have been going on at Johns Hopkins that
theorists and critics in our country have become concerned about the very appli-
cability of the term "mediation." This concern opens to a broader one: the
critic is to concentrate on the person and his vision or self-consciousness that
shines through the literary work, in contrast to the previous, New-Critical obsession with the persona and the "impersonal" vision objectively structured *in* the
work. This has been the source and has supplied the nourishment for both so-
called phenomenological criticism and structuralist criticism as these two movements have—in their different, if not totally opposed, ways—supplanted the
so-called New Criticism or contextualism that went unchallenged for so long. It
was Johns Hopkins that was this country's forum for Georges Poulet; and it is at
Johns Hopkins that we find such productive younger protagonists of these movements as J. Hillis Miller and René Girard, with Paul de Man shortly to arrive as
a brilliant reinforcement. No wonder commentators begin to be tempted to speak
of the Hopkins school.

Let me admit that I offer myself as a new offshoot of that contextualist
movement, now perhaps deservedly displaced among those doing our most adventurous theoretical probings; I hope to find a new life (or at least liveliness) for it
by trying myself to do justice to the serious misgivings about language as
mediation which critics like Poulet have shown to us all. Surely in these late
days criticism can no longer dare to assume the validity or the value of its discrete
analyses of literary works, or of its arguments defending the exhaustive study of
unique forms as unique language systems. As the person of the poet threatens to
undo the persona, so his consciousness threatens to undo the work's telic self-

211

sufficiency: as the person threatens to undo the persona, so his body threatens to undo the word-as-body, so the world threatens to overwhelm the word.

> ... the modern [poet] either does not acknowledge or does not know a mediator for his orphic journey. He passes through experience by means of the unmediated vision. Nature, the body, and human consciousness—that is the only text.[1]

These words are taken from *The Unmediated Vision*, a remarkable volume by Geoffrey Hartman (recently a close colleague and cohort of Paul de Man). It was fitting that in 1966 this early work of Hartman's was at last reprinted and that it appeared with a freshness that suggested original publication. It was not only fitting but seemed to be a necessary accompaniment to the recent flourishing of criticism directed at denying or overcoming the mediating nature of poetry in order to get us to the thing itself. Indeed, in view of all we thought we had learned since 1954 (its original date of publication), and from more recent European writings, we surprise ourselves with the reminder of its date and of its being composed by a young American scholar (though by one clearly indebted heavily to European sources).

We may remember also that our recent fantastic, Norman O. Brown, in his Neo-Freudian apocalyptic plea, *Life Against Death*, recognized in kinship that *The Unmediated Vision* was a revolutionary work of criticism which bypassed the word for the body. He saw that, for Hartman, the poem is no longer to be conceived as "other" or as object; it is to be absorbed into the poet's (and, ultimately, the critic's) self as subject. In the modern world, now bereft of all mediation—of the Christian miracle in which Word did become flesh—there can be no verbal text for our study; instead, "the only text," as Hartman tells us, is "nature, the body, and human consciousness."

It is just the notion of the poem as object, as an "insensible It," that—by way of reaction against it—impels the anticritical crusade of Ihab Hassan, literary follower of Norman Brown. Despite differences between the European phenomenological tradition behind Hartman and our native irrationalist, anti-establishment radicalism, this connection between Hartman and both Brown and Hassan reveals them serving a similar tendency to deobjectify and repersonalize literature. The similarity deserves to be noted, as it has not been, for it points to a common need in our theoretical climate. Neither Hartman nor other phenome-

---

[1] Geoffrey H. Hartman, *The Unmediated Vision: An Interpretation of Wordsworth, Hopkins, Rilke, and Valéry* (New Haven, 1954), p. 155.

212

nological critics are likely to travel with Hassan to the logical extreme of maintaining that action, rather than contemplation, is a "legitimate response to art" once a presence—not depersonalized—has replaced the coldly viewed object as the stimulus of that response. But one might well claim that such an extreme is a proper consequence of those aspects of the neo-romantic theoretical impulse which they share.

These attitudes toward literature, seemingly revolutionary to those of us who grew up under the unchallenged dominance of the would-be classicism of New-Critical analyses of discrete poems, achieve their force and the momentum of their influence through their being a moving alternative to that criticism. Ever since the earlier revolution in the academy effected by the New Criticism, the abundance of discrete critiques in our books, our journals, and our classrooms has prompted the wearied cry "Enough—and too much." So convergent has been the focus on the discrete work that we must have expected, as an inevitable humanistic reaction, the impatient demand to have literature returned to the humane matrix that fosters it and is in turn fed by it. As critical method, fed less and less from a source of theoretical justification, seemed more and more to feed on itself, it multiplied its increasingly mechanical operations and its consequently lifeless products. The living body of the poems it dealt with was made more and more into a corpse: the critic's role, no longer the humanistic one of renewing the vitality of our verbal heritage, was becoming the pseudo-scientific one of post-mortem, dissection become autopsy.

There has, then, been the inevitable reaction against this sort of critical establishment by those determined in their own ways to restore life to literature, to reassert the critic as midwife instead of as coroner. Some would destroy criticism itself by opposing mediation: by seeing its mediating function and the mediating function of poetry as suspect, as precluding life, draining that life from an object left on the dissecting table. This attack on criticism as it is restricted to single works is an attack on the objective hopes and disinterested pretensions of the critical exercise. Under attack here is the detached critic—the critic as analyst and judge—the critic coolly operating a mediating (meddling) enterprise. Distance between the critic and the work is to be destroyed as that which replaces human response with dehumanized analysis: distance creates the space for analysis and, consequently, the claim to a would-be scientific objectivity. But the critic's destruction of space or distance can be accomplished only by his following the precedent of the poet, who must be seen as destroying the distance an "impersonal" theory of creation would impose between him and his work. If the critic (or, rather, anticritic), thus dedicated to process rather than product, must deny the distance between the work and its author, then poetry, too, comes to be seen as the enemy of mediation, of the mediating nature of language. The poem is at war with discourse as mediator. The poem is that paradoxical discourse dedicated to denying its own nature. It is to transmit immediacy, obliterating its own presence, a presence that threatens to deaden immediacy by freezing its dynamic flow into a static object. Instead, the work melts into an instantaneous union of "unmediated vision," shared among work, author, and critic, an undemarcated flowing of the vision among the three. And the spectacular—even apocalyptic—breath of life returns to inspire, as it rehumanizes, our traffic with literature. Thus it is that the central and detached concern with the object as a self-defined structure comes to be rejected because of its flight from the human contact with the object, the human contact that not only comes before and after the object but becomes the object, by merging with it, giving it its life.

The attack on the mediating properties of poetic structure and of the critical language seeking to fix that structure has taken several forms. The so-called phenomenological critics here and in Europe, perhaps most extremely represented by Georges Poulet, who, as Hillis Miller has shown us, is not really phenomenological at all—such critics (let us rather call them critics of unmediated self-consciousness) blur the work into the author's consciousness and ours, substituting a pulsating "interior distance," as subjective as human time, for the flat contours of spatial form, searched out by conventionally "formalistic" critics. Poulet's conception of form as static and dead—as objective—makes his anti-formalism explicit. The disregard for the single work as a discrete whole, as well as the impatience with the critic who painstakingly fusses over such works, must follow—and normally does. The "human" and the "interior" must be made to prevail over the scientific and the fixedly exterior if the vitality of literature is to be ever renewed instead of once and for all stifled. The results of such studies are brilliant, spectacular, even at times persuasively luminous—but not finally very transferable. They superciliously bypass the function of criticism as an educating process. Poems about poems, they impress the imagination more than the understanding.

A visionary critic like Harold Bloom has an even more open disdain for the discrete critique. Behind his treatment of the individual author (all of whose works constitute a single corpus) is an all-unifying, monolithic, transcendent vision that absorbs all works and their authors into itself. The breath of meaning, issuing from the organic life that moves these visions and makes them one, can be received only as we merge work with author (as creative imagination), merge authors into a "visionary company," and merge all with the sublime vision.

Again the objective, as impersonal, as distanced, is rejected in the romantic denial of space, the romantic explosion of distinctions.

Ihab Hassan, we have seen, looks toward another sort of neo-romantic apocalypse, an unmediated breakthrough to body from which the Word is finally excluded. The flesh, then touched in its immediacy, can dispense with the falsely metaphorical illusion that claims the Word-become-flesh. And, when the re-won bodily realities of our instincts can rush in, the middleman of art need not—nay, dare not—enter. The writers who celebrate this "dismemberment of Orpheus," Miller and Beckett and a host of younger novelists, create an anti-art, an anti-word, directed at the extinction of art, at total silence.[2]

To a great extent, then, the attack upon the poem as object and upon criticism as discrete analysis is an attack upon word-worship, upon the mediating function of language and our willingness to settle for the medium, for the empty carton with its generic label. It is also an attack upon form-worship and upon the entire post-Kantian mood of our criticism of the last century and a half. What mediates subjective experience for the more aesthetic of us is not so much mere words as the special forms created by words, the order-producing impositions that become fixed, static objects. In molding chaos, in taming outrage, in directing chance, in rendering the casual into the causal—in other words, by converting all the raw materials of a no longer mediated human subjectivity into the willed perfections of Aristotelian inevitability—humanity has allowed the formal impulse (licensed as an act of freedom by Kant, Schiller, and many who follow) to end by destroying human freedom. For it destroys the subjective freedom of the random, of the unstructured, of the indeterminate, in its service of the formal impulse that was to allow the person, as human, triumphantly to transform the subjective into the objective, thereby redeeming the irrational within himself. But, with its formative impulse, the human is seen as betrayer of its free person.

The formal and classic, then, must come to be seen as stasis, that which arrests the dynamics of temporality in the deadness of shape, of spatial thereness. The still classical *Stürm und Drang* antagonism to Lessing's *Laokoön*, for all its promise of freedom of mingling among the arts, ends by freezing literature into sculpture. Time's jagged unpredictabilities are rounded into place. This may have been enough for Kant and Goethe, Schiller and the post-Kantians—indeed

---

[2] See Hassan's "The Dismemberment of Orpheus: Notes on Form and Antiform in Contemporary Literature," in *Learners and Discerners*, ed. Robert Scholes (Charlottesville, Va., 1964), pp. 135–65; "Beyond a Theory of Literature: Intimations of Apocalypse?" *Comparative Literature Studies*, 1 (1964): 261–71; *The Literature of Silence: Henry Miller and Samuel Beckett* (New York, 1967).

it was their grandly humanistic dream—as they tried to replace the divine mediation by Christ with the human mediator, now granted divinely creative powers. But the modern, with a more radical sense of human freedom, negates them as Mann's Leverkühn negates Goethe's Faust and "takes back" the human hallelujah of Beethoven's *Ninth*. The very formative categories of Kant are rejected in the return to the unformed continuum of the raw "given."

Such a temperament views poetic form as the mediating element, as that totalitarian force that everywhere subdues the wayward to its overwhelming autotelic purposiveness, thus delivering death to our subjective freedom. For form, being contextual, ought to involve the rigorous marshaling of words, the systematic transformation of all that comes to it from without into the "new word" within, whose totality of definition is constituted by its every serving part. All indeterminacies are rendered determinate under an irresistible Hegelian functionalism. The all-unifying human imagination, our gift from Coleridge, and the Kantian and post-Kantian tradition behind him, has, like God, conquered chaos, has used its *fiat* to make it order.

But this sort of human god, imposed by Kant, Goethe, Schelling, Coleridge, or even Nietzsche upon a world no longer mediated by the divine-human paradox authored by the true God, is for Hassan or the early Hartman an inflated phantom bent on depriving the fleshly creature of his newly won freedom from the word, that presumptuous surrogate for body. His body, which he knows in its instinctive immediacy from the inside, no longer need yield to an outside transubstantiating authority. If God, author of mediation, is dead, then the man-god should embrace the truly autonomous, unchartable freedom of the immediate rather than try to impose his own mediation, his own ersatz cosmos in the microcosm of the poem. For the entire notion of cosmos, of microcosm and macrocosm as mutual reflections, is seen as existentially obsolete, whether God-made or man-made. Thus Hassan, looking at the (to him) false mediations of an outmoded literature that seeks perfect speech instead of total silence, characterizes such language as a series of equations which his apocalyptic prophet must shun: language equals sublimation equals symbol equals mediation equals culture equals *object*ivity equals abstraction equals death. As point-by-point apocalyptic alternatives, silence (as the identity of nothingness and the indiscriminate, chaotic all) has as its equations (instead of sublimation) indulgence, (instead of symbolism) flesh, (instead of mediation) outrage, (instead of culture) anarchy, (instead of objectivity) subjectivity, (instead of abstraction) particularity, (instead of death) instinctual life. And the antipoet, who writes his "antibook" for the anticritic with his anti-aesthetic, cultivates the accidental, the indeterminate, the "unstructured or even random element in literature," refusing to absorb it into the authority of form, insisting on its persisting on its own out there, radically autonomous in its caprice, as testimony of its and our own capricious freedom, nurtured in the gratuitous act. Hassan himself tells us that "Apollonian Form finally becomes Abstract Authority" (with the capital letters their emblem of Abstract Authority). From here we can see his Dionysian alternative lurking. True life, in its chaotic subjectivity, has regained its primacy over the trim lines of art. Indeed, art is to obliterate itself into the unmediated terrors of existence, into the rites and mysteries of the orphic act. Orpheus, then, is to aid in his own dismembering. "Imitative form," which is—as Yvor Winters taught us —no form at all but a dissolution into the formlessness of raw experience, yields up all aesthetic pretensions to wallow in the mimetic surrender to human darkness. The *Dunciad* has indeed become the *Inferno*.

I have given myself perhaps too expansively to dealing with Hassan, since I have granted that he is immeasurably more extreme than our more influential anti-mediators. I thought it worth doing because in him I found the neo-romantic impulse against the formal or mediating principle in its purest form. It should be helpful with the less immodest claims of more subtle minds. As a matter of fact, Hassan himself, in his moments of retreat, of recognition of the not-altogether-abandoned poet, is such a more subtle mind. He can at times see the artist's need forever to turn on himself, finally to make even the random element somehow *his* random element, the antibook somehow part of his total (and totally absorptive) book. Thus the act converts to intellectual gesture. Hassan himself can intellectualize even to this extent:

> Literature recoils from the withering authority of the new Apollo, but it does not surrender itself wholly to the frenzy of Dionysus. It only *feigns* to do so. It employs self-irony and self-parody, as in the novels of Mann and Camus; it develops, as in the works of Beckett or Genet, forms that are antiforms. . . . Literature, in short, pretends to a wordy wordlessness and participates in the Dionysian denial of language not with its own flesh, but with the irony of its divided intelligence.[3]

This is a long way from Hassan's more extreme justification of total silence as the last refuge of "the freedom of language to seek some purposeless and indeterminate antiform," or of a language that "becomes indiscriminate, random, fluent beyond words" in its dedication to its "outrageous vision."[4] His more balanced

[3] "The Dismemberment of Orpheus," pp. 148–49.
[4] *Ibid.*, p. 162.

view that has the poet resist total identity with Dionysus in a turning upon himself allows for the poet's turning of the antibook into *his* book. And, of course, this is a reintroduction of aesthetic mediation.

As such it would quite satisfy me as a critic dedicated to return at last to the poem as an object, though enriched by what those suspicious of the mediating nature of language have revealed about the death-threatening tendencies of the word. The would-be objective critic, who wants to defend his art against the skepticism of the anti-mediators by meeting it head-on, must begin by agreeing about the paralyzing consequences of mediation. He, too, must be suspicious of discourse as a mere medium, that which by definition precludes immediacy and which by its action freezes all flow. But, having shared the visionary critic's distrust of the medium, he must yet try to exempt poetry from its deadening powers. Having condemned mediation, he must yet save poetry. He can accomplish this only if he does not deny the poem as object, that is, only if he does not force an immediacy in the poem's relation to its creator by collapsing the poem into consciousness or vision. To make the poem a special object, one without the object's deadly there-ness, its spatial "fix," he must be prepared to ask, "When is a medium not just a medium? How can a medium be free of its pre-destined curse of mediation?" And he must be prepared to earn and to believe his answer: "When it can be the thing itself, holding the dynamism of flux in its coils." For the poem as discourse and thing is motion and is in motion. Yet it is motion in stillness, the stillness that is at once still moving and forever still.[5]

All these are theoretical problems steep and troublesome. As such they demand something beyond the unquestioning, blithe pursuit of discrete explication, the sort of explication that in its late days helped create, and justified, the anti-objective reaction which now demands that we take such theoretical troubles —or else abandon to the visionaries the maintenance of literature as a live art and act.

The theoretical task is easier when the opposition to recent criticism comes from those who would overmediate, those whose impatience with the tentative delicacies of analysis leads to crude interposings. For the tentative delicacies of the critic are his responses to the uniqueness of his objects, his efforts to fit his discourse to ever-new systems that defy his common measures. And it is this uniqueness—the critic's tribute to that unmediating medium, that space-eluding object—which the stubborn overmediator cannot wait to pause over. We have

---

[5] I expand this idea in my essay "The Ekphrastic Principle and the Still Movement of Poetry; or *Laokoön* Revisited," *The Play and Place of Criticism* (Baltimore, 1967), pp. 105–28.

seen that, even if the critic must resist yielding to the anti-mediator who bypasses all form for uninhibited subjectivity, he still must try to preserve the special life of his object by fighting for its immediacy, for the medium *malgré lui*. But the overmediator is finally willing to freeze his object by spatializing its form, universalizing it by absorbing it into common formulas—models—broader than the work (or, in cases, broader than literature itself). This sense of the model is what is placed between the work and our private response, shaping both work and response to our awareness of that model. The deadening effect upon work and response is almost enough to send us, by way of reaction, to the dynamic vitality of the anti-mediator, except that we know of that danger too. But we know we must not surrender his sense of life to paint a frozen model.

When we sweep aside the recently fashionable language of structuralism with its models, we find this very instinct for universalizing the individual work which lay behind the pre–New Critical attitudes, whether socio-historical or biographico-psychological, this instinct which made the New Criticism necessary. The unregenerate overmediator, who preferred to learn nothing from the contextualist revolution, sounds pretty much like those who preceded that revolution, as he tries to adapt the work to extramural commonplaces. For example, the social concerns of Walter Sutton, which move him to keep the lines between literature and culture at once, continually, and broadly open, are not markedly different from the concerns which prompted Ransom, Tate, Brooks, and others—by way of reaction—to make their defense of poetry several decades back.[6] Against such arguments as Sutton's, based as they are on the failure to grasp the organismic assumptions, the New-Critical defense is still valid, although there is now the need to deepen its theoretical basis and extend its theoretical consequences.

Other more subtle forms of overmediation also threaten to preclude the criticism of the poem as a unique language system. They all have their attractiveness to the extent that we cherish the encyclopedist's pretentious hope of unifying our knowledge and our languages. (Nor should we give up the encyclopedist's universal dream of a logocentric utopia, except grudgingly.) But the cost to literature as authentic discourse is high. The structuralist—a Lévi-Strauss or a Jakobson—runs the risk that the peculiarly literary will slip away when poetic structures, general linguistic structures, and anthropological structures come to be juxtaposed, not only as analogous, but even as homologous. Again, the meth-

---

[6] See Sutton's "The Contextualist Dilemma—or Fallacy?" *JAAC*, 17 (1958): 219–29, and "Contextualist Theory and Criticism as a Social Act," *JAAC*, 19 (1961): 317–25. See my comments in "Contextualism Was Ambitious," *The Play and Place of Criticism*, pp. 153–64.

odological issues may not finally be very different from those that brought the New Criticism into existence. It is just this fear of the overuniversalizing, over-mediating tendencies of such latitudinarian structuralism which moves sympathetic observer-participators like Michael Riffaterre and Geoffrey Hartman to their critiques and qualifications.[7] Of course, these suggest structuralist efforts that would preserve the uniqueness of the poetic structure and resist the adaptation to generic models; but they would appear to abandon the distinctively structuralist ambition and would pose no real opposition or alternative to contextualism.

Another variety of structuralism—René Girard's—combines it with something very like Poulet's method of bypassing mediation, as we see the extremes (of anti-mediation and overmediation) meet. In his conclusion to *Deceit, Desire, and the Novel*, Girard finds that all novels end by becoming the same novel: he uncovers at last the "banal" structure hidden in the common conclusions of all novels.[8] But the structural uniformity is a uniformity in the discoveries of self-consciousness in that the single conclusion creates its conversion by having the protagonist at last turn upon his mediator, so that in the end all barriers, all mediation, between the vision of a character and his author (and, as Poulet would extend this, between the author and us) are destroyed. A single pattern creates an always similar break-through in which distinct entities merge into instantaneity and identity. Anti-mediation is found to be the single structural model for the novel. Perhaps Girard can serve to remind us that Poulet himself, for all his antiformalism, for all his anti-mediation that suggests antistructuralism, may strengthen the structuralist impulse by his methodological monism. His work always seems to lead to the glorious identity of consciousness shared by reader, poet, and work, to the collapsing of the distinct categories of time and space in the instantaneous union between every critic and author. The very overcoming of mediation becomes a universal principle of writers, each of whom moves toward becoming Mallarmé or Proust. Or, finally, there is Northrop Frye, who, like the structuralist, works from a model, though in his case it is restricted to a model literary universe; but the overpowering shadows cast by his many-faceted monolithic structure upon the little lonely work have by now often enough been lamented. The overmediation often shrieks its impositions, even as it excites us

[7] I refer to two fine essays in the "Structuralism" double issue of *Yale French Studies*, no. 36–37 (1966): Michael Riffaterre, "Describing Poetic Structures: Two Approaches to Baudelaire's *les Chats*," pp. 200–42, and Geoffrey Hartman, "Structuralism: The Anglo-American Adventure," pp. 148–68.

[8] *Deceit, Desire, and the Novel: Self and Other in Literary Structure*, trans. Yvonne Freccero (Baltimore, 1965), pp. 290–314.

with the monolithic set of forms which structures the common human imagination and its common human dream.

Whatever the alternative critical attitudes that have followed upon the criticism which emphasized discrete analyses of poems as objects, these attitudes have been taken up in part as a reaction against that emphasis; but they have not removed the need for such a criticism and have not overcome the arguments in support of this need. Whether the anticontextualist proceeds from the desire to destroy the poem as a mediating object by seeing through it to the poet's immediacy, or from the desire to destroy the poem's immediacy by burdening it with universalizing mediations, he has not precluded the need to preserve the object as at once object *and* immediate.

But we have noted also the extent to which these responses have been generated by failures within the critical movement and by a flagging of its theoretical impulse to justify what it was doing. Its evangelical mission to save poetry dwindled into the Sunday sermon, moving routinely from text to text. It is this explication for explication's (and ingenuity's) sake that late defenders of criticism must not resort to, must move beyond. If Frye's totally absorptive system is seen as too universal, causing total deprivation to the singular, the critic of the discrete must resist the mere compilation of isolated perceptions as part of an endless bill of particulars. This critic must at least move back to the world from his internalized systems: what has turned inward must at last, and in a special way, open outward; the mutually reflecting mirrors (to borrow a metaphor I have used elsewhere) must be transformed to windows that capture a newly visioned reality. The "new word" that is the poem, still fully released from what the old words had been, yet returns to our common language to enrich it by renewing its powers of reference. And the critic must help, not only in defining that new word, but—perhaps more crucially, if less easily—in tracing its return to its culture and language, illuminating as it goes. If the critic stops with mere explication of the system, if he does not return it to its subtle function in the world of reference, its redefinitions of language and of vision; then he may be sure that his own role will be usurped by the impatient non-contextualist, who will open the language of the poem outward at once and without taking pains, who will make it serve the world of reference in a vulgar way that deprives poetry of those special powers which the critic of the discrete poem should be dedicated to serve and preserve. And he will deserve to be replaced.

It may very well be that only by his taking the theoretical issues very seriously can the critic prevent himself from succumbing to the myopia which his endlessly attractive objects induce in him. He is obliged, at considerable pain, to

convert a terminal experience of a self-sufficient object into an instrumental occasion: he must ask "why?" and "to what end?" even as he accounts for the
"finality" that asks no more. Again we see it is his double need, the need to see
the paradoxical poetic medium at once as immediate and as that which mediates
the general meanings of the world beyond. At stake is the nature of language
generally. The poet may subvert that language, words in their general naming
function, but only to save and serve the possibilities of *his* language, a language
created *pour l'occasion* out of its own general incapacities. This is the stuff that
the rarest of dreams, of visions, are made of—the rarest since, in their ultimate
immediacy, they are not transferable, can occur nowhere but here in this work.
And this work at once denies the power of its words, and yet, by its very being,
denies that denial.

Sir Philip Sidney, in his *Astrophel and Stella* (considerably more than in
his *Apology for Poetry*, where he more properly might have done so), often confronted this very problem of the uses and limitations of language as the poet
must find it and refine it. Perhaps nowhere does he manage this confrontation
more explicitly and more brilliantly than in "Sonnet 35" ("What may words say,
or what may words not say"), a poem which I have treated elsewhere in detail.[9]
In conclusion here I should like to use it only as a sort of allegory of the argument of this paper. For the movement of the sonnet springs (as its first line tells
us) from the poet's awareness of the absurdities of language in its normal uses:
his explicit distrust of language-as-names yields a special sort of anti-nominal
system.

The poem proceeds under the reasonable control that produces and sanctions a series of outrageously irrational compliments, all governed by the initial
confession of the incapacity of words. The paradoxes that follow are made up of
words colliding with themselves in a desperate flight from meaninglessness. Each
key word denies its own meaning, each abstraction obliterates itself by being
itself in a way that identifies it with its opposite. With reason itself supervising
the process, the very possibility of language has been precluded by the reason-
defying perfection of Stella. Yet the unique immediacy of her presence, having
negated language, has become its own language—the language of *this* poem—
which has transcended the emptiness of language that functions only as mediation. Out of the mutual blockages of language, then, the poet has broken through
to his own language, with meaning newly restored out of the accumulated ver-
balistic wreckage of conventional meanings. Further, such a language comes

---

[9] In "The Continuing Need for Criticism," *Concerning Poetry*, 1 (1968): 18–20.

freighted with its rarities of vision, although I cannot pursue them here. Poems like these give us access to immediacies of consciousness as perhaps no other object does (and I say "object" pointedly now, seeing the object in its dynamic freedom).

Is our sense of language or of vision ever quite the same again? "What may words say, or what may words not say" indeed! By denying that words can say anything, these specially empowered words can say it all. My argument has been that it is clearly the role of criticism to listen closely to such words, hearing and overhearing all that they can affirm and deny, and neither to obliterate them in search of wordless vision nor to move through them to the stereotyped visions we had before this configuration of them, this poem, came along. And, while it listens this closely, what many things must it clearly become and continue to be the function of criticism to say? Dare one have the temerity to propose more precisely than these vague notions of mine suggest? In the second part of this essay I shall try to dare. But you will rightly remember that most theorists have uttered such fond hopes before, so that you will not expect too much. And I fear I may give you no more than you expect.

II

Through diverse critical traditions, through many centuries in the history of criticism, the veil has appeared as a metaphorical equivalent of the aesthetic symbol (a variety, perhaps, of the garment figure, although it lends itself to far more ambiguous adaptations). The mediating character of art has thus been implicitly recognized as it has—through the veil—entered the very vocabulary and primary conceptions of the critical theorist. And the ambivalent attitude toward the role and value of the veil, in its relation to whatever reality was claimed to be behind it, is clue to the ambivalence of attitude toward art's mediation itself.

It is all part of the problem—as old as criticism—concerned with the opposition between particularity and universality in art. Or, to convert to more theological terms, it is the opposition between the sensible and the intelligible, the earthly and the transcendently spiritual. It is the problem of the sin, as well as the saving virtue, of art, Augustine's concern over Dido slain, the awesome question that asks whether art, as particular embodiment, is an avenue to heaven or an earthly drag that blocks our upward path. Is the symbol the incarnate thing (i.e., spirit) itself, a substitute needed by imperfect man in his need to find a sensuous equivalent, or is it a perverse substitute that man in his lowliness lusts to place in his own way? Is it a sacred effigy of the true God or a profane idolatry? And so the several Platonisms, Neo-Platonisms, and anti-Platonisms have wrestled with one another through the centuries.

As orthodoxy and heterodoxy struggled through the Middle Ages and Renaissance to find a satisfactory formulation of the role of art, the fortunes of the veil (as synonym for art) fluctuated: now it was the false mediator, purveyor of illusion, of distortion, the obscuring element; now it was the indispensable threshold to the absolute—pure transparency itself. Thus it could be restricted to its frustrating function as replaceable surrogate in the thinness of allegory or it could be expanded to the rich double life of another sort of allegory offered by the typological *figura*: both the pointer and that to which it points, which it bears immanently within itself. But in neither case was there any question about the ultimate reality of that universal, transcendent realm, whether the veil is that which obscures it or is our sensuous access to it.[10]

It is not to be unexpected that, with the revolutionary inversions of the secular world in these last centuries, reality eventually is transformed into the irreducible particulars that are swept along in the flux of experience. This fluid reality is now seen to be veiled by the false, nonexistent universals projected by our anti-existential need for mediation. So, as particulars and the universal exchange places, the concrete sensuous "given" that formerly functioned as veil now is in *its* turn veiled as the universal is revealed as a fraud invented for our comfort. After all, one cannot make an ontology out of the projection of universals by the Kantian categories without anthropomorphically blundering into things-in-themselves; and the universals can claim no further metaphysical authority, no matter how heroic an imposition they may be by man, who in his quest for sanity refuses to surrender to the chaos of sense data. Kierkegaard extends this Kantian notion—after Hegel's vainglorious attempt to restore the illusion of final reality for these universals—to the existentialist extreme of denying all ontology, affirming only subjectivity, only the particular as absolute. Thus the veil of false universals now becomes the veil of Maya, seen by Schopenhauer and Nietzsche as the agent of will which the Bergsonian T. E. Hulme calls upon poetry to strip away. Poetry, then, becomes the anti-mediator, destroying the mediating universal. Kierkegaard had denied this possibility—as his condescending distrust of the aesthetic kept art within the universal, refusing to allow it existential immediacy. For Kierkegaard insisted on the formal incommunicability

---

[10] The role of the veil in medieval and Renaissance theory is usefully and effectively traced in Katherine E. Gilbert and Helmut Kuhn, *A History of Esthetics* (New York, 1939), pp. 149–72.

of the unmediated, accepting it as being by definition incommunicable, as beyond language. He is only a little more denying than Georges Poulet was to be, Poulet who (as we saw in Part I, above) finally must get beyond the aesthetic even if he does not quite go beyond language—as, for example, we saw Ihab Hassan bring us.

A principal aim of the first part of my essay was, similarly, to establish that the universal, as the spatial, is the mediator, hence is the veil, but—unlike Poulet —to put the aesthetic symbol on the other side, as the correlative (hopefully objective) of unmediated particularity. Though it is itself a final object, yet it is to be intimately related to reality as existential and to be differentiated from the universal in experience and language even as the existential itself is.

Let me recapitulate: I granted that the phenomenological and existentialist manners of constructing our world of experience in its immediacy require us to distinguish in our experience between the existential as unmediated and that selection from the existential (in accordance with some principle of order) which creates the universal as the mediated. I granted further that our antiobjective existentialist quest might lead us to transfer this dichotomy between the unmediated and the mediated—between consciousness and its objects—in our experience to a similar dichotomy in language. If we did, we could emerge with poetry as a language of "human time," of "interior distance," a subjective, antiformalistic celebration of the instantaneous flight that bypasses all mediation, with the rest (the frozen world of fixed objects to be related to one another and speculated about) left to the non-poet. Thus the critic involved with unmediated self-consciousness can allow distinctions in experience to reflect themselves directly in language: there is either the language of objects (mediated) or the language of Cartesian preobjective consciousness (unmediated), the latter seeming to be almost an abdication from language as well as an abdication from the formal obligations of poetic discourse. But can language do no more to bridge the gap, language released from its normal bondage? What could a total indulgence in language allow that a total abdication from it would not?

Given the distinction in experience between unmediated and mediated, can we rather distinguish in our language between the poetic (contextually conceived as unique systems) and any other (systematically propositional or ordinary), claiming that only the poetic has access to the existential, from which the latter has removed itself by its generic nature? But, it can be argued by the critic of unmediated self-consciousness, the poem also is a form and formula, a fixed object that in its frozen state incapacitates itself from capturing the immediate. It, too, occurs in a medium and, hence, it is mediate rather than immediate and thus is subject to the anti-mediator's rejection of it and flight from it. Such an argument can be answered, as I tried to answer it in Part I, only by referring to the paradoxical nature of poetic discourse, which thus becomes at once the source and mouth of meaning, at once a fixed form and yet, through its dynamics of interrelations capturing stillness in movement, attaining objective immediacy. It thus converts into a medium that is at war with its role, language that subverts the normal behavior of language in order to attain the character of sacred communion which symbolism has lost in the secular world.

So at least the argument would go that would seek to recover the poem as object without having it forgo the existential immediacy that the contextualist, no less than the anti-mediator, must seek to keep within the poem's unique domain. The veiling function of poetic language, so long viewed ambivalently, is now seen as systematically ambiguous, if not downright miraculous. But the heart of the problem remains, since all we have been offered is a verbal mystique that cannot pretend to be a solution. In what follows I shall see if I can press these issues further.

The very formulation of the problems would seem to preclude our progress. Once we adopt enough of the existentialist stance to distinguish firmly between the immediate and the mediate in experience, how can we hope to capture or transmit the immediate in the mediate forms of language? Does not the very use of language carry with it the abandonment of the immediate to the extent that we commit ourselves to our symbolic systems? How can we justify our belief that our symbols can do better? There is, then, the "given" in experience in its immediacy, and there is the fixed object. How can the latter embody the former without losing the former's existential immediacy? That is to ask, how does the "given" in experience find its way into the vision of the whole work considered as an aesthetic form, a spatio-temporal moving finality?

I am aware that, at a time when "visionary" critics are in the ascendancy, I cannot use the word "vision" as my central term without trying to set off my sense of it from the sense it has commonly been earning—especially when I see the force of its common meaning as separating it from the work's totality even as I try to identify the two.[11] I must see the work not as a projection of a pre-existing vision, formed in the self behind it, but as a dialogistic entity that comes into being out of the dramatic conflict of forces and of language which constitutes its finished form. Thus it was that Leo Spitzer used "vision" as a pre-aesthetic cate-

[11] Perhaps it is for this reason an error for me to employ the term "vision," and indeed I might have searched for an alternative had I known when I began *The Tragic Vision* what the contemporary and subsequent use of "vision" was to do to it.

226

gory that characterized how the author saw rather than how the poem meant, reserving his aesthetic claims for what became of vision when the whole went to work on it by becoming a "work." Though in the spirit of Spitzer, I prefer to use "vision" for what comes out rather than for what goes in.[12]

But it is the construction upon the "given" which creates the forms of a vision that creates, and is created by, its form. So we, too, must begin once more with the "given." In my book *The Tragic Vision* I began with the common assumption that our routine (which is to say pretragic) existence depends upon the universalizing veils (that word again) that our social and moral necessities force us to hold between ourselves and the brawling chaos—the jumble of unique instances—that is actually out there (and within us) ready to show its Manichaean face to any who dare thrust the veil aside to look. And it is that forced confrontation of extremity—the unpalliated series of ineluctable consequences which practicality normally persuades us to shun—which creates the tragic existent and sets his tragic course on its way.

If we assume, then, the existential immediacy of the Manichaean face of reality as irreducibly there for the stricken existent, we assume also the multi-dimensionality of the unique particularity of this experience, now viewed without the universalizing veils that comfort automatically imposed. In its particularity this experience is thus inaccessible to the reducing or abstracting habits of our usual linguistic apparatus, of our rational—or at least propositional—responses which we have so well and universally learned. In its uniqueness (instantaneous because it is not just an instance, but an instant) it resists all but its own unrepeatable, flowing, unadaptable self. It is surely utterly closed, shut off, because nothing else is like it; nothing else can explain it, its conjunction of impossible co-ordinate or simultaneous aspects. But—and here is the Bergsonian paradox—it is also and at the same instant utterly open, because, being instantaneous, it is not even an entity; rather, denying itself any discrete instance, it flows into all other instantaneous non-instances and has them flow into *it*.

Well, then, inner experience is impervious to language, and we are trapped in the linguistic shadow-world of the subjective critic of unmediated self-consciousness (really observer and voice-catcher more than critic), in the manner of Poulet, the commentator who tries to match his introspective, impressionistic language to the elusive structures of mental experience before him. We have

---

[12] Leo Spitzer, "*Explication de texte* Applied to Three Great Middle English Poems," in *Essays on English and American Literature*, ed. Anna Hatcher (Princeton, 1962), pp. 193–247, esp. pp. 216–19.

more than once noted his necessary antipathy to form as the objectifying enemy.[13] Such a literary observer tends to see an unavoidable dichotomy in the options open to all literary observers, so that each must choose either the subjective or objective aspect of the work.[14] For Poulet, the literary work is the representative of the author's thought if we but conceive this thought as physical place, a home for its constituted objects. Thus conceived, the work, like the thought, may seem to those of us not attuned to interior distances to be related most obviously to its objects, those things of the outside world which it presumably is *about*. Being most obvious, this relation gives rise to "objective" criticism as the most usual sort. But the work, again like the thought, with those entities which it houses so commodiously, is related more crucially, if less obviously, to the thinking subject, the self that has "redisposed" those objects, now newly created by mind. This "interior distance" between subject and his thought or work, thus conceived, and the redisposition of the objects in accordance with the housing demands in this inner space, is the less obvious but more urgent sort of criticism which must be practiced if the study of literature is truly to be humanized. It thus brings to light the hidden, dark side of the moon, the Cartesian *Cogito*.

But we cannot help but notice that in his open antiformalism a literary observer like Poulet too easily disposes of all formal matters by ranging them on the side of the "objective" features, as if formal features were of the same order as the external objects that thoughts or works presumably are *about*, external objects to which, in other words, thoughts or works would seem to the naïve critic to refer, objects which—to use the most naïve notion—they would appear to "imitate." In his one-paragraph preface to *The Interior Distance*, Poulet blandly sees the "objective aspect" of literature as including "formal" elements (by which he seems to understand no more than generic elements, the "contours" leading

---

[13] I refer again to that most helpful and precise description of distinctions among critics of this sort in J. Hillis Miller, "The Geneva School," *Critical Quarterly*, 8 (1966): 305–21. Miller carefully traces the differences in the ways they play off the counterattractions of consciousness and of literary forms. Perhaps, in both parts of my essay, I have made my task too easy by choosing as my representative of the Geneva school so extreme a critic as Poulet, whom Miller shows to be the most Cartesian (hence antiphenomenological) and most antiformalistic of the group. The less antiformal, of course, are also less representative of the distinctive character of this critical mode.

[14] The most useful statement of the claims which follow occurs in the preface to Poulet's *Interior Distance*, although I believe that, assumed rather than stated, similar claims underlie many writers in this "school." Again I refer the reader to Miller's essay "The Geneva School" for important differences among these critics which I am forced to blur here.

us to "poems, maxims, and novels, plays") as well as what we have learned to call the referential elements, "accounts" or "descriptions" of "objects." And he promises to turn from both to the subjective side. It is a promise he keeps all too faithfully.

But, if he disposes of all formal matters by ranging them indifferently with what we used to call objects of imitation as equally "objective" features, then perhaps he should be reminded to "redispose" his notion of form (as, after Mallarmé, he has the mind in its "interior vacancy" redispose its world of objects) to make it (as our best critics have made it) more than flat categories so dully externalized. Must we choose between the ineffably subjective and the naïvely objective? If so, are we not being too unsubtle? The external object does not stand in the same relation to the poem as that poem's form does, unless we are restricting ourselves to what has long been an obsolete eighteenth-century notion of form as universal generic mechanics. Clearly, as such it is too flattened out and externalized ever to have a vital existence, ever to do more than deaden through abstraction the particular living work to which it was to apply itself.

What else has literary criticism been about since Coleridge and before, if not to work toward a notion of an organic form which would enable us to talk formally about a work without adapting it to stale generalities, but finding instead a form that is uniquely its own, expressive of its own unrepeatable characteristics? What else have these two essays of mine been about? This effort has led to examinations of the special properties of poetic discourse, its ways of meaning, which can permit it to open vistas of vision which normal discourse, by its very nature, seems determined to shut off. I have been pressing myself to show how the literary medium, though still only the words we all, like Hamlet, despise most of the time, manages to free the subjective, even while freezing it into a permanent form, to make the poem an *im*mediate object rather than a mediate one. For, if the medium is at war with itself in literature, if language refuses to serve as it normally does, its struggle serves the higher fidelity to language that shows him who can master this extraordinary medium how thoroughly it can master the most inward folds of our experience. But still, though a medium rendered immediate, a poem's language works to make the poem an *object* and to that extent external and communicable—and in need of more than subjective observation. The dark side of the moon *is* what we are given, but the firm mastery gives it to us in a way we can hope to secure—for ourselves and others. It is a formal way, though of course "formal" here has so many other-than-formal elements in it if we restrict the term to the archaically formalistic meaning Poulet at times reserves for it.

All of which returns us, but I believe newly armed, to the matter of vision and the way it gets into literature. For I have meant to be claiming throughout that we need not see our inner experience as being, after all, impervious to all language once we remember the inward immediacies that our great poets can force their language to embody. Suppose we begin with the special sort of "given" which I saw the tragic vision assuming about moral experience, and suppose we can characterize that "given" in its extremity as unadaptably unique, at once an indissoluble lump among innumerable other equally autonomous but dissimilar lumps in the stream of chaos, yet at the same time the stream itself, always becoming but never having become, and thus never hardened to lump; then we have begun by seeming to put such a "given" and such experience beyond the generic, freezing powers of language. We can recall my remarks concerning Ihab Hassan's assault on the word, his fear that subjective "outrage" may be fatally compromised by culture's dedication to a mediating "object," with the consequence of abstraction, death. For him this is the necessary and only consequence of the word and its order of beauty, since he does not allow language to be tortured into an object that preserves immediacy and existential vitality, an object that for all its fixed eloquence can preserve a discursive silence. For him, as we saw in the first part of my essay, language must be either eloquent or silent: eloquent in its service of an object for culture (thus violating our "outrage"), or silent in its obedience to outrage (thus deserting all objects).[15]

But I must go further, in order to qualify our fears about the existential incapacities of language, by acknowledging that we have been speaking only of the "normal" powers of language, so that we may find a very abnormal series of possibilities in the history of our greatest literary works.

The subjective flow of the self's awareness of its experience must somehow be preserved, even while being preserved in a fixed object. The death-dealing immobility of the spatial impulse must yield to the dynamic, moving vitality of the temporal, while yet creating that which must persist in an unchanging form: I maintain this need despite those newest critics who claim—against all objectivity—that dynamism must be retained in the ever-changing vitalism of our responses to our inner experience. Despite all that contemporary personalism and existentialism have taught us about objectification (the making into things) as the murderer of the unique, I would want the critic to claim to have found in

---

[15] I repeat what I said in the first part of my essay: that it is undoubtedly unjust to couple Hassan with the Geneva school and its followers, but the dialectic of my argument calls for them to be seen as united on this issue.

the abnormalities of poetic language the one way of having his object without surrendering the immediacy of its data.

There is in the work, as in the "given" of the experience, both the instance and the instant or even instantaneous, with the strange etymological and semantic coincidence of opposition and identity between these: the absolute and irreducible instance, which demands discreteness, a continual awareness of and pausing over the boundaries that constitute it as discrete, cutting it off from all that is not itself; and the absolutely instant or instantaneous, which denies the existence of bounds, of the entity-hood of the moment, in order to get on with the movement, the flow of the moment becoming the next without pausing to be marked. It is the role of poetic discourse to undo the generic tendencies of discourse generally, and so to complicate its context with contingency as to create that language context as its own unique body. Moving dynamically in time, the poem must yet become transfixed into a spatial form.

Hence what I have elsewhere termed the ekphrastic principle becomes the poetic principle in that it invokes "still movement" (in both the Keatsian and Eliotic senses of "still") as the special grace with which poetry is to be endowed.[16] The critic's job is to locate (as it is the poet's job to produce) the spatial orders within the temporal: the circular principle within progression; the freezing principle within the free-flowing; the emblematic as the ekphrastic within that which resists all spatial fixity; the multiple reflections of a mirrorized world of internal relations within a seemingly semantic and syntactic set of relations which, like all language, wants to open outward toward all other language and its referents; the causal and yet—or therefore—the casuistic within the casual; the logical within the chronological; the still recurring within the still moving; the extremities of experience within the compromising muddles of the uncommitted middle. To the extent that our discourse seeks to follow its non-poetic, natural (which, paradoxically, is to say conventional) paths—its "naturally" conventional paths, as it were—it seeks either to be casual and free (in its unsystematic modes) *or* to be causal and frozen (in its non-poetic systematic modes). The poet must have it as both at once: he must create the language as *his* medium by fostering in it the multiple capacities that transform the word into terminal entity, body, effigy, emblem, even as it clearly seems to function in the semantic and syntactic ways that words have as their wont. So the "given" is found in the work, preserved in its density and contingency and not reduced to any conceptual formula, yet preserved and intact by being an utterly formed object once and for all for one and

---

[16] I refer once more to my essay "The Ekphrastic Principle and the Still Movement of Poetry," pp. 105–28.

all. It has a form but is not a formula after all, is constitutive but not conceptual; that is, it gives the forms for our reality but not concepts about it.

If the poem, then (as, alas, all too many poems do), should reduce itself—as the straw-man formalist (attacked by Poulet) would have it—to fixity and only stand still, it would reduce itself to the frozen death of the spatialized discourse of non-poetic systems, losing the empirical dynamism of movement, the flowing vitality of experience in its subservience to universality, that Platonic archetype that levels particularity. But, if the poem should do the reverse, if—as a Poulet would have it—it should be still moving only in the sense of always moving, giving up the paradox of unmoving movement at the heart of the stillness of the Keatsian urn, then it would deny utterly its character as object in an unqualified yielding to the boundless, ceaseless flow of our experience; and we are no better off for art, an art that has given over all in worship of imitative form, form that decries form and cries for formlessness in imitating a formless welter of experiences.

My use of the term "vision" has been shown to be systematically distinct from that of our admittedly visionary critics who seek, in the literary work, signs (often related to signs found in other works) of the author's grasp of his reality as that constituted reality relates to the grasping self. For I seek no vision behind or before the work, though I do seek the vision that comes to be created in the work, *as* the work.[17] Perhaps, to borrow a tired notion from Eliot, it is that the visionary correlative I seek is objective, not subjective, although the fact that it is objective makes it no correlative but the thing itself. In its concern with vision my study is still within what I have called *thematics*, by which I have meant the formal study of an aesthetic complex which becomes more than formal because the complexities that it unifies, as unresolved tensions, reflect the tension of our pre-propositional and extra-propositional experience.[18]

If, unlike Poulet, I insist on the work—for all its elusive subjective churning—as an object, I nevertheless share his fear that the dead hand of objectification can destroy its unique voice by adapting it to alien structures or classes. But

---

[17] In Coleridgean terms, I seek in the work a direct reflection of the secondary imagination, which in its workings with language I must claim to be discontinuous with the primary imagination, "the prime agent of all human perception." Instead of merely being an "echo" of the primary, the secondary "dissolves, diffuses, dissipates" our reality as envisioned for us by our generally constitutive power, the primary. Coleridge uses both descriptions to make up an almost contradictory characterization of the secondary imagination. I choose to see only its character as creator, not that as echo.

[18] See *The Tragic Vision* (New York, 1960), pp. 242ff., for my original definition of *thematics*, together with a discussion of the consequences of that definition.

I believe I voiced my antistructuralist, Crocean antagonism toward the *over-mediators* sufficiently in the first part of my essay.

If my argument has persuaded us to define vision only in terms of the unique work that constitutes it, we still must seek a more precise description of how that work achieves that unique vision, its objective formulation of all in the "given" that in its dynamics resists formulation. This is to ask, how does the infinitely variegated flow of experience achieve an aesthetically transcendent unity? In the midst of experiential chaos, endlessly divisive, we look, as desperately as Gerard Manley Hopkins did, for an aesthetic inscape that will satisfy our thematic craving.

> All things counter, original, spare, strange;
> Whatever is fickle, freckled (who knows how?)
> With swift, slow; sweet, sour; adazzle, dim;
> He fathers-forth whose beauty is past change . . .

Of course, as secular theorists we allow the miraculous metaphor of poetic incarnation to substitute for his theological Word made flesh. We resist Hassan's impulse to obliterate the word in order to embrace the flesh directly, unmediatedly. As I have argued elsewhere, figuratively (that is, in terms of the *figura*) the Trinitarian paradox is the very model of the poet's farthest claim for metaphor as transubstantiating miracle, with its union-in-duality of tenor and vehicle.[19] So there is the aesthetic need and the thematic need to freeze experience in order most fully to feel its flow. With the subjectivity of experience behind and beyond, the work must be created formally as its emblem, a total object; and the work must be created existentially as its vision, the very word "vision" bestowing upon the work the spatial fixity of a thing seen.

How, then, is the poet to play the casual casuist? How is he to realize and master the muddled flow of the confused center of our experience through an aesthetic-thematic symbol? I speak of our experience in its subjective confusion as the "center of our experience" because it resists the purity of definition, the *a fortiori* clarity, of the polar extremes. Experience at its hard edges is no longer confused, though in its extremity it is not where we dare live it unless we are to become polar creatures, tragic existents, ourselves. For, as my examination of the tragic vision was to have demonstrated throughout, the existent cannot embrace at all costs either pole without having it transformed into its antagonist (as, for

---

[19] My book *A Window to Criticism: Shakespeare's Sonnets and Modern Poetics* (Princeton, 1964) rests almost wholly on my attempt to demonstrate the contextually sustained metaphor as the secular substitute for a theologically sustained transubstantiation; see especially pp. 200–204.

example, in the relation of puritanism to sensual debauchery in many works in this thematic genre). Better the safe sanity, the ethical probity—if the visionary blindness—of the inconclusive, compromised middle.[20] But the poet dedicated to aesthetic resolution has to unmuddle the middle through a casuistic play that leads him to summon up and cultivate the extreme. However uncommitted existentially, however aesthetically committed to dialogue alone, he vicariously nourishes the extreme. His method of capturing the extreme (and, with it, all the impurities of the middle he has bypassed and yet, like the alchemist, distilled) is that of converting the endlessly variegated muddle into the terms of his extended metaphor for it. The critic's hypothesis of the work's form is his best guess about what this extended metaphor is, based on all in the work which feeds it.

The repetitive patterns of a work, which give stillness to the movement by freezing freedom, must be read by the critic into his hypothesis of the work's form, as he makes it a reductive metaphor—an emblem, a constitutive symbol—for all the moving life and liveliness of the work. The metaphor, while excluding so much of the middle in its reductive, extremist purity, is in its emblematic fullness at the same time all-inclusive. The hypothesis tests itself by its capacity to account for every aspect of the work, aesthetic and experiential, which is stuffed within it (if it is not being imposed by the overanxious critic). At once puritan and catholic, the reductive metaphor must gather within itself the all of middle existence which it passes by in its pursuit of extremity, as it must gather within its holistic form the varied possibilities sloppily assembled in its tenor. Thus it becomes exclusively all-inclusive—at once existentially (or thematically) and aesthetically (or formally).

It may be helpful at this point for me to quote at length from my extended discussion of the reductive metaphor as both single and double, closed and open, in *A Window to Criticism: Shakespeare's Sonnets and Modern Poetics*.[21]

> The author plays the casuist, dedicated to extremity, by committing himself in the work absolutely to a reduction of one sort of experience to another, to a transfer of properties of one to those of another, a transfer to which every element in the work lends itself totally. Experience of a normal sort—messy, pre-poetic, of mixed and uncertain tendencies, veering in this direction and in

---

[20] This was the antitragic, anti-Dostoevskian, anti-Kierkegaardian plea which the late Philip Blair Rice saw Thomas Mann making, a plea for experience of the center rather than experience at the polar extremes. See Rice's "The Merging Parallels: Mann's *Doctor Faustus*," *Kenyon Review*, 11 (1949): 199–217.

[21] (Princeton, 1964), pp. 209–13.

that, impure in its continual compromise with the totality of definition—is viewed under the aspect of an extremely delimited sort of experience that threatens, momentarily, within its context, to reduce all experience to itself and to read life within its own awesome terms as unbearable and—to a common-sense reason that needs life as mixed—as irrational, even impossible.

Thus, in Mann's *Doctor Faustus*, for example, all forces lend themselves to reveal the generally accepted world of artistic dedication and controlled artistic creativity exclusively under the aspect of the world of disease, to reveal the world of decent austerity and harsh asceticism exclusively under the aspect of the world of license. But the total transfer of properties, the total reduction, is deceptive. The terms I have used in my hasty oversimplification of these worlds should indicate that even as the extremes are poetically equated they remain polarized. In furnishing us a very paradigm of the functioning of extremity, Mann allows no mediation between extremes, but forces one to support the other, even to reflect the other, finally to become a mask for the other. Mann's extreme necessarily bears its opposite within itself by the very nature of its seemingly singleminded purity. The ill-defined, mixed components of the life he deals with follow the path of their most dangerous tendencies to extremes that are at once polar and reversible, opposed and identical. For the equation of the two worlds, the reduction of one to the other, becomes a substantive metaphor. As such it turns on itself, asserting for common sense the duality of its terms, the distinctness of their properties, even as it works the miracle of transubstantiation. Everything in the work—character, incident, language, style —contributes to the collapsing of the broad and mixed world to the narrow and pure one and thus to the creation of the work as a total metaphor, except that, even as the transfer becomes dramatically complete, the separateness of elements asserts itself to our rational, less totally committed selves.

I could go on from *Doctor Faustus* to discuss the reductive metaphors, at once transubstantiating and skeptically self-denying, in others of the novels I treated as fully tensional bearers of the tragic vision. For example, we can too briefly characterize Gide's *The Immoralist*, in which all forces lend themselves to transfer the drive to assert the freedom of the self from the bonds of ethical restraint to its appearance exclusively under the aspect of a total enslavement to the senses. Or Malraux's *Man's Fate*, in which all forces lend themselves to transfer the ethical drive to merge the self with social betterment to its appearance exclusively under the aspect of the demoniac drive to the violence of uninhibited self-expression. Or Melville's *Pierre*, in which all forces lend themselves to transfer the moral devotion to well-meaning self-sacrifice to its appearance exclusively under the aspect of a total perversion at the service of monstrous desires.

235

Or Kafka's *The Trial*, in which all forces lend themselves to transfer the amoral routine of *quotidien* existence to its appearance exclusively under the aspect of blind and unmitigated, moment-by-moment guilt. Of course, the half-innocence in K.'s stumbling half-pursuit, his essential ignorance, proclaim the absurdity of this absolute transfer of properties even as they help us marvel at the nothing-left-out character of Kafka's contextual inclusiveness that allows him to "work" his metaphor. But so it is with all of these and other examples. Always the transfer is complete; the "aspect" under which we are forced to see *is* imposed exclusively. And yet, and yet . . . The polarities rebound; the muddled center reasserts itself; despite our utter captivation by the Word, our sensible selves skeptically reassert the recalcitrant world that resists all transfer and insists on doggedly, dully remaining itself. Still, the magic is never quite dispelled. We have it and we do not, we believe it and we do not, are hypnotically trapped and yet move freely in and out.

I now return to the passage from *A Window to Criticism*:

> . . . I see Mann's version of extremity as a paradigm that allows us to consider the poet's casuistry more broadly, so as to turn it into a generic literary strategy that can serve us with lyrics as well [indeed, even more easily, thanks to the obvious manipulation of devices of control in the lyric. Recall my comments on *Astrophel and Stella* 35, with the transfer of categories between the particular breathing lady and personified abstractions of universal virtues]. To use another obvious example . . . I can cite Donne's lovers in *The Canonization*, whose absorption by earthly love—which is shown in its normal state to be woefully mixed and incomplete in its nature—we are forced to view under the aspect of the total and unworldly dedication that earns sainthood. Everything in the poem, in the fullness of its contextual interrelations, works to bring off the equation, to complete the metaphor in its transfer of properties from tenor to vehicle (from earthly lovers to saints), even though the tenor and vehicle seem opposed to one another. Nevertheless this step-by-step extension of the metaphor carries along with it the covert guide of rationality that asserts the absurdity, even the speciousness, of this extension. It is not that the identity produced by the metaphor is being denied, since such a denial would lead us outside the context and its mutually dependent terms, but that the miracle can be asserted as miracle only by continually recognizing its impossibility, by continually acknowledging the intransigence of the materials and oppositions being mastered, though they are never destroyed.

Such a miracle of substantive identity should of course not be viewed as a propositional truth claim (*A* is *B*) any more than it is a dramatic demonstration of a propositional moral claim (*A* ought to be *B*). With its context totally working to create it, it is rather a total and totally committed incarnation, an effigy of mixed and intransigent experience which has been substantively transferred into, or rendered within, an extreme, unmitigated reduction of one pure and narrow aspect to whose sway all cooperates or conspires in order to make the transfer complete—even as the miracle asserts itself as such by urging an awareness of its denial. Like Shakespeare's Phoenix and Turtle, like my mirror and window, like the *in* and the *through* of contextualism, but perhaps most like Clarissa's scissors which the baron manipulates in *The Rape of the Lock,* the miraculous metaphor divides even while it joins. [That miraculous poem itself works, like the scissors, to divide as it joins, if we consider how thoroughly it creates its vision of the heavy prosaic world of flesh and blood under the aspect of the airiness of the pure world of absolute play.]

In its simultaneous performing of its dividing and joining functions, its opening-out and closing-in functions, the dual nature of the extremity that leads to miracle—but a special sort of miracle at once assertive and denying—can correct an unfortunate over-emphasis that has for good reason bothered students of recent criticism. From Aristotle onward, critics, in insisting on the unity of the literary work, have insisted upon its convergent movement toward a unitary, sharply pointed conclusion and conclusive meaning. The *Poetics* traces, in the development of the literary work, the gradual, inevitable elimination of the multiple probabilities with which it began until, when the climax turns the complication into the dénouement, only the one way that—though hidden to us and to the protagonist—has been inescapably there all along is left and is pursued to its end. It has been hard to improve upon this classic formulation in its convergent simplicity. Thus it could not help seeming dangerously perverse to find recent critics [perhaps our best or most extreme example here would be William Empson] rather emphasizing almost exclusively the divergent meanings of literary works. While also insisting upon unity, they dwell upon the *organic* nature of that unity, upon the *variety* which is being unified. They celebrate the ambiguous instead of the unilinear, the unresolved tensions among centrifugal forces instead of the crowning assertion of the all-dominating centripetal force. At their more reckless moments they may seem to be claiming for the work no more narrowly unified a precision than that of a shotgun blast. And yet they have on the whole been persuasive about the many voices with which even an apparently simple poem may often speak. I am suggesting that literary extremity and its miracle, with the completeness of their absorption of alien, resistant, and incomplete materials together with the completeness of the unbridgeable separateness of these elements, can allow for the combined emphasis on the divergent and convergent natures of literary movement and

237

meaning, the density and plenitude on the one side, the rarity and the order on the other. It can insist on the centrifugal thrust of a work only while placing its control within the pressing and uncompromising union of its finest and most centered point. The impossible combination of identity and polarity can make a total view of the object possible: the perspective is reduced to a single point even as, at the same time, the range of possibilities multiplies endlessly —thus the consequence of the object as both single substantive world and as bodiless reflection of multiple worlds beyond.

The reductive metaphor can in its closedness open an *imm*ediate access to reality's figures, which is to say the way reality becomes "figured" for us, "figured" in the double sense of Auerbach: at once the concrete symbol of the single instance, instantaneous, and—while holding to this character—the *figura*, its ultimate human meaning for us, its allegorical representativeness that exceeds itself, but only by thoroughly being itself. Hence we come upon the vision, but not any vision that pre-existed the work in an individual psyche or in a culture's "*humanitas*" or in a normative structure held in potentiality for individual entities to fulfill; rather the vision that is attained figurally by cutting so fine a verbal figure *as* the work. Yet it *does* become the culture for the moment and for the minds that so constitute it metaphorically. The extremity of total transfer, of metaphor, becomes window to the reduced moment of vision which characterizes the reality created for a culture (created *as* the culture) by its most symbolically gifted seer-makers.[22]

The hypothesis of the work's reductive metaphor thus becomes the formal opening to the work's existential vision. All of its directionless (because all-directional) experience, all of its "dappled," "pied" beauty, utterly ungraspable, is reduced to the emblematic unity that enables us to grasp its movements in a vicarious moment of vision. We are given this way (which neither precludes nor contradicts other ways) of seizing upon it as an entity we may perceive in its discrete entity-hood. It neither precludes nor contradicts other ways, because it gives us no propositional claim about the experience, a claim that would reduce it in another way, a logical way that would cheat it of its uniqueness and integrity by

---

[22] See my discussion of Eliseo Vivas' terms, "subsistence," "insistence," and "existence" (from "The Object of the Poem," *Creation and Discovery* [New York, 1955], pp. 129–43), as I try to relate the poetic context to the existential context in *A Window to Criticism* (pp. 59–63, 214–15). "For it is this metaphor, this total substitution, that allows us to see what an historical moment, in the privacy of hidden, personal inwardness has, in its most daring creations, in the total metaphors of its single, reduced moments of vision, dared to make of its world."

making it serve a universal law, reducing it to cipher, an enslaved particular that is therefore particular no longer. Instead, the metaphorical, visionary grasp gives us the particularity which the *poiesis* helps us to see as *one*, but as no more than one and as translatable to no others. Thus the metaphor, as the formal enabling cause of our vision, its source and its mouth, in the self-enclosure of its extremity, resists all propositional extrapolation, its persistent drama countering every would-be propositional claim with its antagonistic anticlaim.

The very reductive and yet all-embracing nature of the metaphor claimed by the critic's hypothesis must shout the rational denial of its absolute nature, the denial it bears within itself. It must force us to see nothing less than an identity between the muddle of its tenor and the pristine extremity of its vehicle. But the equation it proclaims as a self-enclosing metaphor it must proclaim in awareness of our skepticism. To be metaphor it must insist on the miracle by which things change their nature, become other than themselves, their substance dissolving into other things. It must, with the unrelenting tightness of a total aesthetic control exercised with equal pressure everywhere within its domain, create the vision that sees the messy center of our experience *becoming* its own purified reduction at the hard edge. For our vision it assumes a guise that alters the thing itself, thus proclaiming, however irrationally, the destruction of discrete entities, the blurring of the bounds, the limits, that create the property and propriety of entity-hood. Thus it achieves the fullness of capacity that (in the late Sigurd Burckhardt's terms) corporealizes itself and so attains the totality of definition of metaphor.

But, despite all such seeming magic, discourse—even poetic—remains only discourse, no matter how bent it may seem to be on subverting its own common nature as an open structure that leads us in and out, relating to other discourses and to the world that comes before and after all discourse (or so we assure ourselves in the naïve realism that is our common sense of how things go with us). And we, as prosaic users of discourse (even as we are the victims of the subversive perfection of its involutions in poetry), stubbornly retain the openness of our relations to it and the world, persisting in an anti-Kantian confidence that sees us and our world as pre-existing our symbols. So there must be that in the poem which we find comforting to our anti-aesthetic resistances, our recalcitrance to the miracles of language fully, if too trickily, endowed. The poem's patterned turnings upon itself end by allowing a part of us to turn on *it*, or to turn it against its most contextual pretensions. Our more rational selves find hidden within the poem, for all that would make it a new word, the comforting assurances that our sense for distinction and for property—which is to say propriety—may yet be preserved. It is nothing less than the comforting assurance that it all has been but a verbal game; and we try to set at rest that apocalyptic challenge to make the word into the Word, which is to say the fleshly world.

But of course this challenge, so persuasively urged by the closing, all-reducing action of the all-inclusive metaphor, still remains to possess us. This is to say that the rational covert guide that threatens to undo the mask by revealing it as no more than mask undercuts the miracle of metaphor by proclaiming it not as equation but as miracle, with all the inspiration of awe—and of skepticism—which the notion of miracle engenders. It is no fact; it is no proposition; indeed, fact and proposition flatly deny it. It is but an *im*position upon our vision, sanctioned only by the daring leaps sponsored by the delicate play of language. As no more (but no less) than miracle, it can be held only in the teeth of all rational denials. For it goes without saying that, if we can believe in it as a rational possibility, it is no miracle. By definition its very existence for us as miracle depends upon that part of us which knows it cannot happen—except in a way that passes understanding, an understanding we cannot altogether yield up.

Thus it is that, even as the enclosing metaphor captures the motley variety of experience's soft center within the hard edge of its extremity, thereby reading all of life within its own closed visionary system, there is something else at work in the countermetaphorical motion: in the skeptical denial that restores distinction (that restores our sense of duality where there are two entities), there is an opening outward beyond the miracle (the metaphor, the work, and the world of its words) to the world we know and what that world refuses to permit. An ironic self-doubt arises from the state of dialogue in the work that comes to terms with itself and yet, on the sly, proclaims itself as play; this self-doubt finally can lead even beyond the still-limited visionary dialogue of the single work to the ultimate catholicity of vision that is the proper end of the contemplative life.

The expansion of consciousness I have been urging, the dual awareness, the dialogistic sense that returns with a furtive openness to what has been closed, sealed off, may seem to echo the claims for the anti-poem of neo-romantic critics like Hassan. Let me remind you of this more moderate passage of his which I quoted in the first part of my essay:

> Literature recoils from the withering authority of the new Apollo, but it does not surrender itself wholly to the frenzy of Dionysus. It only *feigns* to do so. It employs self-irony and self-parody, as in the novels of Mann and Camus; it develops, as in the work of Beckett or Genet, forms that are antiforms....

Literature, in short, pretends to a wordy wordlessness and participates in the Dionysian denial of language not with its own flesh, but with the irony of its divided intelligence.[23]

If Hassan would concede more to what closed form can permit, this might seem a helpful way to indicate the Janus-faced character of the work. Its very closedness, its absolute commitment to its metaphorical reduction, its compression into its constitutive symbol, into its emblem—all are accompanied by its prompting our common-sense denial that dissolves its miracles and drags it to earth. All poems must covertly contain their anti-poems, must transcend themselves and their closed limits, transform themselves into *genera mixta*. I quoted earlier my claim that my argument must reconcile those traditions which characterize poetic form as convergent (as in Aristotelian unity) or as divergent (as in Empsonian ambiguity). The centripetal emphasis on an exclusive unity and the centrifugal emphasis on an inclusive variety, simultaneously asserted, are further reflections of the strange commingling of openness in the aesthetic closedness of the literary object. I mean to remind you here of my discussion of the paradoxical co-existence of openness and closedness in our discrete experience viewed at once as instant and instance.

I move on, in conclusion, to suggest some existential consequences of these claims. The extreme situation is that which, forgoing the ameliorations of the center, forces confrontation at the edge; but the existent who would confront is also the creator of the extreme situation. Buried in this circularity is the notion that the mess in the soft center of our experience is a mess that most of us have to create in order to muddle ourselves and preserve our sanity, to keep going as social animals who do not want to look too deeply into mirrors or into another's eyes. Our pursuit of endlessly diversified experience, veering in its infinitely various and self-aborting directions, our blunting the points we have sharply shaped, our lurching and starting and slowing and gliding and leaping, by turns, all are ways we hide from confrontation of what we dare not confront. As in Kafka's *The Trial* we must accept the ambiguous duality of K.'s having been seized for arrest gratuitously *and* K.'s having chosen the state of being arrested, so in this literature generally we must acknowledge both that extremity is there beckoning for him who would cast off all palliative veils to dare confront it and that extremity is a creation of those so willful as to choose the confrontation. The visionary courage—which is to say, the metaphorical courage—of those whose fear of blindness will not permit the diversion of their confronting impulse must be

---

[23] "The Dismemberment of Orpheus," pp. 148–49.

matched by the self-conscious insanity that forces them to wrestle—and to watch themselves wrestling—with casuistic phantoms instead of joining the rest of us in the center, going round and round in the dizzying dance of life. As we stop to look at them as our surrogates, if we observe closely enough, we find their struggle—combined with their consciousness of struggle—to have the purity and perfection of ballet. After such a vision, with what self-consciousness, with what new and corrective sense of our aimless heavy-footedness, do we return to make our motions?

Index

Abbondio, 143, 145, 147, 151
Abrams, Meyer, 126–27, 179, 181–82, 189, 190
Achilles, 161
Action, tragic, polarity of, 118
Adam, second, as Christ, 78
Adamites, sect of, 78, 89
Adams, G. K., 49
Adams, Parson, 171
Adventure novel, 166
Aediles, 29, 31
Aegyptiades, and dominance of Danaides, 114
Aegyptos, sons of, and daughters of Danaos, 114
Aequi, wars against, 29
Aeschylus: ambiguity in, 113–14, 120; and the city, 111; and civic ideal, 108; and *Oresteia*, 108; and *The Suppliants*, 115; tragic tensions between gods and man in, 119
Agamemnon, 120–21
Akenside, Mark, 179
Alalia, battle of, 11
Alba Longa: institutions of, 16; as religious center, 18
Alessandro, passion of, 139
Alfieri, Vittorio, 125
Alföldi, A.: 2, 5, 8, 14, 18, 21, 34; on classes, 22; on Claudii, 26; on Etruscan rule, 12; on federal army, 30; on literary tradition, 7; on Mezentius, 11; on military, 23; on Olus, 12; on temple of Ceres, 31
Allegorism, romantic, irony absent from, 192
Allegory: analogical suppressed in, 190; antithetical to symbol, 173–74; in English romanticism, 188; linked with irony, 203; mechanical form of, 177; past and future in, 207
Almaengien, Jakob von, 78
Amadís of Gaul, 155, 159, 166
Amadís of Gaul, 165
Ambiguity: in art, 102; of authority, 115; in Bosch's painting, 79; of crime, 108; in divinity, 111; in dramatic language, 117; of imagery, 53, 205; of perception, 47; of reality, 121;

in *The Trial*, 241; in universe, 107
American Dream, The, 164
Ames, Adelbert, Jr., 42
Analogy, between mind and nature: 179; replaced by monism, 180
Anderson, M. D., 87
Anderson, M. J., 113
Andrén, Arvid, on terra cottas, 33
Anti-art, 215
Antichrist, Bosch's painting of, 77, 79
Antiforms, 217, 240
Antigone: and authority of gods, 115; and conflict with Creon, 116; on *nomos*, 117
Antigone, 117
Antiheroes, 136, 162
Antimony, between symbol and allegory, 175
Antipoet, 216
Aphrodite, and Peitho, 114
"Apocalypse," 93–94
Apollo, 109, 217, 240
Archetype: in *Fermo e Lucia*, 134; Platonic, 232
Areopagus, 109–10
Argos, men of, 111
Aricia, battle of, 6
Aristocracy: in early Roman Republic, 21; in Latin cities, 29; revolutionary, 17
Aristodemus, 6, 9
Aristotle: on actors, 110; on ambiguity of crime, 109; on *ethosdaimôn*, 113; and irony, 192; theory of tragedy in, 105; 158; on tragedy as imitation of action, 118, 158; *The Poetics*, 237
Army, Roman, 13
Arnobius, on Olus, 12
Art: and form, 67; kinetic, 68; mediating character of, 223; particularity in, 223; universality in, 223
Artemis, Iphigenia and, 121
"Astrophel and Stella," 222
Athena: in *Oresteia*, 108; on Respect and Fear, 109–10
Athens, purification of, 110
Atrides, crimes of, 121

Attica, goddesses in, 110
Auerbach, Erich, 176, 238
Augustine, 223
Aulus. *See* Capitolium
Aulus Vibenna, 12. *See* Olus
Authority, definition of, 115
Automatism: in interpretation, 57; process of, 96–97
Automatisms: of perception, 67; of response, 57
Aventine, reserved for *plebs*, 30

"Balcony," 55
Baldass, Ludwig von, 77
Balzac, H. de: 169; on history, 154
Barthes, Roland, 173
Basileidai, of Ephesus, 16
Baudelaire, Charles: 200, 202, 204, 206, 207; correspondence of, 180; and falling man, 205; on irony, 193–94; and *le comique absolu*, 195; and *Les Chats*, 220
Beauty, incarnate and ideal, 174
Beckett, Samuel, 215, 217, 240
Beethoven, Ludwig van, 216
Beholder's Share, 40
Bellow, Saul, on *Quijote*, 165
Beloch, K. J., 18
Benardete, J., 162
Benjamin, Walter, 173, 176
Bergson, Henri, 40, 227
Berkeley, George, on vision, 43
Bernardi, A., 18
Bertram, Ernst, 98
Betrothed, The, 123
Bible: Christian symbolism in, 80; depictions of, 75 ff.; echoes of, 137; Koberger, 95; language of, 126
Biedermeier, world of, 139
Blake, William, allegory in, 188
Blasco Ibáñez, and Dostoevski, 158
Blood, obsession with, 150
Bloom, Harold, 179, 214
Boa Constrictor, 71, 86, 103
Boas, George, 82
Bond, James, 166
Bondage, Greek hatred of, 32
Bonis, Giacomo, on Forum, 2
Books, Sybilline, 32

Designed by Edward D. King

Composed in Fairfield Text with Umbra Display
by Monotype Composition Company, Inc.

Printed offset by Universal Lithographers, Inc.,
on Warren Olde Style

Bound by L. H. Jenkins, Inc., in Toro Black Grandee, paper over boards
with spine in Riverside Vellum